SECULARISM, CATHOLICISM, AND THE FUTURE OF PUBLIC LIFE

D1453521

SECULARISM, CATHOLICISM, AND THE FUTURE OF PUBLIC LIFE

A Dialogue with Ambassador Douglas W. Kmiec

Edited by Gary J. Adler, Jr.

OXFORD
UNIVERSITY PRESS

OXFORD
UNIVERSITY PRESS

Oxford University Press is a department of the University of Oxford.
It furthers the University's objective of excellence in research, scholarship,
and education by publishing worldwide. Oxford is a registered trade mark of Oxford
University Press in the UK and in certain other countries.

Published in the United States of America by
Oxford University Press
198 Madison Avenue, New York, NY 10016,
United States of America

Library of Congress Cataloging-in-Publication Data
Kmiec, Douglas W.
Secularism, Catholicism, and the future of public life : a dialogue with Ambassador
Douglas W. Kmiec / edited by Gary J. Adler, Jr.
    p. cm.
Includes index.
ISBN 978-0-19-020542-3 (hardback : alk. paper) — ISBN 978-0-19-020543-0
(pbk. : alk. paper) 1. Secularism. 2. Christianity and politics—Catholic Church.
3. Democracy—Religious aspects—Catholic Church. 4. Church and state.
I. Adler, Gary J. Jr., editor. II. Title.
BL2747.8.K55 2015
261.7—dc23
                            2014036743

1 3 5 7 9 8 6 4 2

Printed in the United States of America on acid-free paper

CONTENTS

CONTRIBUTORS

J. Bryan Hehir
Parker Gilbert Montgomery Professor of the Practice of Religion and Public Life
John F. Kennedy School of Government, Harvard University

Gary J. Adler, Jr.
Director of Research
Institute for Advanced Catholic Studies
University of Southern California

Douglas W. Kmiec
Caruso Family Chair
Pepperdine Law School
US Ambassador (ret.) to Malta

Michael Anderheiden
Professor
Institute for Constitutional Law, Theory, and Philosophy
University of Heidelberg

Geoffrey R. Watson
Professor of Law
Columbus School of Law
The Catholic University of America

Hans Joas
Ernst Troeltsch Professor for the Sociology of Religion
Theological Faculty, Humboldt University of Berlin

Massimo Franco
Political Columnist
Corriere della Sera

Erin K. Wilson
Director, Center for Religion, Conflict, and the Public Domain
University of Groningen

Stephen Calleya
Director, Mediterranean Academy of Diplomatic Studies
University of Malta

PREFACE

A preface can fulfill different functions. Typically, it can serve as an introduction to the contributions that follow, touching on each briefly. (Dr. Gary Adler's contribution to the volume fulfills that function with precision and clarity.) A different role for a preface is to highlight the significance of a publication for a variety of audiences. This will be my emphasis here. In publishing Douglas Kmiec's essay along with several strong commentaries, the Institute for Advanced Catholic Studies at the University of Southern California has added another contribution to its library of engaging volumes on topics of vital importance to the role of religion generally and Catholicism specifically in contemporary society.

The questions engaging secularity, modernity, and civil society (within states and transnationally) are of universal significance. States and cultures of very different histories, political traditions, and religious traditions have confronted and/or will confront some version of the issues which Kmiec and his commentators discuss in this work. Moreover, the universal significance of these themes does not suffer from emphasis provided at various points in the work on the Catholic and Western history of engaging secularity. As a complement, not a critique, to the following contributions, I propose here an addendum to the meaning of secularity and then two areas of application for the religion-secularity relationship, both of which have been addressed by Kmiec. He and his colleagues use the distinction between secularization and secularism to enter discussion of secularity. In this they reflect a wider body of literature that involves this dyad. I initially encountered these distinctions in Harvey Cox's *The Secular City* (1965). Personally, today, I would begin with the idea of "the secular." This move modifies some of the analysis in Kmiec et al., but not dramatically.

THE SECULAR

The secular/sacred antedates both the evolution of secularization and the rise of secularism. The secular/sacred distinction is cognate to the spiritual/temporal distinction that takes us back to at least the fifth century. The secular, as I read the term, refers to space and legitimacy. There is a secular space and sacral space in history, and within each there resides offices, functions, and authorities whose actions are presumptively legitimate and whose space should be respected. Viewed in these limited terms, the concept of the secular is a fundamental way to define social existence, and the concept is not inherently or intrinsically hostile to religion. There is some value in emphasizing this "neutral" concept of the secular because in the United States at least, a surprising amount of religious discussion begins with the premise that the secular is a hostile idea. This is surely not the understanding of the term or the reality in Catholic thought and history. As Kmiec indicates, the Pope Gelasius was an original source for the idea we now call secular.

SECULARIZATION

Secularization refers to a historical process through which spheres of activity (in the West) which once were the province of the Church became independent and were assumed by other institutions in society, most often by the state. The process usually was not total, evolving over centuries and finding its present status with a different balance within different countries. It reached an extreme in the twentieth century with totalitarian states of various forms suppressing any independent sectors of activity. The principal areas of activity impacted by secularization involved education, healthcare, and social services. The idea of the secular takes us back to the early history of the Church; secularization as a process has roots in the late Middle Ages and advanced rapidly in the modern era following the seventeenth century. The differentiated outcome of the process can be seen by comparing states within the West (Europe, the United Kingdom, and the United States) and then looking at selected examples in Asia (Japan, Singapore, Indonesia), and the patterns that evolved in post-colonial societies. Like "the secular," the process of secularization is not inherently opposed to the role of religion in society. However, an appropriate definition of religious freedom should include the right of religious communities to establish institutions of education, social services, and healthcare, if they can provide these services competently and in accord with reasonable standards. An aggressive conception of secularization that seeks to bring all forms of these activities exclusively under state control turns a legitimate process into a hostile atmosphere for religious communities, especially for those who see social engagement and service of the poor as obligatory dimensions of their faith. It also can rob civil society of creative and productive relationships between the modern state and religiously based social institutions.

SECULARISM

A key theme in Kmiec's essay is a distinction of two types of secularism (inclusive and exclusive). I do not find myself in a wholly different position from Kmiec, but, in my view, the move from a secular state to the idea of secularism needs further assessment. Unlike the neutral concept of the secular or the historical process of secularization, I would define secularism as a philosophical-legal position that acknowledges the realm of the sacred and the communities within that space but denies them public influence or significance. Secularism has a logical corollary, a "sacristy conception" of religion, that is, it has personal significance but not public standing. Secularism in this sense finds a corollary in aggressive secularization. It also renders "the secular" in a totalizing fashion. The Catholic tradition can live and has lived creatively and harmoniously with "the secular" and "secularization"; it cannot passively abide secularism as a fundamental concept for organizing society. There are ways to respect secularity and also provide a role for the public dimensions of faith.

RELIGION, LAW, POLITICS

The various forms of secularity find a central expression in the shaping of civil law. Law is the expression of the authority of the state, binding all members of a society. Particularly in pluralistic societies, with multiple moral and religious convictions among the citizenry, determining the content of civil law is a test of how secularity functions. The US example, its domestic law and policies, is a test case for determining the relationship of the secular state and the moral content of law and policy.

While an adequate treatment of this topic would require some survey of the classical categories of legal positivism and natural law conceptions of the validity of civil law, a more modest goal here is to structure the religion-politics relationship through the medium of civil law. This does not exhaust the secular/sacred (religion/politics) relationship, but it does address a major component of these terms covering a broad range of issues (bioethics, family and marriage, censorship, and art). In determining the respective spheres of religion and politics, the two terms do confront each other directly; in this encounter issues of religious freedom arise as do the legitimate scope of state authority involving policing power, taxation, and issues of safety, security, and equal treatment before the law. In the West these have been the classical "church-state" issues.

The sphere of the moral content of civil law, which governs everyone in society, raises different questions for religion and the state. Precisely because of the pluralistic nature of modern society, the direct transposition of religious conviction about doctrine into the positive law of society is highly problematical if not dangerous. Debates about the *religious meaning* of civil law rarely yield consensus. The *moral content* of civil law, however, offers a different mediating term between religion and politics. Moral discourse can be rooted in either religious or secular soil; in principle, therefore, the *moral content* of civil law can be argued publicly in either religious or secular terms. But the religious argument confronts the reality of pluralism, as does the purely secular argument. Civil law fits in the secular sphere of societal space. In shaping its normal content, the standard for all participants should be that wherever a moral position is rooted, it must be argued in terms that are comprehensible across the religious-secular divide. Appeals in public policy debate to the *dignity* of the human person engage a wider constituency than appeals to the *sacredness* of the person (even though our Christian discourse about dignity is grounded in sacredness). In socioeconomic debates about equality and fairness, Aquinas's invocation of Aristotle's categories of distributive and legal justice can evoke broader support than the direct transposition of the Hebrew prophets or the Sermon on the Mount into American political debate.

RELIGION, SECULARITY, AND WORLD POLITICS

The context for the previous example was US domestic society and the role of civil law. In that setting, respecting the secular character of the Constitution, the state and civil law is appropriate and most likely to move toward consensus. When the context changes from domestic policy to foreign policy some adaptation is needed. It is not that US foreign policy should be connected to a religious mission. It is rather that a global power, like the United States, must understand that what seems instinctively necessary domestically may, in other parts of the world, seem alien, intrusive, or threatening to deeply held religious or cultural values and customs. The highly structured secular/sacral (religion and politics) pattern in the United States cannot be the assumed model of analysis for understanding other parts of the world today. A form of secularity prevails in many states today and in global institutions (the United Nations, the International Monetary Fund, etc.) as well, but the *degree* of secularity assumed in US policy, in a secular press, in major academic institutions in the United States cannot be assumed in relating to others. A "strict separation" approach to religion and the state, a rigorous secular logic in civil law may miss a conception of society that other states and cultures possess and intend to sustain. Secularity is a pervasive force in the world, but it is embedded in cultures that pre-date the rise of modern philosophers of the secular. The United States has found a uniquely successful workable model for relating secular/sacral and religion/politics themes in its society. Kmiec usefully points out that interfaith dialogue has assumed new significance in a globalized world today. Such dialogue can help US policy to understand, respect, and engage quite different (often ancient) ways of adjudicating the sacral/secular relationships.

The Institute for Advanced Catholic Studies' volume should be welcomed today within religious communities and within the academic and policy communities where the meaning, content, and influence of secularity must be measured across a broad range of issues.

J. Bryan Hehir
Harvard Kennedy School of Government
July 2014

SECULARISM, CATHOLICISM, AND THE FUTURE OF PUBLIC LIFE

PART ONE

SECULARISM
AND CATHOLICISM

Introduction

Secularism, Democracy, and Catholicism

GARY J. ADLER, JR.

Rome and Jerusalem. The history of relations between institutions of religion and organs of the state is long, complex, and contested. Constantine's resolution—merging the projects of state-building with universalization of the Christian faith—held for a long time, setting a standard for stability. Nevertheless, recent centuries have been marked by episodes that demonstrate the complex diversity of institutional and legal "solutions" to religion-state relationships: the Westphalian division of Europe into homogenous confessional states, the rigid separation of faith from government by Ataturk after the Ottoman Empire's fall, and the two clauses of the US First Amendment.

For portions of the past century, the tensions undergirding this relationship seemed almost non-existent to most social scientists and to many American Catholics. The former, captive to a theory that predicted the unidirectional effects of modernity on religion, expected a reduction in belief and the collapse of religious behavior. The latter, celebrating the Second Vatican Council's *Dignitatis Humanae* and John F. Kennedy's public pacification of religious mistrust, exemplified by his talk to the Greater Houston Ministerial Association, enjoyed a new moment of freedom for a Church often burdened by its own machinations in state politics.

Needless to say, both social scientists and American Catholics now see vivid tensions between Church and state. The momentum of recent historical events fills headlines, from *Roe v. Wade* to the Arab Spring, from legal same-sex marriage to the Religious Right, from US health-care reform implementation to *hijabs* in Europe. The first part of each dyad in the previous sentence provides an example of state action—whether judicial, legislative, or executive—that changed the shape, and in some cases moral tenor, of public policy. The second part of each dyad provides an example of what José Casanova termed "public religion": the action of religious groups to transform the public sphere.[1] This brief list of issues and episodes, however, defies easy categorization, either about the direction of "religion" in this millennium or about the state insti-tutional arrangements that fit diverse political and ethnic situations. As some legal theorists and historians argue, the metaphor of "church-state" separation in the United States no longer captures the complexity of judicial interpretation on these matters; worse, it mis-states a complex history.[2]

How should we think about secularism and religion in democracy, in both the United States and abroad?

SCHOLAR, PUBLIC SERVANT, AND CATHOLIC: A CAREER OF RELIGION AND SECULARISM

In the fall of 2011—before the public conflict between Catholic offi-cials and the Obama administration over the contraceptive provision in United States healthcare reform—Douglas Kmiec was invited by the Institute for Advanced Catholic Studies at the University of Southern California to give a lecture that forms the basis of this book.

Kmiec has a long record of scholarship on constitutional law and public service, so his engagement with these topics is not new or super-ficial. Prior to holding his current position of the Caruso Family Chair at Pepperdine School of Law, Kmiec taught with distinction at Valpara-iso University School of Law, Notre Dame University Law School, and the Catholic University of America Columbus School of Law. He has served in the Office of Legal Counsel for presidents Ronald Reagan and George H. W. Bush and more recently as the US Ambassador to Malta for President Barack Obama. Serving three presidents and two political parties in an era of elite polarization and religious partisanship poses unusual challenges.

The back story does not disappoint. In early 2008, during the presidential campaign, Kmiec, a lifelong pro-life Republican, came out in public support of the Democratic senator Barack Obama. Kmiec's political endorsement led to controversy and personal suffering in the Catholic Church, including the denial of Communion to Kmiec by a priest during mass in Ventura County, California. After Obama's election, Kmiec was appointed US Ambassador to Malta in 2009. With this posting to a majority-Catholic country sitting astride the Southern European-Northern African border, Ambassador Kmiec undertook, with the explicit support of the president, a number of initiatives to encourage diplomatic engagement with communities of faith. After a public rebuke by the Inspector General of the State Department for this activity, Kmiec resigned on May 31, 2011. In the wake of his resignation, *Los Angeles Times* editorial writer and personal friend Timothy Rutten noted that

> over the last few years, Kmiec has emerged as one of this country's most important witnesses to the proposition that religious conviction and political civility need not be at odds; that reasonable people of determined good conscience, whatever their faith or lack thereof, can find ways to cooperate in the common good.[3]

On September 13, 2011, just after the ten-year anniversary of the 9/11 terrorist attacks on the United States, Kmiec gave the lecture that opens this book. In the chapter that emerged from that lecture, Kmiec marshals his broad experience as scholar, lawyer, ambassador, citizen, and Catholic. The Institute for Advanced Catholic Studies then asked other scholars from the United State and Europe to respond to Kmiec's argument.

UNDERSTANDING SECULARISM, DEVELOPING CATHOLICISM

Kmiec's chapter covers a broad range of legal issues and democratic theory quandaries. At moments he links then Pope Benedict XVI's vision of faith in public life with that of President Barack Obama; at others he reviews constitutional thought across three continents and two religious traditions. We invited each of the respondents to reflect on Kmiec's argument, doing so in a way that drew from their specific expertise and context. Together, Kmiec and his respondents raise several very important questions:

Is secularism alive?

Is secularism good for religion, for democracy?

Is the relationship of religion and state a matter of prudential tweaks, or is a substantial development needed in the jurisprudence of existing democracies?

What responsibility do religious actors have toward the common good when secular policy clashes with religious belief?

What contributions can the Catholic tradition make, if any, to the current regime of state-religion engagement in the United States?

The authors of these chapters approach these questions through different disciplines. However, they all do so in the midst of two important developments: a productive burst of scholarship on secularism, democracy, and religion and a Catholic Church facing fast-moving political and policy challenges. The contributors write with two voices: as analysts of secularism and religion, and as interlocutors with the Catholic tradition. These two components should make this volume's reflections useful not only to those interested in the topic of secularism but also those who wish to see the Catholic tradition contribute to the common good. Thus, the authors provide a snapshot view of topics related to church-state jurisprudence, sociological changes in religion, and foreign policy issues. They also suggest ways to deepen Catholic thought in an era after John Courtney Murray, when the scope of Catholic debate on "social issues" has been too narrowly defined (e.g., homosexuality, birth control, and abortion) and when the institutional Catholic Church struggles to renew social trust in the wake of its own sexual abuse scandal.

A brief review of recent scholarship on secularism and the state of the Catholic Church regarding such matters will enrich the reading of these chapters.

The strict "secularization thesis" of the twentieth century, which aligned the rise of modernity with the necessary collapse of religion, has died. *Requiescat in pace*. In its absence, affirmations of peaceful religious pluralism and poorly evidenced arguments about the natural "marketplace" of religious demand have given little insight into the complex existence of religious meaning, ritual, and identity in modernity.[4]

The chapters in this volume take a different direction. They directly address a central component of modern life in many nations, including most Western nations: *secularism*. Secularism stands in relationship to the cognates secular, secularity, and secularization.[5] Charles Taylor, in his widely discussed book, *A Secular Age*, delineated three forms of secularity.[6] That book focused primarily on what Taylor termed "secularity 3," the conditions of belief characterized by the Western social imaginary, a mode of experience that marginalizes transcendence and prioritizes the immanent aspects of social life. What Taylor termed "secularity 1" is the main topic here—the place of religion in public space and life. José Casanova, whose scholarship helped to loosen the grip of classic secularization theory, similarly notes that secularism can have a number of internal meanings. This volume focuses on one such meaning: "different legal-constitutional frameworks of separation of state and religion."[7]

Secularism so defined stands for the historical product of institutional differentiation: the separation (to varying degrees) of religious and sociopolitical institutions from each other. In national and social spaces characterized by secularism, political authority is no longer (or at least not fully) grounded on religious charisma or revelation. The mundane aspects of common life in a secular society—taxes, security, education, social welfare—are, to greater or lesser extents, organized by non-religious criteria. Secularism recognizes, at least implicitly, the priority of conscience and consequently stands in tension with political projects that attempt to homogenize belief. Secularization—the removal of religion *tout court*—is not an inevitable outcome of a society that incorporates secularism, understood as a commitment to the institutional separation of state and religion.

The social phenomenon of secularism can entail numerous dimensions: individual, organizational, cultural, and national. These dimensions have only recently been systematically investigated. Under the classic theory of secularization, they hardly seemed important: why attend to something that was exiting stage right? Today the creation, maintenance, and institutional boundary conflicts that constitute secularism are objects of intense research.[8] Ironically, scholars may have required confirmation of the relative *absence* of secularization in order to pay close attention to the social actors, movements, interest groups, practices, rituals, and mindsets that comprise the ongoing practice of secularism.[9] Secularism now usefully refers to those juridical norms, political institutions, political rights, religious rights, political behaviors, and religious behaviors that make up the wide array of state-religion regimes.

In a recent review of research on secularism, Gorski and Altinordu note that one product of events in the Islamic world is that the structures and processes behind the secularism within which Westerners, especially, live have been made more visible.[10] Contrary to facile claims about the disappearance of European religion, Casanova observes that "European societies may be highly secular, but European states are far from being secular or neutral."[11] The historical process that has produced the West's "secular age" is riddled with contradictions, a "zig-zag [path] . . . full of unintended consequences."[12] As Taylor argues regarding the West, the urges to organize society and reform religion, once unleashed, contributed in unanticipated ways to both the institutional location of religion in Western societies and the personal experience of believing in an era of many options.

Versions of secularism may compete or succeed each other across time within a country or a region, such as the "West." Elizabeth Shakman Hurd has shown that two versions of secularism—laicism and Judeo-Christian—structured much of the political life in the West over the last two centuries.[13] The developmental path of these secularisms, though, was not only the result of internal cultural shifts or political decisions. Hurd argues that the very concept of the "secular" in the West developed from an othering of Islam. The result, especially today, is that engage-ments between political life and Islam are seen in the West as "a threat to the privileged status of the private sphere and as a step towards theocracy."[14]

In this context, the Arab Spring is a vexing topic for many ob-servers who, in a pattern familiar to analyses of pre-1960s American Catholicism, predicted the incompatibility of a robust religious faith with democratic governance.[15] Concerns about state capture by anti-democratic forces through democratic means are real, particularly in cases where religious groups have ideologies that challenge state independence.[16] Yet, the exaggerated focus on this outcome as an either-or probability underplays real differences in democratic prac-tice that already exist in many countries, and that may come to exist as majority-Islamic societies navigate new waters.[17] To those who claim that the Western path is normative, the global patterns of state neu-trality and religious pluralism can be surprising. In India, a project of "principled distance" between religious authority and political power involves the reanimation of secularism in a moment when groups re-animate religious identities to constitute homogenous religious par-ties.[18] Craig Calhoun observes that "postcolonial societies around the world have given rise to most of the regimes of religious pluralism and religious tolerance" as states have managed co-existence amid reli-gious diversity.[19]

With this diversity in mind, "knowledge of the various forms of sec-ularism, with their attendant advantages and dilemmas, would be useful knowledge indeed."[20] The contributors to this volume wholeheartedly agree that such clear analysis is needed, but they add an important addi-tional dimension which, in their minds, makes a key contribution to this entire discussion: the internal self-reflection of the Catholic tradition. In other words, it would also be good to know how Catholic religious actors and institutions do and should think and act regarding the dy-namics of secularism.

In probing this, our contributors are immediately confronted with an opinion, among some anti-religious voices and some overly reli-gious ones, that religious belief and activity are necessarily opposed to secularism. Their approaches to the topic, though, give voice to a lively debate within the Catholic tradition, particularly about its intellectual resources for supporting certain configurations of secularism. Their contributions reveal different strands of Catholic thought and practice. The Catholic tradition, broadly understood, could be a multi-century rolling collection of case studies regarding historical relations between religion and state. In this regard, is it too much to say that Catholicism is similar to secularism: diverse, contested, and changing?

In the United States and Europe, the Catholic concerns of an earlier era included, respectively, state intrusion into private religious practice and the dismantling of clerical influence over national political life. Today, many concerns of the institutional Catholic Church in Europe and the United States hinge on claims about the morality of certain behaviors and state policies that make such behavior legal. Recent arguments from the Catholic hierarchy against same-sex marriage, for example, are not simply moral claims about the topics of homosexuality and marriage but are intertwined with an array of issues in Catholic life, such as the locus of moral teaching and different theological approaches to understanding sexuality.

The controversy that erupted from the Obama administration's January 2012 implementation of contraceptive coverage in healthcare reform highlights these very issues. Many observers might agree that agents of both state and religion stumbled in that argument. Was the quick deployment of religious conscience protection as the trump card in the disagreement the only Catholic response? After all, Catholic organizations in a number of states were already abiding under equivalent healthcare regulations. Was this church-state conflict an indicator of an aggressive state secularism, as the United States Conference of Catholic Bishops seemed to suggest with the "Fortnight for Freedom"? Either way, the episode did not bode well for careful negotiation of state-religion relationships. Our contributors step into this moment, bringing reflections that stretch both the democratic and Catholic traditions. In doing so they make better sense of secularism, not as a unidirectional structural process or political ideology, but as a process of institutional negotiation lodged in contexts of religious, cultural, and national diversity.

INTRODUCING THE CONTRIBUTORS' CHAPTERS

Chapter 1: Douglas W. Kmiec

Prompted by a high-profile 2011 decision from the European Court of Human Rights (*Lautsi and Others v. Italy*), which upheld an Italian mandate to display the crucifix in public school classrooms, Kmiec begins with a startling claim: that secularism has been crucified. In his opening pages, Kmiec suggests that "secular" Europe may be more hospitable to state engagement of religion than the "religious" United States and that President Barack Obama, who has been continuously confronted by US Catholic bishops, might be in close agreement with Pope Benedict XVI's vision of religion in democracy. He writes, "Obama, like the Holy Father, thus squarely challenges secularism and those who would urge that religion be banished from the public square." With such startling comparisons in tow, Kmiec provides a tour of core issues in religion-state relationships.

Kmiec claims that secularism is not necessarily anti-religious, but that the concept "secularism" contains a bewildering variety of tensions. He writes for an American, and Catholic, public that knows little about Islam and is distrustful of whether Islam is compatible with democracy. The worries about Islam, according to Kmiec, may grab headlines, but these tacit concerns about compatibility, tolerance, and inclusiveness regarding Islam (and Sharia) are best understood by delving into an analysis of actually existing religion state relationships and trajectories of thought within religious traditions.

Kmiec presents a spectrum of religion-state relationships that ranges from compelled theocracy to compelled atheism, both of which he rejects as anti-democratic. To understand the overwhelming majority of countries that lie in between, Kmiec introduces a distinction: whether the state's jurisprudence tends toward excluding or including religion. The *Lautsi* case shows the complexity of his project. When the European Court of Human Right's over-turned a lower court ruling, the Italian government was able to retain crucifixes in public classrooms. According to Kmiec, this stands in strong contrast to recent decades of US Supreme Court jurisprudence that interpreted the First Amendment's establishment clause to mean distant separation. As presented here, Europe and the United States have taken different approaches: Europe is inclusionary as to religious display, allowing the symbols of faith on equal terms. The United States is exclusionary as to religious displays. With this case as evidence, is it possible that secularism in Europe is dead, but run amok in the United States?

Not quite. Kmiec discusses how Islamic plaintiffs have fared in recent European cases. According to him, not well. While state establishment seems unproblematic for Christian faiths in the eyes of European Courts, many rulings express skepticism about the democratic propensities of Islam, with the effect of limiting Islamic practices and political parties.

For the United States, Kmiec's answer may disappoint some who see recent state-religion conflicts as signaling the decline of religious influence in the United States. For Catholic thought on these topics, the age of simply assuming a feasible congruence between natural law–derived public policy goals and actual political outcomes is long over. Yet, Kmiec claims to coincide with both the Pope and the president when he writes, "The relation between church and state cannot easily be hidden behind any wall, no matter how high, because the relation between law and morality within us is commonly inseparable from religious instruction."

Surprisingly, Kmiec suggests that religious groups have a large responsibility for the preservation of secularism in society. And so, in the latter portion of his chapter, he arrives at a long reflection about how Catholics should consider their involvement in democratic life. Here, Kmiec inserts a series of principles and criteria into a line of Catholic thought about democracy and political life. Reviewing Gelasius, Pope Leo XIII, and John F. Kennedy, Kmiec suggests the observance of prudent and sensitive lines between public and private spheres of responsibility. Different religions, including Catholicism, should enforce their distinct doctrines within the private sphere on those who have voluntarily joined the religious community. Regarding the public sphere, though, Kmiec is cautionary about how Catholics in an imperfect democracy should act in regard to a law that conflicts with their morality.

Kmiec writes that an "overstated claim of conscience . . . [is] expecting democracy to always coincide with one's own understanding, or our Church's understanding, of moral truth." Tacking a middle course, Kmiec continues by noting that the "perfect coincidence of ... [democracy and the Church's truth] would not be democracy but a theocracy or heaven itself." If the Catholic Church fails *through democratic means* to establish its morality into law, this is not in itself a moral evil. Further, the Church's public voice should recognize these limits, which would prevent culture war rhetoric. "No one of us can presume either to have government enforce the Catholic view on others or that Catholics will be exempted from a generally applicable law."

It is helpful to keep in mind that Kmiec actually wrote this text *prior* to the January 2012 contraception policy debate and the "Fortnight for Freedom" campaign in the United States. With this breadth of provocative thoughts based in jurisprudence, international comparison, Catholic thought, and democratic theory, Kmiec begins a stimulating conversation.

Part Two: Relations between Church and State

CHAPTER 2: MICHAEL ANDERHEIDEN

Dr. Michael Anderheiden, a professor at the Institute for Constitutional Law, Theory, and Philosophy at the University of Heidelberg, directly engages Kmiec's spectrum of ideal-type relationships between religion and the state. Anderheiden was invited to introduce the work of his late mentor Winfried Brugger, a recognized scholar on constitutional law, theory, and religion on both sides of the Atlantic.

As reviewed by Anderheiden, Brugger's work contributes a conceptual clarification about religion-state relationships. Brugger's starting point is not the assumed existence of two spheres, one religious and one political. Instead, he begins from the assumption of democracy: that democracy is a public good that should continue. From the unlikely starting place of the French tripartite motto *liberté, égalité, fraternité*, he draws out three models of relationship between religion and state. Each model displays a different depth of religion-state connection, solving some problems but causing others. In contrast to Kmiec's scheme, there is decidedly more uncertainty about how to categorize countries given Brugger's use of historical instead of juridical criteria.

None of his three models have *a priori* clear advantages, but "all three models of church-state relations ... ask for a minimum of religious tolerance for political reasoning." This chapter not only sparks discussion of the best categorization scheme for religion-state relationships, but reinforces the importance of pragmatic principles of political participation as discussed by Kmiec.

CHAPTER 3: GEOFFREY R. WATSON

Geoffrey Watson is a friend of Kmiec and is the other constitutional scholar represented in the volume. As his title notes, though, these affinities do not stop Watson from critical engagement with Kmiec. Watson, a Canadian by birth, is a professor of law in the Columbus School of Law at the Catholic University of America. Watson clerked for the chief judge of the US Court of Appeals for the Fourth Circuit and was attorney-advisor in the Office of the Legal Adviser of the US Department of State. He has written widely on legal topics, and his books include *The Capability Problem in Contract Law* (New York: Foundation Press, 2004) and *The Oslo Accords: International Law and the Israeli-Palestinian Peace Agreements* (Oxford: Oxford University Press, 2000).

Watson makes an important distinction between the United States and European legal settings, showing that in Europe, no legal architecture exists that parallels the US First Amendment's establishment clause. Thus, the *Lautsi* outcome should not be interpreted as a surprise and is thus no clear "win" for religion over secularism. Reviewing a range of European cases, Watson suggests that the differential treatment of Islam by the United States and Europe described by Kmiec may not be so clear. He cites evidence of European court decisions against Christian religious groups that are similar to decisions against Islamic groups.

Recent years have seen a wide literature suggesting typologies of state-religion relationships. To this literature, Watson suggests a scheme oriented around the two poles of free expression and establishment. Referring to a Rawlsian method of the "original position," he argues that establishment issues are not as important as free exercise issues: individual persons in any society would likely be more concerned about the latter than the former. If establishment issues are not so important, then, court rulings about establishment, like *Lautsi,* do not reveal much about the state of secularism (or religion).

Part Three: The Catholic Church, Moral Authority, and Secularism

CHAPTER 4: HANS JOAS

Hans Joas, the Ernst Troeltsch Professor of the Sociology of Religion in the Theological Faculty at Humboldt University of Berlin, and a Member of the Committee on Social Thought at the University of Chicago, engages Kmiec's discussion about recent American Catholic involvement in political life. Joas does so through simultaneous reflection on the religious and democratic thought of a leading member of the American Catholic hierarchy, Francis Cardinal George of Chicago. Joas has written widely on social theory, religion, and pragmatism; his books include *Faith as an Option: Possible Futures for Christianity* (Palo Alto, CA: Stanford University Press, 2014), *The Sacredness of the Person: A New Genealogy of Human Rights* (Washington, DC: Georgetown University Press, 2013), and *Do We Need Religion? On the Experience of Self-Transcendence* (Boulder, CO: Paradigm, 2008).

Writing with a European experience in mind, Joas puzzles at the state of American Catholic democratic engagement. "Is secularism really the enemy of democracy?" he asks. He suggests that some Catholics see a French-like exclusion of religion from the public sphere coming in the near future to the United States. For Joas, then, one of Kmiec's contributions is the pragmatic yet principled way that Kmiec discusses the role of religious organizations or persons whose conscience is threatened by social or political developments. Instead of withdrawal and conflict in these situations, more engagement, respect, and dialogue are needed because of the reality of diversity and the dangers of coercion. Secularism is a good, not an evil, and the main way to construct and tend that good is through democratic engagement. Joas suggests, too, that this engagement will require transformations in Christian self-understanding, transformations that are in significant tension with current modes of Catholic thinking and practice. Finally, he concludes with a social scientist's eye to the diversity of religious life, citing Ernst Troeltsch's colorful description of "Catholicism," which is anything but homogenous.

CHAPTER 5: MASSIMO FRANCO

Massimo Franco is a political columnist for *Corriere della Sera* and author of *The Crisis in the Vatican Empire: From the Death of John Paul II to the Resignation of Benedict XVI: Why the Church Has Become the New Global Culprit* (New York: Open Road, 2013); *Parallel Empires: The Vatican and the United States, Two Centuries of Alliance and Conflict* (New York: Doubleday-Random House, 2009); and *C'era una volta un Vaticano-Perché la Chiesa sta perdendo peso in Occidente* (*Once there was a Vatican: Why the Church is losing influence in the West*) (Segrate, IT: Mondadori, 2010). With extensive journalistic experience covering the Vatican, Franco writes a provocative account of how to understand the Vatican's anxiety about European culture and the Vatican's power given the sexual abuse scandal.

According to Franco, the new millennium began with a situation in which loud European Christian voices were primarily intolerant ones, claiming a "Western identity" that was more ethnic and nationalistic than religious. This portrayal aligns with Kmiec's concern that Islamic practice is unfairly treated in Europe. However, Franco continues this cultural analysis in an organizational analysis of the Vatican. Soon after Islamic worries began, the sexual, fiscal, and diplomatic scandals of the Vatican erupted into public view.

In this context, Franco holds that secularization of the Vatican's authority and voice occurred because of the "secularization of sin." With this controversial phrase, Franco suggests that the Vatican's reaction to the sexual abuse scandal reveals that it has not changed, but that the times have. During the Cold War the Vatican anchored a moral cause and was beyond reproach. Today, that is no longer the case. The sexual abuse crisis—and subsequent revelations of organizational failure—is not seen as an unfortunate mistake by a privileged social institution but a crime over which the state should have authority. As Franco writes, "The 'moral unipolarism' of the Vatican is deeply under scrutiny . . . if not over."

Addressing Kmiec's portrayal of *Lautsi* as a victory against secularism, Franco thinks it is a pyrrhic one. The government briefs in the *Lautsi* case had to do with Western identity, not Catholicism. The roster of countries submitting briefs shows an East-West divide, in which the formerly Communist countries of Eastern Europe argue for a (Western) religious identity that seems unsupported by actual Western European countries. Can the Vatican re-claim its moral authority? Will the Vatican be able to address a new cultural context? Can European religious identity avoid the pitfalls of nationalism and xenophobia? For these questions, Franco writes, "Kmiec acts as a rhabdomancer to discover how our societies' values will be shaped by religion, or by the lack of religion in the next years."

Part Four: Secularism and International Affairs

CHAPTER 6: ERIN K. WILSON

Erin K. Wilson is the director of the Center for Religion, Conflict, and the Public Domain at the University of Groningen. A scholar of Australian origin, Wilson's writings on democracy, human rights, refugees, and global justice provide a theoretical structure for making sense of religion within a complex process of globalization without relying on the facile assertions of earlier writing on secularization. Wilson's published works include two recent books, *After Secularism: Rethinking Religion in Global Politics* (New York: Palgrave Macmillan, 2011) and *Justice Globalism: Ideology, Crises, Policy* (Thousand Oaks, CA: Sage, 2013).

Wilson begins by noting that Kmiec's discussion of secularism tends toward a focus on state institutional processes, especially those engagements with religion governed by judicial decisions. Wilson argues that an important turn in scholarship on secularism focuses on its Western ideological structure, which portrays religious belief and practice as irrational, unimportant, and corrosive to political life. Consequently, the effects of secularism cannot be easily hemmed in by political and institutional arrangements. This ideological structure is especially pernicious because it portrays itself as neutral, universal, "public," and exportable despite its deep historical and cultural connection to specific contexts.

Somewhat ironically, the success of another ideological force—neoliberal globalization—has provided evidence of how the reigning ideology of secularism is inadequate for fully understanding religion in the contemporary world. Religious groups and ideals have been at the forefront of efforts, especially transnational ones, to push back against the inhumane economic and political outcomes of neoliberalism. They often work outside global institutions in which the secular ideology is embedded and which are thus suspicious of religious motivation and uncomfortable with religious actors outside of "official" religious structures.

Wilson's respect for the power of religious ideals and the role of religious groups in modernity is very similar to Kmiec's, but the analysis of the current situation leads to very different conclusions. For Wilson, the secular state project as it currently exists imperils religion. The *Lautsi* decision reflects how the state, with secular ideology, retains power over religion by supporting only those religious groups that further secular state goals. So what can be done? Wilson briefly reviews some possible ways forward, suggesting that "the boundaries between public and private do not need to be more clearly delineated but instead done away with entirely and new forms of understanding the entanglement of the religious and secular, sacred and profane, immanent and transcendent explored."

CHAPTER 7: STEPHEN CALLEYA

Stephen Calleya is the director of the Mediterranean Academy of Diplomatic Studies and associate professor of International Relations at the University of Malta. During Kmiec's ambassadorial appointment to Malta, Calleya and Kmiec hosted a number of meetings and discussions around issues related to religion, immigration, security, and the Arab Spring. Calleya's works include *Regionalism in the Post–Cold War World* (Surrey, UK: Ashgate, 2000) and *Evaluating Euro-Mediterranean Relations* (London: Routledge, 2005).

Calleya presents a portrait of the intricate international relations occurring through the space of the Mediterranean. Malta is on the geographic boundary of two continents, situated between various religious traditions, states, and economic forces. From this vantage point,

Calleya demonstrates that the forces that drive many of Europe's cultural "crises," such as immigration and Islamic diversity, are inadequately addressed by European states. Islamic immigrants are poorly engaged by receiving countries. This situation, along with cultural exclusion, creates new problems.

With this detail, Calleya gives a twist to Kmiec's notion of inclusionary secularism. Such a legal regime should not merely include "religion." In a situation where "religion" is increasingly constituted by multiculturalism, the appropriate strategy is to include cultural and ethnic diversity alongside religious diversity.[21] Written a year after Kmiec's original lecture, Calleya's chapter takes advantage of that time span to provide additional thoughts about the Arab Spring. Noting the lack of coherent engagement by European countries with the deep issues of the uprisings, Calleya writes that it is "astonishing to see the EU adopt a navel gazing attitude towards the historic moment taking place in the Mediterranean." Calleya agrees with Kmiec that if Europe were to take up greater engagement, there is quite a bit of inclusionary work with Islam to be done.

NOTES

1. José Casanova, *Public Religions in the Modern World* (Chicago: University of Chicago Press, 1994).
2. Philip Hamburger, *Separation of Church and State* (Cambridge, MA: Harvard University Press, 2002); Michael W. McConnell, "Reclaiming the Secular and the Religious: The Primacy of Religious Autonomy," *Social Research* 76, no. 4 (2009).
3. Timothy Rutten, "A Voice for Faith-Based Diplomacy Is Muffled," *Los Angeles Times*, April 13, 2011, http://articles.latimes.com/2011/apr/13/opinion/la-oe-0413-rutten-20110413.
4. Philip S. Gorski and Ateş Altinordu, "After Secularization?" *Annual Review of Sociology* 34 (2008).
5. José Casanova, "The Secular, Secularizations, Secularisms," in *Rethinking Secularism*, ed. Craig Calhoun, Mark Juergensmeyer, and Jonathan Van Antwerpen (New York: Oxford University Press, 2011), 66.
6. Charles Taylor, *A Secular Age* (Cambridge, MA: Belknap Press, 2007).
7. Casanova, "The Secular, Secularizations, Secularisms."

8. Philip S. Gorski et al., eds., *The Post-Secular in Question: Religion in Contemporary Society* (New York: Social Science Research Council and New York University Press, 2012).

9. James A. Beckford, "SSSR Presidential Address: Public Religions and the Postsecular: Critical Reflections," *Journal for the Scientific Study of Religion* 51, no. 1 (2012).

10. Gorski and Altinordu, "After Secularization?"

11. Casanova, "The Secular, Secularizations, Secularisms," 70.

12. Taylor, *Secular Age*, 95.

13. Elizabeth Shakman Hurd, *The Politics of Secularism in International Relations* (Princeton, NJ: Princeton University Press, 2008).

14. Ibid., 119.

15. Gorski and Altinordu, "After Secularization?"

16. Nancy J. Davis and Robert V. Robinson, *Claiming Society for God: Religious Movements and Social Welfare in Egypt, Israel, Italy, and the United States* (Bloomington: Indiana University Press, 2012).

17. Abdullahi Ahmed An-Na'im, "Islam and Secularism," in *Comparative Secularisms in a Global Age*, ed. Linell E. Cady and Elizabeth Shakman Hurd (New York: Palgrave Macmillan, 2010).

18. Rajeev Bhargava, "The Future of Secularism," in *The Future of Secularism*, ed. T. N. Srinivasan (New York: Oxford University Press, 2007); Rajeev Bhargava, "Rehabilating Secularism," in *Rethinking Secularism*, ed. Craig Calhoun, Mark Juergensmeyer, and Jonathan Van Antwerpen (New York: Oxford University Press, 2011).

19. Craig Calhoun, "Rethinking Secularism," *Hedgehog Review* Fall (2010): 42.

20. Gorski and Altinordu, "After Secularization?" 76.

21. Tariq Modood, "Is There a Crisis of Secularism in Western Europe?" *Journal for the Scientific Study of Religion* 73, no. 2 (2012).

Chapter 1

Secularism Crucified?

DOUGLAS W. KMIEC

RELIGION AND POLITICS—YET AGAIN

The late Henry Hyde is the senator whose name is on the Hyde Amendment limiting federal funding in the United States for most abortions; he once gave a talk at the Notre Dame Law School at my invitation in the run-up to the 1984 presidential election. The senator began his talk by quipping: "Someone has remarked that this must be an election year. Everyone's talking about theology."[1] The theology buzzword for some time in American politics has been secularism.

It is not surprising, therefore, that the Holy Father would have raised the issue of secularism on a number of occasions.[2] In his first visit to the United States in April 2008, Pope Benedict XVI urged that the

Editor's Note: The original version of this chapter was delivered as a talk by Ambassador Kmiec on September 13, 2011, as part of the Robert and Elizabeth Plumleigh Speakers Series at the Institute for Advanced Catholic Studies at the University of Southern California. This chapter was completed in late 2011. For extension into numerous political, diplomatic, and religious developments since that time, please see the final chapter. A law review citation style is used for this chapter to reflect its style of legal argumentation.

1. Henry Hyde, Congressman, Address at the University of Notre Dame Law School: Keeping God in the Closet: Some Thoughts on the Exorcism of Religious Values from Public Life (Sept. 24, 1984), transcript *available at* http://archives.nd.edu/research/texts/hyde.htm (last visited Oct. 13, 2011).
2. *Editor's Note:* As of 2015, Pope Benedict XVI is Holy Father *Emeritus*.

practice of Catholicism more greatly infuse public policy.[3] This sentiment was urged as well by presidential aspirant Newt Gingrich. In a 2011 prayer breakfast presentation, Gingrich agreed with Pope Benedict—which is likely a good thing for a newly converted Catholic to do.[4] He bemoaned the attempt to exclude God from American culture, using such examples as the banning of school prayer; repeated efforts to have the courts strike "one nation under God" from the Pledge of Allegiance; and Supreme Court decisions disallowing overt references to religion in public life.[5]

However, following the pope's instruction as Mr. Gingrich would see it would seem disagreeable to Bill Keller, now-former executive editor and continuing columnist of the *New York Times*. In a preelection column, Keller likened a presidential candidate who relies on faith in public matters to a candidate who might believe that "space aliens dwell among us."[6] The column was cleverly, if irreverently, written, with Keller stating that such a belief "might not disqualify the candidate out of hand.... But I would certainly want to ask a few questions. Like . . . does he talk to the aliens? Do they have an economic plan?"[7]

In his column, Keller argued that we should not be "squeamish" about asking faith questions when a candidate has relied on faith to win public approval.[8] This is a fairer proposition than that faced by the late John F. Kennedy (JFK), who—at a time when Catholicism made one suspect in the American political milieu—went about declaring that he

---

3. Pope Benedict XVI, Responses of His Holiness Benedict XVI to the Questions Posed by the Bishops (Apr. 16, 2008), http://www.vatican.va/holy_father/benedict_xvi/speeches/2008/april/documents/hf_ben-xvi_spe_20080416_response-bishops_en.html.
4. Newt Gingrich, Address at the National Catholic Prayer Banquet (Apr. 27, 2011), transcript *available at* http://www.washingtontimes.com/blog/watercooler/2011/apr/27/transcript-gingrich-addresses-national-catholic-pr/ (last visited Oct. 13, 2011).
5. *Id.*
6. Bill Keller, *Asking Candidates Tougher Questions about Faith*, N.Y. TIMES, Aug. 25, 2011, http://www.nytimes.com/2011/08/28/magazine/asking-candidates-tougher-questions-about-faith.html?_r=1&scp=1&sq=%22space+aliens%22&st=nyt.
7. *Id.*
8. *Id.*

would not rely on his faith to make public decisions, and that he would not expect Church officials to tell him what to do.[9]

Mr. Keller has a number of questions for so-called believer candidates such as Mr. Gingrich, the most essential of which was whether they elevate "the Bible, the Book of Mormon (the text, not the Broadway musical) or some other authority higher than the Constitution and laws of this country."[10] Keller explains that it would matter to him "whether a president respects serious science and verifiable history [and that he also cares] if religious doctrine becomes an excuse to exclude my fellow citizens from the rights and protections our country promises."[11]

Article VI of the US Constitution provides that "no religious Test shall ever be required as a Qualification to any Office or public Trust under the United States."[12] It is not a violation of this Clause to make reasonable inquiry of personal belief. The Clause is aimed at precluding a religious Test instituted in law to qualify for office; it does not preclude informed inquiry by voters.

So what specifically might Mr. Keller wish to ask a candidate?

The key question, from the text of his column, would seem to be this: If there is a conflict between the candidate's faith and the Constitution, how would the candidate resolve it? Presumably the right answer here, to Keller, is to give preference to the Constitution as the "Supreme Law." Yet Catholics and other people of faith in Europe and the United States nourish the idea of "conscientious exception," remembering the good example of Thomas More and the tragic consequences of the Holocaust

9. In a famous speech to the Greater Houston Ministerial Association in 1960, while campaigning for president, John F. Kennedy Jr. stated: "I believe in an America where the separation of church and state is absolute—where no Catholic prelate would tell the President (should he be Catholic) how to act, and no Protestant minister would tell his parishioners for whom to vote—where no church or church school is granted any public funds or political preference—and where no man is denied public office merely because his religion differs from the President who might appoint him or the people who might elect him." Senator John F. Kennedy, Address to the Greater Houston Ministerial Association (Sept. 12, 1960), transcript *available at* http://www.jfklibrary.org/Research/Ready-Reference/JFK-Speeches/Address-of-Senator-John-F-Kennedy-to-the-Greater-Houston-Ministerial-Association.aspx (last visited Oct. 13, 2011).

10. Keller, *supra* note 6.

11. *Id.*

12. U.S. CONST. rt. VI.

in disregard of limits of positive law to discharge our duty to fellow man. Curiously, Mr. Keller also wants to know from Texas governor Rick Perry and other "believer" candidates whether they think that the United States is a Judeo-Christian nation (and if so, what that would mean in practice?); and whether a candidate would have any hesitation about appointing Muslims or atheists to public office.[13]

The last question is particularly interesting because, in the context of the *New York Times* article, Mr. Keller's implication is that open-mindedness would not exclude the appointment of a Muslim citizen to public office. Intuitively, a believer in religious pluralism and interfaith dialogue, such as myself, would tend to concur.

A Preliminary Inquiry into Islam's Compatibility with Democracy

What is to be made of the fact that the European Court of Human Rights (ECHR), a respected, effective, and on occasion progressive court, has reached the conclusion that Sharia (Islamic law) is essentially incompatible with "the fundamental principles of democracy"?[14] As the ECHR saw it in its 2001 decision of *Refah Partisi v. Turkey*, the inconsistency stems from the fact that Sharia, when faithfully applied, reflects the rules of the past embedded in a particular religious tradition that is "invariable."[15] By contrast, the court reasoned, democratic systems thrive on pluralism and the constant evolution of public freedoms and their redefinition or expansion.[16] Beyond that, the ECHR also found that Sharia diverges from values of the European Convention on Human Rights with respect to criminal law and procedure, the legal status of women, and the regular interventions of Sharia into all spheres

---

13. Keller, *supra* note 6.
14. Refah Partisi v. Turkey, App. No. 41340/98, 35 Eur. H. R. Rep. 56, 87 (2001). The 2001 judgment, handed down by a Chamber of the Third Section of the ECHR, affirmed the constitutionality of the dissolution of the Refah Partisi political party in Turkey. The decision was later referred to the Grand Chamber of the ECHR, which affirmed the Third Section's judgment. *See* Refah Partisi v. Turkey, App. No. 41340/98, 37 Eur. H. R. Rep. 3 (2003).
15. Refah Partisi v. Turkey, App. No. 41340/98, 35 Eur. H. R. Rep. 56, 87 (2001).
16. *Id.*

of private life on the basis of religious precept.[17] While it can be argued that the ECHR decision—a case affirming the ordered dissolution of the Islamist political party, Refah, in Turkey—might be valid only in the context of the sensitive and specific situation as it exists in Turkey,[18] the court's considerations have been repeated elsewhere, especially insofar as Sharia would seem to contest the essential equality of men and women that is at the core of European Convention jurisprudence.[19]

Of course, nothing in theory would preclude an Islamic believer from serving in public office by denying—à la John F. Kennedy—any desire to impose Islamic belief on non-consenting fellow Americans. Yet the validity of such a denial cannot just be assumed, as passages in the Qur'an proclaim the Sharia to govern all of life.[20] Indeed, the idea that law can be separated from morality vis-à-vis Islamic belief has been described as "devilishly off track."[21] The positivist notion that law is merely

17. *Id.*
18. The Turkish government has pursued implementation of particularly "exclusionary . . . policies toward religion" which have been argued to be "products of dominant assertive secularist ideology." AHMET T. KURU, SECULARISM AND STATE POLICIES TOWARD RELIGION: THE UNITED STATES, TURKEY, AND FRANCE 163 (2009).
19. According to the European Court of Human Rights, "Gender equality [is] recognised by the European Court as one of the key principles underlying the [European] Convention [on Human Rights] and a goal to be achieved by Member States of the Council of Europe. . . ." Sahin v. Turkey, App. No. 44774/98, 41 Eur. H. R. Rep. 109, 133 (2005). Many authors, however, have commented on Sharia's seeming incompatibility with democratic ideals, including the notion of gender equality. *See,* e.g., ELIE KEDOURIE, DEMOCRACY AND ARAB POLITICAL CULTURE 5–6 (1994) ("The idea of representation, of elections, of popular suffrage, of political institutions being regulated by laws laid down by a parliamentary assembly, of these laws being guarded and upheld by an independent judiciary, the ideas of the secularity of the state, of society being composed of a multitude of self-activating, autonomous groups, and associations—all these are profoundly alien to the Muslim political tradition."); Ziba Mir-Hosseini, *Muslim Women's Quest for Equality: Between Islamic Law and Feminism,* 32 CRITICAL INQUIRY 629, 629 (2006), *available at* http://www.smi.uib.no/seminars/Mir-Hosseini/Questforequality.pdf ("Muslim jurists claim, and all Muslims believe, that justice and equality are intrinsic values and cardinal principles in Islam and the sharia. If this is the case, in a state that claims to be guided by the sharia, why are justice and equality not reflected in the laws that regulate gender relations and the rights of men and women? Why do Islamic jurisprudential texts—which define the terms of the sharia—treat women as second-class citizens and place them under men's domination?").
20. RAJ BHALA, UNDERSTANDING ISLAMIC LAW (SHARIA), xxi (2011).
21. *Id.*

the command of the sovereign is to a Muslim "puzzling, absurd, or even heretical."[22] In any event, Islamic adherence to Sharia law would pose exactly the problems of compelled Christian theocracy about which Mr. Keller seems most concerned with respect to the Republican primary candidates. An Islamic scholar directly likens this aspect of Sharia to the thought of Augustine, Aquinas, and Dr. Martin Luther King Jr., all of whom took the view that "a secular law that violates God's law is no law at all."[23]

From these considerations and comparisons, therefore, we should not indulge the notion that Muslims are more suspect than Christians in terms of their possible service in public office. At a minimum, it may be sacrilegious, but nevertheless accurate, to say that every person is in some sense his or her own religion; as in Christian practice, each individual ends up being the keeper of his or her own conscience. (Such a statement is not in contradiction of the Holy Father, who makes the different point that we cannot be our own life project. Our existence, purpose, and meaning are wholly dependent upon our Creator.[24] The textual point is merely that discovering the full meaning of God's ownership of us is something for which we are individually responsible.)

In modern times, religious enforcement mechanisms in Christianity are weak—deliberately so, for we are to remove the beam from our own eye before finding the splinter in our neighbor's?[25] Can we assume this is true of Muslim believers as well, with regard to any sanctions or instructions imposed by their own faith? Admittedly, the scope of Islamic enforcement methods is not as clear as in Catholicism, especially as we factor in geographic space. For example, in Islam, drinking alcohol (*shrub al-khamr*) is considered a crime against Allah (praise be unto him).[26] However, the punishment for such a crime can vary widely; in Saudi Arabia, both Muslims and non-Muslims would be subject to the

22. *Id.*

23. *Id.*

24. Pope Benedict XVI, Message of the Holy Father Benedict XVI on the Occasion of the Twenty-Fifth World Youth Day (Mar. 28, 2010), *available at* http://www.vatican. va/holy_father/benedict_xvi/messages/youth/documents/hf_ben-xvi_mes_ 20100222_youth_en.html.

25. *See Matthew* 7:5.

26. BHALA, *supra* note 20, at 1237.

sanction of flogging.[27] By contrast, in the Islamic country of Jordan, alcohol is easily obtainable.[28] The various ways in which Muslim belief either directs or prohibits or sanctions departures from orthodoxy have to be sensitively evaluated before we can reach a conclusion that Islam is categorically antagonistic to democracy writ large.

Walls of Separation—Do They Resolve or Worsen Religious Controversy?

The conundrum of faith versus obedience to laws contrary to faith is not easily resolved. Indeed, one of the strongest temptations for a high wall of separation between church and state is the expectation that this bright line or high wall resolves these clashes. That is illusory, however; rather, this line merely hides them and uses the blunt edge of secularism to suppress the true nature of the faith of the believer. What would be lost in a wholly secular state is well captured in the June 5, 2011, World Atheist Convention Declaration on "Secularism and the Place of Religion in Public Life."[29] While a close reading of this declaration shows that its statements coincide with some of the recommendations of the author to reduce unnecessary clashes among religious believers,[30] exclusionary secularists as well as some atheists go well beyond eliminating potential for divisiveness. One atheist objective is to attempt to suppress believers' yearning to know human purpose in a transcendent sense. This creates another source of division. In this regard, the World Atheist Convention Declaration indulges the idea of censoring faith-based arguments out of public policy debate.[31]

27. Adli Hawaari, *Getting a Drink in Saudi Arabia*, BBC News, Feb. 8, 2001, http://news. bbc.co.uk/2/hi/middle_east/1160846.stm.

28. *Id.*

29. Michael Nugent, *Dublin Declaration on Secularism and the Place of Religion in Public Life* (June 8, 2011), Atheist Ireland Blog, http://www.atheist.ie/2011/06/ dublin-declaration-on-secularism-and-the-place-of-religion-in-public-life/.

30. *Id.* ("Freedom of conscience, religion and belief are private and unlimited. Freedom to practice religion should be limited only by the need to respect the rights and freedoms of others. . . . The state should be strictly neutral in matters of religion and its absence, favouring none and discriminating against none.").

31. *Id.* ("The State should be based on democracy, human rights and the rule of law. Public policy should be formed by applying reason, and not religious faith, to evidence.").

Rejecting the preceding suggestion, the US Supreme Court is adamantly opposed to government censorship of content. The Court expresses that opposition by demanding that any attempted censorship survive strict scrutiny through a so-called compelling justification for limiting speech on matters of public concern. In a few cases, the Court has carved out a limited number of narrowly defined[32] categories of low or no value speech—for example, hate speech[33] or so-called fighting words or obscenity. However, even within categories of unprotected speech, the Court is watchful for regulation that creates uneven suppression of ideas.

The powerful protection enjoyed by political speech today is perhaps best illustrated by the extent to which speech that is almost universally disdained (e.g., the symbolic burning of the national flag or loud, repulsive homophobic shouting outside the funeral service for a member of the military)[34] has been protected under our Free Speech or First Amendment jurisprudence. The US Supreme Court refuses to permit government to be selective in the punishment or civil liability even for

32. In some cases, the categories survive without any modern example.
33. *See* R.A.V. v. City of St. Paul, 505 U.S. 377, 382–383 (1992) ("From 1791 to the present ... our society, like other free but civilized societies, has permitted restrictions upon the content of speech in a few limited areas [such as defamation, obscenity, or 'fighting words'], which are 'of such slight social value as a step to truth that any benefit that may be derived from them is clearly outweighed by the social interest in order or morality.'") (quoting Chaplinsky v. New Hampshire, 315 U.S. 568, 572 (1942)).
34. In Snyder v. Phelps, the US Supreme Court held that hateful speech conveyed on signs displayed by the Westboro Baptist Church, while they picketed the funeral of a soldier which took place on public property, fell within the scope of First Amendment protection; this shielded the group from tort liability. Snyder v. Phelps, 131 S. Ct. 1207, 1220 (2011). Although the speech caused pain to the family of the deceased soldier, the content of the group's signage "plainly relate[d] to ... matters of public import," such as "the political and moral conduct of the United States and its citizens, the fate of the Nation, homosexuality in the military, and scandals involving the Catholic clergy. . . ." *Id.* at 1216–1217. In his opinion, Chief Justice John Roberts wrote that, while "speech is powerful ... [and] can ... inflict great pain, as a Nation we have chosen ... to protect even hurtful speech on public issues to ensure that we do not stifle public debate." *Id.* at 1220.
    In contrast, while Article 10 of the European Convention on Human Rights provides that "everyone has the right to freedom of expression," ECHR case law has established that hate speech is "not protected by Article 10 ... and therefore can be restricted by governments [[of Europe] in their national law." COUNCIL OF EUROPE, FACT SHEET: HATE SPEECH (Nov. 2008), at 1, www.coe.int/t/DC/Files/Source/FS_hate_en.doc.

hateful speech that, absent that selectivity, would fall outside constitutional protection. In the United States, government censorship is to be avoided even at the cost of leaving hurtful expression un-remedied.[35]

An important question arises: If even forms of articulated hatred are shielded from government censorship, why exclude faith-based expression from the public debate, which is often the highest form of speech to a believing individual? In this respect, when we expansively protect freedom of expression, should we not also find the free exercise of religion to be strengthened?

As one author has put it:

> Pope John Paul II spoke for Christians and Muslims alike when he said: "Even if some are reluctant to refer to the religious dimension of human beings and human history, even if others want to consign religion to the private sphere, even if believing communities are persecuted, Christians will still proclaim that religious experience is part of human experience. It is a vital element in shaping the person and the society to which people belong."[36]

If John Paul II was correct, an exclusionary understanding of the separation of church and state—or secularism—cuts deeply against human experience itself; it is asking men and women to deny their essential being. To the extent that one's beliefs of faith seek to influence or transform the law (and most, if not all, do), restraining that yearning for reform comes at a high cost.

Resolving Religious Conflict Necessitates Interfaith Understanding

The difficulty of reconciling faith with public law is compounded by how little we know of each other's faiths or religious practices. One of the

---

35. Snyder, supra.
36. BHALA, *supra* note 20, at xxii (quoting Pope John Paul II, Address of the Holy Father at the Exchange of Greetings with the Diplomatic Corps (Jan. 13, 2001), *available at* http://www.vatican.va/holy_father/john_paul_ii/speeches/2001/documents/hf_jp-ii_spe_20010113_diplomatic-corps_en.html).

most attractive features of Barack Obama, as a candidate in past senatorial and presidential election contests, was his appreciation of this difficulty. It was my privilege to be appointed by President Obama as US Ambassador to the Republic of Malta in 2009 with the special purpose of exploring ways in which we could learn more about each other's faith traditions, and then utilize this greater knowledge to mitigate cultural clash by faith-informed diplomatic means. The need for promoting interfaith understanding is great; for instance, a Pew Forum Study in 2010 showed that many Americans are ignorant about major world religions, even including their own.[37] The situation is not much better in Europe, where there have been recommendations for greater inclusion of religion-focused education in classrooms.[38] In survey work done through the US Embassy in Malta, we ascertained that less than 5 percent of American secondary schools engage in any form of comparative religious curriculum. The number is not much better in Europe, tending to fall somewhere between 10 and 15 percent.

While I was ambassador, significant embassy efforts sought to enhance interfaith dialogue and to ascertain whether faith-based methods could be successful in reducing conflict while at the same time observing our own constitutional commitment to the freedom of religion. Unfortunately, the stranglehold of secularism within the Department of State was compounded by a mistaken (really out of date) understanding of existing Establishment Clause jurisprudence by the legal advisor, and an inspector general either unaware of or unwilling to defer to a presidential directive. Admittedly, the State Department was being asked to accept a somewhat novel role for an ambassador; and

---

37. PEW FORUM ON RELIGION & PUB. LIFE, *U.S. Religious Knowledge: Survey* (Sept. 28, 2010), http://pewforum.org/Other-Beliefs-and-Practices/U-S-Religious-Knowledge-Survey.aspx) ("Large numbers of Americans are uninformed about the tenets, practices, history and leading figures of major faith traditions—including their own.").

38. *See,* e.g., INSTITUT EUROPEEN EN SCIENCES DES RELIGIONS, RELIGION IN EDUCATION: CONTRIBUTION TO DIALOGUE 3 (Mar. 19, 2009), *available at* http://www.iesr. ephe.sorbonne.fr/docannexe/file/5592/policy_rec_version_c_2_final_20_03_09. pdf ("At a European level we suggest making room in the classroom for dialogue and discussion about and between different religious (and non-religious) worldviews. . . . Education policy development and implementation need to focus on the transformation of abstract (passive) tolerance into practical (active) tolerance.").

despite White House efforts to establish this unusual line of authority, it was not observed. This led the inspector general to throw up her hands and proclaim that the interfaith initiative was outside the interests of government.[39]

This should only be a temporary setback. The director of the White House Faith-Based Office retains the president's confidence. There is far too much at stake for bureaucratic interference to be permitted to undo the positive application of the president's thoughtful analysis given at Cairo University in June 2009 of the relations between Islam and the United States. The president's powerful words deserve to be quoted directly:

> So long as our relationship is defined by our differences, we will empower those who sow hatred rather than peace, and who promote conflict rather than the cooperation that can help all of our people achieve justice and prosperity. . . . This cycle of suspicion and discord must end.
>
> I've come here to Cairo to seek a new beginning between the United States and Muslims around the world; one based upon mutual interest and mutual respect; and one based upon the truth that America and Islam are not exclusive and need not be in competition. Instead, they overlap, and share common principles— principles of justice and progress; tolerance and the dignity of all human beings.
>
> I do so recognizing that change cannot happen overnight. . . . No single speech can eradicate years of mistrust, nor can I answer in the time that I have all the complex questions that brought us to this point. But I am convinced that in order to move forward, we must say openly the things we hold in our hearts, and that too often are said only behind closed doors. There must be a sustained effort to listen to each other; to learn from each other; to respect one another; and to seek common ground. As the Holy Koran tells us, "Be conscious of God and speak always the truth." That is

---

39. *See* Tim Rutten, *A Voice for Faith-based Diplomacy Is Muffled* L.A. TIMES, Apr. 13, 2011, http://articles.latimes.com/2011/apr/13/opinion/la-oe-0413-rutten-20110413.

what I will try to do . . . to speak the truth as best I can, humbled by the task before us, and firm in my belief that the interests we share as human beings are far more powerful than the forces that drive us apart.[40]

The president had long made a similar observation in the domestic context.[41]

Two Essential Insights for Democracy to Be Compatible with Faith

Given President Obama's message at home and abroad acknowledging the significance of faith to better cultural understanding and greater trust across disparate populations, we can resolve to advance the compatibility of democracy and faith recognizing two propositions. First, a democracy unattached from moral truth is a "thinly disguised totalitarianism."[42] And second, from practical reasoning, it follows that overstated claims of conscience by the believers of any faith tradition can destroy democracy and the common ground of community that democracies depend upon to flourish.

What is an overstated claim of conscience? Just this: expecting democracy always to coincide with one's own understanding, or our Church's understanding, of moral truth. Perfect coincidence of the two would not be democracy but a theocracy or heaven itself. Those who

40. President Barack Obama, Remarks by the President on a New Beginning (June 4, 2009), *available at* http://www.whitehouse.gov/the-press-office/remarks-president-cairo-university-6-04-09 [hereinafter Obama, Remarks on a New Beginning].

41. *See* Senator Barack Obama, Keynote Address at the Call to Renewal's Building a Covenant for a New America Conference: Faith and Politics (June 28, 2006), transcript *available at* http://www.nytimes.com/2006/06/28/us/politics/2006obamaspeech. html [hereinafter Obama, Call to Renewal], (last visited Oct. 13, 2011) [hereinafter Obama, Faith and Politics] ("But over the long haul, I think we make a mistake when we fail to acknowledge the power of faith in people's lives—in the lives of the American people—and I think it's time that we join a serious debate about how to reconcile faith with our modern, pluralistic democracy.").

42. Pope John Paul II, Encyclical Letter, Veritatis Splendor, para. 101 (Aug. 6, 1993), *available at* http://www.vatican.va/holy_father/john_paul_ii/encyclicals/documents/ hf_jp-ii_enc_06081993_veritatis-splendor_en.html [hereinafter Veritatis Splendor].

confuse earth with heaven will seldom be satisfied with a democratic outcome. To preserve the essential aspects of democracy, disappointed faith adherents should not be thought to have an entitlement to any of the following:

1. A constitutionally mandated exemption from a generally applicable law.
2. A justification for civil disobedience with respect to the law.
3. An insistence that those who share in the faith-related disappointment with the law as it exists break off political relations with others of different faiths who believe differently.

While democratic supposition denies entitlement to these, the aspiration for mutual respect and understanding ought not to be a signal for democratic withdrawal but for enhanced democratic engagement. A willingness to continue in dialogue with those who see matters differently, in terms of moral truth in the democratic process, is not a matter of treachery but a necessity for the formation of community. Rights and duties have long been seen as correlative. The right of mutual respect is correlative of the duty of democracy to be sensitive to ways to accommodate dissenting faith belief. So, too, the right to have religious dissent accommodated is hinged on the duty to avoid overstated religious objection. For example, it would be an overstatement to find oneself in complicit cooperation with an act viewed by the Church as an intrinsically evil act, simply because that act has gained protection under law.[43] In Catholic moral traditions, intent, will, and object are the matters

---

43. *Editor's Note:* Some of the conceptual terms used here (evil, good, intent, will, conscience) may be unfamiliar to non- or lay-Catholic readers. Kmiec uses these terms both as a way to argue within the Catholic tradition and as a model of using, not abandoning, religious language in the "public square." This language has developed over centuries from philosophical and theological traditions, so they may strike the modern reader as foreign. Evil, in this technical moral language, refers not to a force that lies outside of human agency and directs an act, but to the moral nature of a situation's or act's propensity to negate virtue, violate natural law, and/or propagate harm. An "intrinsically evil act" is understood by the *magisterium* (the teaching authority of the Church located in the hierarchy) as an action without the potential of good, no matter the nature of intent or will by the agent. The classic example is abortion.

reviewed by conscience to determine good from evil.[44] While the object is most important, intent and will cannot be disregarded. Where there is no intent to advance an intrinsic evil and no steps have been taken to perform it, the mere fact of adoption or permission of an evil action under law cannot make a citizen complicit in it solely by means of citizenship, or by a vote for a supporting candidate.[45]

A determination of formal cooperation[46] is more likely in those places where an individual act is evaluated by voters under a single-subject referendum. Intrinsically evil acts, one hopes, will not be the usual subject of legislative effort; although, given the long-running dispute over abortion and now embryonic stem cell research, we cannot ignore the possibility. Were it to become commonplace for a legislature to regularly legalize that which is intrinsically wrong, the availability of exemption or opt-out subject to alternative regulation becomes important. Prudence would recommend that where a significant majority group views the object of a proposed law as intrinsically evil, the law should not be enacted unless a compelling governmental interest was present.

---

44. *See* Catechism of the Catholic Church, §1757–1761, *available at* http://www.vatican.va/archive/ccc_css/archive/catechism/p3s1c1a4.htm.

45. In 2004, Cardinal Joseph Ratzinger (now Pope Benedict XVI) wrote: "A Catholic would be guilty of formal cooperation with evil, and so unworthy to present himself for Holy Communion, if he were to deliberately vote for a candidate *precisely* because of the candidate's permissive stance on abortion or euthanasia. When a Catholic does not share the candidate's stance in favor of abortion or euthanasia, but votes for the candidate for other reasons, it is considered remote material cooperation, which can be permitted in the presence of proportionate reasons." GEORGE WEIGEL, ETHICS AND PUBLIC POLICY CENTER, CARDINAL RATZINGER AND THE CONSCIENCE OF CATH-OLIC VOTERS (Sept. 29, 2004), http://www.eppc.org/publications/pubID.2177/pub_detail.asp (quoting a letter by Ratzinger to US bishops). As one author has noted, such a stance on what constitutes "cooperation with evil" does not properly address such matters as "the actions of individuals and small groups in relation to larger social structures . . . . We need to develop new ways of analyzing the involvement of individuals in systemic structures of complicity." M. Cathleen Kaveny, *Catholics as Citizens: Today's Ethical Challenges Call for New Moral Thinking*, AM. MAG., Nov. 1, 2010, http://www.americamagazine.org/content/article.cfm?article_id=12531.

46. *Editor's Note*: In the Catholic moral tradition, formal cooperation refers to the participation of an individual in the immoral act of another while sharing the intention of the other.

In 2006, then-Senator Obama noted that during his 2004 Senate campaign, his opponent, Alan Keyes, said that "Jesus Christ would not vote for Barack Obama."[47] Obama gave what he called the "typically liberal response": that as a member of a pluralistic society, it was impermissible for him to impose his religious views upon another.[48] He "was running to be the U.S. Senator of Illinois and not the Minister of Illinois," he quipped.[49]

Had Senate candidate Obama left it at that, voters could easily have written him off. But the insufficiency of his answer later nagged at him. He realized the insufficiency of an exclusionary secularist understanding of government in addressing the inescapable relationship between public law and morality, including the multiple ways in which different faiths express moral truth.[50] Barack Obama's subtle and sensitive understanding of these competing considerations was the principal reason that moderate and progressive Catholics came to his side in the 2008 presidential election.[51]

The neglect of the president's party to maintain this inquiry about faith, morality, and civic life may have cost the party dearly in the 2010 midterm election.

Barack Obama's understanding of both the necessary relation between law and morality and the limits that must be observed between

47. Obama, Faith and Politics, *supra* note 41.
48. *Id.*
49. *Id.*
50. *Id.* ("Mr. Keyes's implicit accusation that I was not a true Christian nagged at me, and I was also aware that my answer did not adequately address the role my faith has in guiding my own values and my own beliefs.").
51. *See*, e.g., PATRICK WHELAN, THE CATHOLIC CASE FOR OBAMA 2 (2008), http://www. catholicdemocrats.org/cfo/pdf/Catholic_Case_for_Obama_booklet.pdf ("Americans seem tired of being pitted against one another over issues of race, disparity of wealth, and religion. Senator Obama has made bringing Americans together to solve common problems the central theme of his campaign, which focuses on restoring the pride Americans once felt about our country being a moral leader among all nations."); *see also* PEW FORUM ON RELIGION & PUB. LIFE, *How the Faithful Voted* (Nov. 10, 2008), http://pewforum.org/Politics-and-Elections/How-the-Faithful-Voted.aspx (noting that Catholics supported Obama in the 2008 presidential election by a nine-point margin over Republican candidate Senator John McCain, compared to Catholic support for Republican incumbent George W. Bush over Democratic candidate John Kerry in the 2004 election.).

the two to keep a democratic system responsive to diverse people with diverse faiths was well-put when he said in 2006 that the greatest political division in America today is "not between men and women, or those who reside in so-called Red States and those who reside in Blue, but between those who attend church regularly and those who don't."[52] He also recognized that some conservative leaders "exploit this gap" by reminding evangelical Christians that Democrats "disrespect their values and dislike their church."[53] The truth hurts; but, of course, pointing fingers at Pat Robertson, Karl Rove, or today Rick Perry would still not have merited positive Catholic notice. But Obama kept talking. He didn't just criticize those on the right who used religion as a wedge issue; he also directed a healthy amount of criticism to the left and his own party. Democrats, he said, avoid engaging the substance of religious values by falsely claiming that the Constitution bars the subject.[54] Even worse, some far-left liberals paint religious Americans as "fanatical" rather than as people of faith.[55] (Regarding the manner and substance of our questions on the strength of religious values, it is best for us to remember that while we are entitled to ask them, we are not entitled to do so with the glint of mocking disapproval.)

Barack Obama in 2006, and as a presidential candidate in 2008, was a public figure who actually understood that for millions of Americans, faith "speaks to a hunger that's deeper than . . . any particular issue or cause."[56] Obama reflected on how neither of his parents were actively religious, and yet he found himself "drawn . . . to be in the church."[57] He could engage in community organizing for the poor, but without faith he would always remain "apart, and alone."[58] Faith did not mean the absence of doubt, said Obama, but it did mean hearing God's spirit beckoning.[59]

52. Obama, Faith and Politics, *supra* note 41.
53. *Id.*
54. *Id.* This erroneous claim is what derailed the interfaith initiative begun in the US Embassy in Malta.
55. *Id.*
56. *Id.*
57. *Id.*
58. *Id.*
59. *Id.*

Obama, like the Holy Father, thus squarely challenges secularism and those who would urge that religion be banished from the public square. Calling as his faith witnesses Abraham Lincoln, Martin Luther King Jr., Frederick Douglass, and Dorothy Day, Obama would tell his audiences that it is an "absurdity" to insist that morality be kept separate from public policy.[60]

Having urged liberals to see how much of American life is grounded in the Judeo-Christian tradition, Obama did have a request for conservatives—namely, that they try to fully understand the liberal perspective on the separation of church and state. Not the infamous "wall of separation" that bizarrely mandates exclusionary secularism disguised as neutrality,[61] but the perspective (according to Obama) that separation more readily protects church from state than the opposite. Moreover, more readily keeping the church community intact supports the needed underlying structures for the development of social mores, and, if not the resolution of division, at least the toleration of difference.

This sentiment—unlike the exclusionary view invented by the late Justice Hugo Black in the late 1940s[62]—contains the wisdom of Alexis de Tocqueville, who cautioned churches against aligning too closely with the state for fear of sacrificing "the future for the present."[63] "By gaining a power to which it has no claim," Tocqueville observed, "[the church] risks its legitimate authority."[64]

Obama's conception in 2006 of church-state relations was informed and intelligent. It merited the high honor accorded him in the form of an honorary degree from the University of Notre Dame in 2009. With due respect to my colleague Mary Ann Glendon, her refusal to appear on the same platform with the president was an example of the ethical

---

60. *Id.*
61. In a 1947 US Supreme Court decision, Justice Hugo L. Black wrote: "In the words of [Thomas] Jefferson, the [First Amendment] clause against establishment of religion by law was intended to erect 'a wall of separation' between Church and State. That wall must be kept high and impregnable." Everson v. Bd. of Educ., 330 U.S. 1, 18 (1947).
62. *Id.*
63. ALEXIS DE TOCQUEVILLE, DEMOCRACY IN AMERICA 155 (George Lawrence trans., Scott A. Sandage ed., HarperCollins 2007) (1966).
64. *Id.*

overstatement to which I alluded earlier; it was more promotive of division than of dialogue.[65]

Obama's thoughts in 2006 rejecting exclusionary secularism, moreover, could have been seamlessly added to Mitt Romney's thoughtful "Faith in America" speech without significantly changing its meaning.[66] (The Romney speech unfortunately did not moderate the shameless mocking of the Latter Day Saints [LDS] faith by other Republican primary candidates in the 2008 primaries. The LDS faith is one of strong family and missionary commitment—no aspect of which, as modernly articulated—has ever been shown to rend or test the limits of religious tolerance by the body politic any more than other faiths).

As already noted, as reflected in the 2001 judgment of the European Court of Human Rights in *Refah Partisi*, some do believe that the limits of tolerance of Islamic Sharia for other religious beliefs have been reached.[67] This ECHR judgment begs important reexamination, however. In particular, it did not take into account how the import of Sharia changes depending on time, place, and people. For example, in some countries, Sharia law applies to Muslim and non-Muslim alike, prompting serious encroachment upon religious freedom; however, in other countries, such as Jordan, there is an Islamic majority but a wholly

---

65. Glendon, a former US ambassador to the Vatican, refused to accept the Laetare Medal (the University of Notre Dame's highest honor) at the university's 2009 commencement when she learned that President Obama would be present at the ceremony to receive an honorary degree and to speak to graduates. Katharine Q. Seelye, *Obama's Notre Dame Visit Is Still Drawing Criticism*, THE CAUCUS: THE POLITICS AND GOVERNMENT BLOG OF THE TIMES, N.Y. TIMES, (May 11, 2009, 2:01 PM), http://thecaucus.blogs. nytimes.com/2009/05/11/obamas-notre-dame-visit-is-still-drawing-criticism/.

66. In a 2007 address, Romney addressed religious liberty—a topic he believed to be "fundamental to America's greatness"—and "perspectives on how [his] own faith would inform [his] presidency, if [he] were elected." *See* Mitt Romney, Address at the George Bush Presidential Library: Faith in America (Dec. 6, 2007), transcript *available at* http://www.npr.org/templates/story/story.php?storyId=16969460 (last visited Oct. 13, 2011).

67. Refah Partisi, 35 Eur. H. R. Rep. 56, 60 (2001) ("It is difficult to declare one's respect for democracy and human rights while at the same time supporting a regime based on sharia, which clearly diverges from Convention values, particularly with regard to its criminal law and criminal procedure, its rules on the legal status of women and the way it intervenes in all spheres of private and public life in accordance with religious precepts.").

secular legal system.[68] In still other countries such as India, the secular constitution allows for a separate Islamic family law system to apply to the Muslim community.[69] Indeed, marriage and family law questions are most likely to highlight the divide between Sharia and secular laws. Can these differences be reasonably handled with a constitution within a Constitution? There is some positive historical assessment of both formal and informal, but separate Islamic family law systems. Indeed, there may be something of a preference for informal methods of conciliation that has resulted when Muslims have withdrawn from state institutions and developed their own methods of dispute resolution. While there are real costs in terms of a society not having a uniform rule of law from a common source, there are also costs to insisting on uniformity from multivariate sources. Moreover, accommodating Islamic separateness shows respect which can be—and historically has been— reciprocated, supplying your mutual active understanding a different source of mortar for maintaining a community as a whole. In A.D. 628, for example, the prophet Mohammad (praise be unto him) clearly established a tradition known as *Sunnah* promoting tolerance toward Christians. This was established in a historic promise made in St. Catherine's Monastery located at the foot of Mount Sinai.[70]

The relation between church and state cannot easily be hidden behind any wall, no matter how high, because the relation between law and morality within us is commonly inseparable from religious instruction. Commonly inseparable, yes, but not incapable of separation—or at least the advocates of secularism would insist. Indeed, we saw in the writing of *New York Times* editor Bill Keller that even in the United States, where the founding generation repeatedly linked morality and religion, the modern American mind puts a higher burden of justification on those persons framing laws or engaging in political discussion who readily and overtly draw on religious belief to derive moral principle. The no establishment clause may buttress this effect.

Currently, it is thus asserted, and generally accepted, that religion is not the sole source of morality. Fundamentalist believers of any of

68. BHALA, *supra* note 20, at xxix.
69. *Id.*
70. Bhala, *supra* note 20, at xxv.

the Abrahamic faiths necessarily must concede as a simple empirical matter that not everyone is in agreement that a nation's legal system or its larger culture be linked to a concept of religious-grounded morality as opposed to a morality or ethical system derived from a wholly secular measure. Indeed, as Bill Keller's witty essay discloses, there is a greater tolerance for those who make the effort to exclude religious belief—or at least to get beyond their own parochial sensibilities—in the derivation of morality than those who on principle find that their moral systems necessarily involve some religious understanding. It is as if a sign read: "As you contemplate the general laws, thank you for not praying," in the same way that we are grateful to our neighbor for not contaminating the air in a restaurant with cigarette smoke. Religiously grounded morality no longer holds the advantage of our institutional presumptions. Recall, though, that Justice William O. Douglas, one of the most progressive members of the US Supreme Court, matter-of-factly declared that the American institutions "presuppose the existence of a Supreme Being."

All of the discussion to this point has assumed that speaking of law and morality does not mean solely focusing on the relationship between law and religious doctrine. By definition, there are numerous secular value systems or frameworks with moral claims. For example, to evaluate the consequences of human action in relation to efficiency, compatibility with the human environment, and an increase in happiness for the greatest number would be to undertake to identify a given nonreligious value (economic evaluation, environmental harmony, and relative levels of joy and sadness). Ideally, morality derived from religion and morality derived from humanism, economic efficiency, or other nonreligious value ought to be able to co-exist harmoniously.

In the next part, we take a closer look at exclusionary and inclusionary forms of secularism. After examining these, it will be possible to lay out five different forms of church-state relationships and the types of governments associated with them. The governments will range from the extremes of compelled theocracy to compelled atheism, with three consent-based and thus democratically acceptable governmental forms: a democratically acceptable form of confessionalism (as in Malta); a democratically acceptable non-confessionalist, inclusionary model (favored by the European Court of Human Rights with respect to the public display of religious symbols, but exclusionary and favoring Christianity as to substance); and a democratically acceptable form of exclusionary secularism (which exists in the United States as to the treatment of religious symbols but is tempered by a nondiscrimination principle that neither favors nor disfavors a particular faith tradition). An understanding of these forms of secularism, together with thoughts on how Islam views secularism, will enrich our understanding of the recent European Court of Human Rights decision upholding the mandatory display of the crucifix in public school classrooms in Italy.

THE DIFFERENT FORMS OF SECULARISM

Secularism in Relation to Public/Private Spheres of Decision Making

Secularism defines the separation or distance between religion and the governing institutions of a nation. When the term was originally coined in the nineteenth century, it was advancing the proposition that certain questions of morals are best decided only within the private sphere.[71] For that time, it is fair to perceive secularism as protective or respectful of religious belief—in essence, cordoning off public interference from a matter of considerable individual significance. Curiously, secularism takes on an almost opposite meaning in the present; namely, that from rational thought it is claimed to be possible to achieve a life well-lived without making reference whatsoever to religious belief.[72] In other words, the original concept of secularism was not seen as hostile either to religion or to religiously grounded argument in the private sphere.[73]

71. TALAL ASAD, FORMATIONS OF THE SECULAR: CHRISTIANITY, ISLAM, MODERNITY 23–24 (2003).
72. *Id.* at 5 (noting, however, that the "place of religion varies" even among modern nations that deem themselves secular. For instance, the United States has a secular federal government but a largely religious population; while in France, both the state and its citizens are secular.); *see also* Elizabeth Shakman Hurd, *The Political Authority of Secularism in International Relations*, 10 EUR. J. INT'L REL. 235, 238 (2004).
73. *Id.* at 6 n. 6.

Quite the opposite, the faith nourished in private was to be respected in the same sense as family privacy.

Once faith was tucked away, however, there was less sharing of religious sentiment or insight—at first, because it was impolite to question a person's religious sensibilities (Jefferson noted in bolstering the idea of religious freedom at America's founding, for example, that matters of faith were of delicate sensibility.) Over time, however, having put faith off limits to protect sensibility, proponents of secularism had greater opportunity to question the necessity of religion in the public sphere for a well-ordered society, especially if that public sphere had been sufficiently narrowed in scope.[74]

Thus, the division of public and private spheres also came to reflect the desire to protect Enlightenment rationality from being obscured or muddled by particularistic religious myth, the pejorative characterization of faith common among atheists or agnostics. The pejorative is regularly employed today by the so-called new atheists, of whom Richard Dawkins is perhaps most prominent. It is not always apparent, however, whether Dr. Dawkins is decrying the persistent influence of faith on public discussion or on Islamic belief. The Dawkins view, whatever its motivation to one side, reveals that the separation of religious argument and inquiry was less necessary for its own good than to ensure the operational functionality of institutions which, if bogged down in metaphysical or spiritual argumentation, would be less capable of accomplishing their prosaic tasks. It is necessary, so the argument proceeds, for the public sphere to be free of religious dispute since faith is premised not on empirical proof that can be replicated but on intensely held matters of ideology.

The defense of this mutated and faith-hostile understanding of secularism depended on a narrowing of the public sphere. This understanding initially could be argued as respectful of the importance of religious belief and the need to give it adequate breathing space. Yet public space

---

74. See Nikki R. Keddie, *Trajectories of Secularism in the West and the Middle East*, 6 GLOBAL DIALOGUE 23, 23 (2004) ("In the nineteenth century . . . 'secular' c[a]me to be associated with 'secularists' who espoused a doctrine of 'secularism'—the belief that religious institutions and values should play no role in the temporal affairs of the state.").

seldom remains within paper fences very long. Soon religious belief en-countered Enlightenment trespassers pointing out that faith was inca-pable of coming up with answers that would be persuasive across the pluralism of *Christian* belief occupying the seats of power.

Confining religion to the private sphere did not make the public sphere safe for religion. America today brags of robust religious freedom for all—believer and non-believer alike. This was not the original under-standing, as Justice Joseph Story recounts in his legal treatise. Religious freedom in America did not extend even to all Christians, as the histori-cal suspicions and suppressions of Catholics reveal. There will always be a price to pay for failing to acknowledge the diversity of religious beliefs and it will come in the form of an argument for the censorship of reli-gious speech in the public square.

Among other intolerances, the Anglican split from the Catholic Church was enough to show that the public space no longer had the ca-pacity for universal values. In North America it was only a bit of sleight of hand that would preserve the notion of particular faith beliefs to the well-being of the Republic. The truth of matters would be boldly declared, and not only declared, but characterized as "self-evident." Critically, this self-evidence was nominally traced to the hand of the transcendent "Creator," a divine power of supreme vagueness. The claim of self-evidence would over time be its own form of intellectual self-censorship, and instead of enriching a multiplicity of unique belief in the Divine, these ideas were sequestered into the private sphere. As William Connolly writes, building on the work of Jürgen Habermas,

> The best hope for a peaceful and just world under these new circumstances was institution of a public life in which the final meaning of life, the proper route to life after death, and the divine source of morality were pulled out of the public realm and depos-ited into private life.[75]

75. WILLIAM E. CONNOLLY, WHY I AM NOT A SECULARIST 21 (1999). The seminal work on this topic is JÜRGEN HABERMAS, THE STRUCTURAL TRANSFORMATION OF THE PUBLIC SPHERE: AN INQUIRY INTO A CATEGORY OF BOURGEOIS SOCIETY (Thomas Burger & Frederick Lawrence trans., 1991) (1962).

In this way, Jürgen Habermas conceived of a public sphere of deliberation about common affairs.[76] It was a medium of conversation and talk as it related to the basics of internal civil order and defense from external threat.[77] Such a conception of the public sphere could not be normative, however, after the Reformation. Religion is specific and hardly a common affair, so secularism had to be understood as greatly reducing, if not banishing, religiously grounded argument in the public sphere.

Normative arguments that often draw upon religion constitute a hallmark of decision making in the private sphere; this allows mediating institutions, notably church and family, to deal with the most highly sensitive questions in our lives. There is some sense to this as fathers or mothers reveal in rejecting the common adolescent refrain anchored in a rough majority rule that "everybody" is staying out past curfew or getting their body parts tattooed. By contrast, when we focus on the question of how large a police force to have, and whether its officers should carry weapons, we do not apply religious doctrine to resolve these matters of budgeting, efficiency, and effectiveness. In the best case, secularism keeps public decision making out of faith and family matters (intra-family abuse or other harm excepted), reserving those matters to the faith community of the family's choosing. Being deposited somewhere kept faith on life support, and if parents, families, and religious instruction would only ensure its vibrancy, faith of some type might be called on for a public encore when it had something uniquely powerful to say. Permanently sequestering faith to private space was unsatisfying.

Notice that the division of the public and private spheres, while something of a concession to the public to be free of imposed religious belief, is nevertheless a better compromise than dismissing religious considerations from having public influence altogether. Noah Feldman refers to this moderate position as dividing religion from public decision making, but not from influence on culture and society as a whole.[78] The eminent Jesuit theologian John Courtney Murray made a similar observation in his emphasis and confidence in a natural law–informed culture

76. See Habermas, *supra* note 75, at 1–2, 27.
77. *Id.*
78. Noah Feldman, Divided by God: America's Church-State Problem—And What We Should Do about It, Farrar, Straus & Giroux, 2005.

that would distinguish the heavy hand of the state from the hands of moral formation derivable from society. By this means of subtle cultural formation, religion secured its position against the concentrated power of the state, which then had to stay awake to human need to retain its influence.

The differences between understanding secularism to confine religion to the private sphere as opposed to denying the significance of religion to cultural formation and value can be illustrated by a recent referendum legalizing divorce in Malta.[79]

Prior to passage of the referendum, Malta had been the only European Union (EU) country prohibiting divorce.[80] In a country where 95 percent of Maltese are Catholic,[81] the issue had been previously well handled by canon law courts that applied the different considerations applicable to annulment, which, if decreed, expunges the marriage as being without proper intent in its formation.[82] The referendum, however, passed because the Church panels were not seen as addressing, or addressing with the right sensitivities, the issue of domestic abuse which, according to published reports, is experienced by a quarter of Maltese women.[83]

Of course, the proponents of divorce sought to make a wider case applicable to marital failure generally, but in doing so, they needed to be seen as not withdrawing too much authority from sacred sources or from the private sphere.[84] As a consequence, the referendum gave approval to divorce only when certain rigorous conditions were met—specifically,

79. Lisa Abend, *Malta Says "We Do" to Legalizing Divorce*, TIME, June 1, 2011, http://www.time.com/time/world/article/0,8599,2074721,00.html. The referendum passed on May 29, 2011, by 53 percent to 46 percent. *Id.*

80. *Id.*

81. *Id.*

82. *Id.* Other options for ending a marriage in Malta previously included filing for a legal separation that would prevent later remarriage or going abroad for a divorce that could later be legally registered in Malta.

83. *Domestic Violence "One of the Main Reasons for Divorce,"* TIMES OF MALTA, May 6, 2011, http://www.timesofmalta.com/articles/view/20110506/local/domestic-violence-one-of-the-main-reasons-for-divorce.363951.

84. Some in Malta saw the pro-divorce agenda not as a rejection of Catholic beliefs, but instead as a reflection of a growing belief that some issues should be decided by civil law and others by the Church. Abend, *supra* note, 79.

after a lengthy four-year period of counseling and separation, where all hope of reconciliation was seemingly absent, and children of the marriage were provided for and "adequate maintenance [was] guaranteed."[85] Virtually no one challenged these pre-conditions because the authority of the Church and her courts was deeply embedded. The authority of the canon law courts in Malta will be diminished by the referendum but not eliminated. Proper legislative drafting implementing the referendum will likely be pressed to recognize the historic and continuing role of the Church and seek a transfer into the public sphere of only those matters that cannot be handled well in the private sphere.[86]

Whether one construes secularism as confined to the public sphere or as a device to diminish religious influence altogether, it is interesting to contemplate from its history that secularism is of distinctly Christian origin. Recent scholarship argues that the original concept from the Greek intended only to differentiate that which belonged to this world from that which one could anticipate in the next.[87] Paying attention to the Christian influence begs the question of what that influence meant for the concept of secularism. It is one thing to say that the Christian Bible directs us to give to Caesar what is Caesar's and to God what is God's; it is quite another thing to know with certainty how God and Caesar divide the pie. Interestingly, the sphere to be subjected to religious influence at present is greatly expanded if one indulges a fundamentalist conception of faith, whether or not that conception is anchored in Christianity or Islam.

If secularism is construed to mean that a nation cannot keep most moral questions in the private sphere, and thereby allows faith—be it Christian or Islamic or some other—to continue to have broad influence, the problems of public governance multiply quickly. For example, because of the wider scope assumed by the public sphere when moral questions are sought to be answered in that locus, there will be a need

85. Mario Cacciottolo, *Malta Reacts to Historic Vote to Introduce Divorce*, BBC NEWS, May 29, 2011, http://www.bbc.co.uk/news/world-europe-13589320.
86. The Maltese Parliament approved divorce legislation in July 2011; the law will come into force in October 2011. Kurt Sansone & Lawrence Vella, *Historic Vote Ushers in Divorce*, TIMES OF MALTA, July 26, 2011, http://www.timesofmalta.com/articles/view/20110726/local/Historic-vote-ushers-in-divorce.377401.
87. Craig Calhoun, *Rethinking Secularism*, HEDGEHOG REVIEW, Fall 2010, pages 35–48.

to translate religious argument into a secular presentation. In the translation, much in the way of spirituality and non-rational justification is lost. When John Rawls argues for the exclusion of religious speech from the public square, it is quite obvious that freedom of speech as well as religion is diminished.[88] Arguably, when the line between the public and private spheres is not well drawn, complex issues of power sharing within the governing democratic structure become great as well, with one example being the ECHR opinion affirming the dissolution of Islam's Refah party.

As this is written for publication, the issue of whether democracy and Islam are compatible is coming into greater focus. Gaddafi is dead in Libya[89] and the first real democratic electoral activity in Tunisia and Egypt has taken place.[90] The Tunisian elections chose 217 members of a new assembly that is charged with, among other responsibilities, drafting a new Tunisian constitution.[91] Eighty political parties vied for attention in Tunisia.[92] However, given the present discussion on the proper

88. *See,* e.g., JOHN RAWLS, THE LAW OF PEOPLES; WITH, THE IDEA OF PUBLIC REASON REVISITED 143–144 (1999) ("To engage in public reason is to appeal to one of . . . a family of liberal political conceptions—to their ideals and principles, standards and values—when debating fundamental political questions. This . . . still allows us to introduce into political discussion at any time our comprehensive doctrine, religious or nonreligious, provided that, in due course, we give properly public reasons to support the principles and policies our comprehensive doctrine is said to support.").

89. Col. Muammar el-Qaddafi (also spelled Gaddafi), who ruled an autocracy in Libya for nearly forty-two years, was killed on Oct. 20, 2011, by rebel fighters. Kareen Fahim et al., *Violent End to an Era as Qaddafi Dies in Libya*, N.Y. TIMES, Oct. 20, 2011, http://www.nytimes.com/2011/10/21/world/africa/qaddafi-is-killed-as-libyan-forces-take-surt.html. On Oct. 23, 2011, the transitional Libyan leadership declared that a new government would be established, with Islamic tenets at its core. Adam Nossiter and Kareem Fahim, *Revolution Won, Top Libyan Official Vows a New and More Pious State*, N.Y. TIMES, Oct. 23, 2011, http://www.nytimes.com/2011/10/24/world/africa/revolution-won-top-libyan-official-vows-a-new-and-more-pious-state.html?scp=13&sq=libya&st=cse.

90. In January 2011, civil resistance in Tunisia led to the overthrow of President Zine El Abidine Ben Ali, who had been in power for twenty-three years. *Tunisia Profile*, BBC NEWS AFRICA, Oct. 24 2011, http://www.bbc.co.uk/news/world-africa-14107241. Ben Ali's loss of power resulting from popular uprising inspired the "Arab Spring," the term for a subsequent series of popular revolts across the Middle East against other autocratic rulers. *Id.*

91. *Id.*

92. *Id.*

scope of secularism, the party of greatest interest is the one headed by Rachid al-Ghannouchi, whose Islamist Renaissance Party (al-Nahda or Ennahda in Arabic) hoped to win a majority.[93] It is reported that the secularists are greatly fearful of such a result and anticipate that with the victory of an Islamic party will come highly illiberal laws on marriage, divorce, and inheritance.[94] Obviously, they are applying a concept of secularism that does not recognize the possibility that most of these questions could be resolved by leaving them to the private sphere: within the teachings of Islam for Muslims, and within the Catholic Church to the extent that it speaks to these subjects. Of course, there will always be a border between what is public and private, and determining the size of the respective spheres will require a level of equal treatment (which the ECHR has not always shown toward Islam).

Concerns about the legacy of unequal treatment, the need for minority inclusion, and the dangers of political favoritism are not insurmountable, but they are present in different ways and degrees in each of the Arab Spring nations. For example, with far too broad a conception of the public sphere, suspicions in Tunisia ran high that democracy would just become a vessel to impose a different level of authoritarian control for a politically favored group.[95] Thus, it was reasoned that if a dominant minority, al-Nahda, fulfilled its own projections of winning a majority of seats, it would have power and be in a position to hold parliament hostage in case of deadlock.[96] Of course, one can see in the

93. Anthony Shadid, *Islamist Imagines a Democratic Future for Tunisia*, N.Y. TIMES, Oct. 21, 2011. http://www.nytimes.com/2011/10/20/world/africa/rachid-al-ghannouchi-imagines-democratic-future-for-tunisia.html?scp=1&sq=political%20islamist%20faces%20moment%20of%20reckoning&st=cse.

94. *Id.*

95. *Id.*

96. *Id.; see also The Islamist Conundrum: Secular Tunisian Voters Remain Wary of the Islamists' Growing Appeal*, THE ECONOMIST, Oct. 22, 2011, http://www.economist.com/node/21533411 (noting that some observers independently projected that al-Nahda could win 20 or more percent of the vote, giving the party a "controlling bloc" in government that many have deemed would be "disastrous."). The elections were held on October 23, 2011; as of October 25, 2011, al-Nahda had won a plurality of preliminary votes (about 40 percent). David D. Kirkpatrick, *Moderate Islamist Party Heads toward Victory in Tunisia*, N.Y. TIMES, Oct. 24, 2011, http://www.nytimes.com/2011/10/25/world/africa/ennahda-moderate-islamic-party-makes-strong-showing-in-tunisia-vote.html?pagewanted=all.

founding of the United States similar devices to consolidate power, as in the "winner-take-all" feature of the electoral college. And as for holding a "do-nothing" legislative branch accountable, examining the record of Harry Truman or engaging Barack Obama in conversation will likely affirm an occasional need to awaken legislative energies.

The public discourse by al-Nahda in the run-up to the election in Tunisia sought to connect its approach to larger questions of global economic structure and motivation. The old ways wholly dependent on capitalism are eroding, says the party, which put emphasis on morality and obligations to community.[97] Islam and Christianity are certainly not at odds on this criticism, as both have raised similar objections to the evaluation of human life only in terms of its consumption habits. Pope Benedict XVI called for a modification of the ideology of Adam Smith.[98] The question in the balance is whether

97. Shadid, *supra* note 93.

98. In 2009, Pope Benedict XVI had issued an encyclical letter, Caritas in Veritate, calling for economic activity to be "directed towards the pursuit of the common good" (italics removed), and not just to be "conceived merely as an engine for wealth creation." Benedict XVI, Encyclical Letter, Caritas in Veritate, para. 36 (June 29, 2009), *available at* http://www.vatican.va/holy_father/benedict_xvi/encyclicals/documents/hf_ben-xvi_enc_20090629_caritas-in-veritate_en.html). On October 24, 2011, the Pontifical Council for Justice and Peace issued a document, "Towards Reforming the International Financial and Monetary Systems in the Context of Global Public Authority," which has been described as a "practical extension" of Benedict's 2009 encyclical. Amy Sullivan, *The Vatican's Radical Ideas on Financial Reform*, TIME SWAMPLAND BLOG (Oct. 24, 2011), http://swampland.time.com/2011/10/24/the-vaticans-radical-ideas-on-financial-reform/. The Pontifical Council's document, which "hammered the values of the financial world" by criticizing an "'economic liberalism that spurns rules and controls,'" is a "fierce denunciation of . . . free-market theology. " *Id.* (quoting Pontifical Council for Justice and Peace, "Towards Reforming the International Financial and Monetary Systems in the Context of Global Public Authority."). The document recommended forming a global political authority to oversee the global economy in order to "bring more democratic and ethical principles to a marketplace run amok." Elisabetta Povoledo, *Vatican Calls for Oversight of the World's Finances*, N.Y. TIMES, Oct. 24, 2011, http://www.nytimes.com/2011/10/25/world/europe/vatican-calls-for-global-oversight-of-the-economy.html?_r=1&ref=romancatholicchurch. *But see* John L. Allen Jr., *Vatican Note on Economy the First Ripple of a Southern Wave*, NAT'L CATH. REP., Oct. 25, 2011, http://ncronline.org/news/vatican/vatican-note-economy-first-ripple-southern-wave (noting that the document, written by a African cardinal, is less likely to reflect the social and political thought of Catholics in the West; instead, it is more reflective of a so-called southern consensus in the Catholic world that reflects the more progressive economic views of Catholics in Africa, Asia, and Latin America.).

Islam can abide whatever public/private sphere split is agreed to democratically; and whether, in terms of the private sphere over which Islam would retain influence over its own membership, it could impose penalties or other means of enforcement far more severe than in Christianity without a public outcry to protect Muslims from the discipline of their own faith.

The US Constitution's First Amendment protection of religion is imperfect, but it works only because it is *not* a devious way either to impose a favored belief on those who do not consent nor is it the suppression of belief by those who would seek to insinuate secularity under the guise of neutrality. The American Constitution accords religious freedom of practice and belief to all believers of every faith, not because we have determined every faith to be without error or equally capable at conveying transcendent understanding of our human existence but because in a Kantian sense, the freedom to believe or not believe without coercion is the only means by which we can honor the dignity of another human being. In establishing a rule of law that treats the voluntary faith inquiries of all persons as ends worthy of respect, we have fashioned a standard by which there is a real possibility that the words in the Koran—"And He is oft Forgiving, full of love"—will place Christian, Jew, and Muslim on the common ground of peace. But are there models of secular understanding that would likewise be capable of achieving such common ground?

Muslim conceptions of what is secular differ from the idea of secularism of the West—the latter more susceptible to the chimera that all is reason. Secularity in the Islamic tradition does not abandon reason, as often occurs in strains of Wahhabism. To the contrary, much Islamic teaching manifests respect for reason that is infused with spirituality. The unanswered question is whether reason dressed in the spirit is tolerant only of the scrupulous believer or also of the non-believer, or also of those who believe as a matter of human right in the freedom to find their own way in matters of faith and religion.

By now the reader has determined that some bad news is around the corner and it is just this: Not every strain of Muslim belief seeks to find a harmony of philosophy and religion. The differences among Islamic believers mentioned here is nonetheless further reason to be concerned about the unnuanced rejection of Islamic belief as being incompatible with democracy (e.g., the *Refa* decision in the European Court of Human Rights). The potential for harmonizing philosophy and religion thus becomes a corollary for how democracy, the reasoned exercise of governing by consent, may come to be reconciled with at least some of the necessary aspects of its functioning, such as religious pluralism and equal treatment for men and women.

With regard to the harmony of philosophy and religion, it is said that Muslim intellectuals can be divided into three groups: (1) those who believe in the complete harmony of philosophy and religion, such as Al Kindi, Farabi, and Averroes; (2) those who believe in the partial compatibility of the two, such as Ghazzali, in spite of his open attack on philosophy and philosophers; and (3) those who reject the doctrine of harmony between philosophy and religion altogether, such as the Sunni and Shiite.[99]

The doctrine of harmony potentially allows for greater theoretical common ground between faith and reason, perhaps even yielding a conception of Sharia law that is more tolerant of religious pluralism. Most Western assessments of democracy's potential in nations with majority Islamic populations assume a definition of secularism that is itself Western and unharmonious. Unlike the Islamic pursuit of harmony as an aspect of pluralism and secularity, the Western conception of secularism modernly pushes toward exclusion.

Whether democracy is perceived as compatible with an Islamic nation may well turn on whether a Western or Islamic conception of secularism is the method of analysis. Indeed, where the doctrine of harmony informs the Islamic faith tradition there would arguably be less need for public and private spheres to diverge. Nevertheless, because of Western unfamiliarity with Islamic natural law, there has been little interfaith understanding of how the doctrine of harmony might have supplied a foundation more tolerant and more open to the competing ideologies that guide the nascent governments in the Arab Spring. Of course it was in that context that the Muslim Brotherhood exercised

99. A. Ezzati, *Islam and Natural Law*, London, UK, Islamic College for Advanced Studies Press, 2002.

political boldness to write into its new constitutional system an explicit, and invariable, standard of Sharia as the authoritative measure for legislation. To the Western ear uninformed by the doctrine of harmony, that seemed entirely one-sided and unacceptable. On the flipside, exploring this doctrine of harmony for its potential to accommodate religious difference is important because it stands foursquare in opposition to the anti-rationality of Wahhabi-ism, the strain of Islamic belief most closely associated with terrorist activity.

Overall, it would seem that from the Middle Ages to the present, Islam did not separate reason and revelation; indeed, quite to the contrary. Like John Paul II's encyclical *Fides et Ratio*, faith and reason are seen, at least outside fundamentalist Islam and its anti-rationalism, to be walking hand in hand without contradiction—at least ultimately. At any given time, one might argue that science or reason disputes faith, but this negating tendency is understood as only the dimness of the human mind in comparison to the divine intellect.

Exclusionary and Inclusionary Secularism

Before outlining possible models of government associated with secularism, I should note that the type of secularism of great concern to the Holy Father is that which leaves little to be resolved in the private sphere, and on the public side sees itself as an opponent or antagonist of religious reference—with the view that religion or religious practice is actually harmful to the well-being of individuals.[100] (This type of secularism shall be termed "exclusionary secularism.")[101] This view seeks

---

100. *See* Pope Benedict XVI, Address at Audience with H. M. the Queen and State Reception (Sept. 16, 2010), *available at* http://www.vatican.va/holy_father/benedict_xvi/speeches/2010/september/documents/hf_ben-xvi_spe_20100916_incontro-autorita_en.html ("More aggressive forms of secularism no longer value or even tolerate . . . traditional values and cultural expressions [such as in religion].").

101. *See, e.g.*, Gregory C. Sisk, *John Paul II: The Quintessential Religious Witness in the Public Square*, 45 J. CATH. LEGAL STUD. 241, 242 (2006) ("With the turn in certain sectors of American society toward an aggressive and exclusionary secularism in the latter part of the twentieth century . . . [came] the emergency of resistance and even some intolerance toward expression of religious sentiments on issues of public moment.").

to convince modern philosophy and politics that religion principally offers an occasion for hate and division rather than for finding common ground or an increase in mutual understanding and accommodation.[102] Also within this category of exclusionary secularism are nation-states that selectively target one or more faiths for exclusion. In contrast, secularism that reasonably reserves to the private sphere normative questions on how to live a good life compatibly with moral reality, and within that sphere also shows no favoritism toward one faith tradition over another, is inclusionary secularism.

Drawing the line between exclusionary and inclusionary secularism is a matter of high importance for believers and secularists alike—that is, all of us. Arguably, it is the generosity of mind implicit in inclusionary secularism that permits a defensible concept of the secular at all. By contrast, when exclusionary secularism pushes through, the first casualty is the freedom to believe, followed by a loss of freedom to speak and act with religious motivation. More than faith, then, is oppressed by exclusionary secularism, or, pardon the metaphorical reference, crucified. Without the subtle explanatory power of different religions to explain humanity to itself, the secular goods of civil order and initiative diminish. In brief, exclusionary secularism in crucifying religious belief engenders conditions that invite the undoing of a range of social goods. The limitations on freedom to inquire into religious matters or to be inspired by them leaves far too much to the unsatisfying inducements of power, wealth, and ideology.

SECULARISM IS THE ANOMALY

Because of the need for secularism to operate in inclusionary harmony with faith, exclusionary secularism is the exception, not the rule. Religious teaching has guided the structure and decision making of many modern states or nations. In this regard, the anomalous state or nation

---

102. *See,* e.g., KURU, *supra* note 18, at 2–3 ("[One view of secularism] argue[s] that people should participate in democratic deliberation by putting aside their religious doctrines, which impede[s] consensus due to their dogmatic aspects.").

is the one that has neither reference to a particular religion nor a generic faith in a transcendent being. David Smolin observes:

> Americans tend to conflate the no-establishment and religious liberty principle, [but] international human rights principles necessarily separate them, as the mere existence of a state church or officially-sanctioned or favored religion does not of itself violate any norm of international law. Democracy, human rights, and the rule of law have frequently co-existed with state churches and established religions.[103]

Five Church State Relationships

Consider the five most common relationships between religion and law (or church and state, if you will) that one finds on the map.

1. DEMOCRATICALLY UNACCEPTABLE: COMPELLED THEOCRACY

The basic feature of theocracy is a general understanding that the government is receiving divine guidance through ruling clergy or other governmental officials serving with clerical approval. God is perceived as head of either government or state, or of both.[104] Nevertheless, theocracies may be differently organized; some have a hierarchy that reflects the religious hierarchy itself, and some operate with a separate governing hierarchy that is fully controlled by religious belief. A theocracy should be distinguished from a government in which one or more religions are given preference as an established or confessed religion of the state.[105]

---

103. David Smolin, *Exporting the First Amendment? Evangelism, Proselytism, and the International Religious Freedom Act,* 31 Cumb. L. Rev. 685, 689 (2000–2001) (citing Nathan A. Adams IV, *A Human Rights Imperative: Extending Religious Liberty beyond the Border,* 33 Cornell Int'l L.J. 27–32, 64–65 (2000)).

104. *See, e.g.,* Central Intelligence Agency, The World Factbook [hereinafter CIA World Factbook], *Government Type,* https://www.cia.gov/library/publications/the-world-factbook/fields/print_2128.html (last visited Oct. 13, 2011).

105. *See* section "Democratically Acceptable Confessionalism" of this chapter.

In modern terms, Islamic states are most likely to be perceived by the West as theocracies, to the extent that Sharia is the "law of the land," affecting both private behavior and all aspects of public life.[106] Saudi Arabia, Libya, and Iran are examples of virtual or actual theocracies.[107] In Iran, for instance, ultimate political authority is vested in a Supreme Leader, or a learned religious scholar, who is accountable to an eighty-six-member body of clerics (called the Assembly of Experts).[108]

Also excluded from this classification would be countries where Islam is a majority religion, but where Sharia does not affect aspects of everyday life. One example is Nigeria, which is 50 percent Muslim; there, states may elect (but are not required) to use Sharia laws and courts, and non-Muslims are not required to submit to Sharia jurisdiction.[109]

Comparably, Israel is not a theocracy; Judaism is the majority religion, but the country classifies as a "parliamentary democracy" because of its legislature elected by popular vote.[110] Nevertheless, it is quite apparent in any visit to Israel that many religious teachings cover interactions within the culture, and that the legal authority frequently relies upon religious sources to maintain order.[111]

---

106. *See* BHALA, *supra* note 20, at xxx; *see also* Carlos Fraenkel, *Theocracy and Autonomy in Medieval Islamic and Jewish Philosophy*, 38 POL. THEORY 340, 340–341 (2010) ("Can a theocracy—a political community ruled by God—promote the autonomy of its citizens? As citizens of modern liberal democracies we find such a claim hard to reconcile with our basic intuitions. Religions like Islam . . . seem incompatible with concepts of autonomy proposed from the Enlightenment onward. Does not a divine Law lie at their heart—in the broad sense of sharia in Arabic . . . which prescribes what we may and may not do, promising reward for obedience and threatening punishment for disobedience?").

107. *Id.; see* CIA WORLD FACTBOOK, *Saudi Arabia*, https://www.cia.gov/library/publications/the-world-factbook/geos/sa.html (last visited Oct. 14, 2011); CIA WORLD FACTBOOK, *Libya*, https://www.cia.gov/library/publications/the-world-factbook/geos/ly.html (last visited Oct. 14, 2011); CIA WORLD FACTBOOK, *Iran*, https://www.cia.gov/library/publications/the-world-factbook/geos/ir.html (last visited Oct. 13, 2011).

108. CIA WORLD FACTBOOK, *Iran, supra* note 104.

109. *Id.;* U.S. DEPARTMENT OF STATE BUREAU OF DEMOCRACY, HUMAN RIGHTS, AND LABOR, *Nigeria: International Religious Freedom Report 2006*, http://www.state.gov/g/drl/rls/irf/2006/71318.htm.

110. CIA WORLD FACTBOOK, *Israel*, https://www.cia.gov/library/publications/the-world-factbook/geos/is.html (last visited Oct. 14, 2011).

111. Israel's legal system is mixed, integrating English common law, British Mandate regulations, and religious laws (including Jewish, Christian, and Muslim). *Id.*

Following the re-election of George W. Bush to the US presidency in 2004, a communist, anti-Christian blog predicted that America would become a theocracy due to the rise of the Christian political right.[112] This broadside is, of course, hyperbole and should be treated as such. Normally, I would not dignify such commentary with inclusion in a scholarly essay; however, the entry starkly illustrates the importance of sensitivity and reasonableness (or in this case the lack of it) in challenging perspectives associated with another person's faith or religion.

2. DEMOCRATICALLY ACCEPTABLE CONFESSIONALISM

Modern confessional states or nations have an official or dominant religion, with clergy who have a certain level of political autonomy but must still answer to secular political institutions.[113] However, governing is not based directly on revelation or divine authority, but usually on some form of democratic means. Some countries recognize Roman Catholicism as the official religion, including Liechtenstein and Malta.[114] There are also countries that lack an established state religion but have laws that are influenced by or specially recognize Catholicism. Examples include Argentina, Italy, and Poland.[115]

---

112. Larry Everest, *The Rise of the Christian Fascists: The Specter of a U.S. Theocracy and Why the People Must Stop It*, Rev. Worker # 1263 (Dec. 26, 2004), http://rwor. org/a/1263/rise-of-christian-fascists.htm ("The agenda of Bush and the Christian right is not limited to criminalizing abortion, outlawing gay marriage, forcing children to recite prayers in school, and mandating the teaching of Biblical creationist ignorance. Their ultimate goal is Christian fascist theocracy. Now, following the election, they feel emboldened—and compelled—to take their theocratic project to a whole new level. They want to see a religious rule in this country.").

113. Kimitaka Matsuzato and Fumiko Sawae, *Rebuilding a Confessional State: Islamic Ecclesiology in Turkey, Russia and China*, 38 Religion, St. & Soc'y 331, 332 (2010).

114. CIA World Factbook, *Liechtenstein*, https://www.cia.gov/library/publications/ the-world-factbook/geos/ls.html (last visited Oct. 14, 2011); CIA World Factbook, *Malta*, https://www.cia.gov/library/publications/the-world-factbook/geos/ mt.html (last visited Oct. 14, 2011).

115. Ch. 1, §2, Constitution Nacional [Const. Nac.] (Arg.), *available at* http://www. argentina.gov.ar/argentina/portal/documentos/constitucion_ingles.pdf(last visited Oct. 14, 2011) ("The Federal Government supports the Roman Catholic Apostolic religion."); Art. 7 Constituzione [Cost.] (It.), *available at* http://www.senato.it/ documenti/repository/istituzione/costituzione_inglese.pdf (last visited Oct. 14, 2011) ("The State and the Catholic Church are independent and sovereign, each within its own sphere."); Constitucion de la Republica del Paraguay, June 20, 1992,

In addition, a number of countries give special preference and recognition to faiths other than Roman Catholicism, and they include Greece (which gives special recognition to the Eastern Orthodox churches); Denmark, Iceland, and Norway (which recognize for preference the Lutheran Church); and the United Kingdom (where the two established state churches include the Church of England [Anglican] and the Church of Scotland [Presbyterian]).[116]

3. DEMOCRATICALLY ACCEPTABLE INCLUSIONARY SECULARISM

The third category describes much of modern Europe in terms of religious display following the 2011 ECHR decision in *Lautsi v. Italy*, where many countries—such as Italy—understand religious symbols as having educational and cultural value beyond mere recognition of a particular religion.[117] With the notable exception of France, religious

art. 82, *available at* http://www.servat.unibe.ch/icl/pa00000_.html ("The role played by the Catholic Church in the historical and cultural formation of the Republic is hereby recognized."); KONSTYTUCJA RZECZYPOSPOLITEJ POLSKIEJ [Constitution], art. 25 (Poland), *available at* http://sejm.gov.pl/prawo/konst/angielski/kon1.htm ("The relations between the Republic of Poland and the Roman Catholic Church shall be determined by international treaty concluded with the Holy See, and by statute.").

116. Constitution of Greece, art. 3, *available at* http://www.unhcr.org/refworld/docid/4c52794f2.html ("The prevailing religion in Greece is that of the Eastern Orthodox Church of Christ."); Constitution of Denmark, June 5, 1953, ch. 1, §3, *available at* http://www.unhcr.org/refworld/docid/3ae6b518c.html ("The Evangelical Lutheran Church shall be the Established Church of Denmark, and as such shall be supported by the State."); Constitution of the Republic of Iceland, June 17, 1944, art. 62, *available at* http://www.government.is/constitution/; NOR. CONST., art. 2, *available at* http://www.stortinget.no/en/In-English/About-the-Storting/The-Constitution/ (recognizing the Evangelical-Lutheran religion as the official religion of Norway); US DEPARTMENT OF STATE BUREAU OF DEMOCRACY, HUMAN RIGHTS, AND LABOR, *International Religious Freedom Report 2005: United Kingdom, available at* http://www.state.gov/g/drl/rls/irf/2005/51589.htm (last visited Oct. 14, 2011).

117. In response to the 2009 ECHR decision in *Lautsi v. Italy*, originally finding that the public display of crucifixes in classrooms violated human rights, twenty European countries joined Italy's subsequent appeal to the Grand Chamber of the ECHR to "openly defend the legitimacy of Christian symbols in society, particularly in the classroom." EUR. CENTER FOR L. & JUST., *ECHR Crucifix Case: 20 European Countries Support the Crucifix* (July 21, 2010), http://www.eclj.org/Releases/Read.

symbols are included in the public sphere on an open, inclusionary basis. Oddly, however, ECHR opinions that touch on the application of laws against hate speech or the freedom to wear religious apparel indicate an exclusionary, or less protective, stance toward Islam than toward Christianity.[118]

4. DEMOCRATICALLY ACCEPTABLE EXCLUSIONARY SECULARISM

In some respects and at some points in its jurisprudential history, the United States fits this category. That often surprises European citizens who are more likely to know the reference to the Creator and the declared self-evident truth of the Declaration of Independence. At least in comparison to the jurisprudence of the European Court of Human Rights, which (as is apparent from its 2011 decision in *Lautsi*) more readily accommodates religious displays in public places, the United States has transformed a commitment to neutrality into a commitment of exclusion of religious reference and display from the public square.[119]

---

aspx?GUID=983c3dd3-9c17-4b70-a016-37851446ec0e. These countries included Armenia, Albania, Austria, Bulgaria, Croatia, Cyprus, Greece, Hungary, Lithuania, Malta, Monaco, Moldova, Poland, Romania, the Russia Federation, San Marino, Serbia, Slovakia, and Ukraine. *Id.* They joined Italy's side to "affirm the social legitimacy of Christianity in European society . . . [including in national] identities, cultures, and . . . traditions." *Id.*

118. *See,* e.g., Choudhury v. United Kingdom, App. No. 17439/90, 12 HUM. RTS. L.J. 172 (1991) (declaring inadmissible the application of a Muslim British citizen who sought to prosecute Salman Rushdie under Britain's anti-blasphemy law, on the grounds that Rushdie's *Satanic Verses* constituted an attack on his religion.); Dogru v. France, App. No. 27058/05, 49 Eur. H. R. Rep. 179 (2008) (holding that the expulsion from school of a Muslim secondary school student in France, due to the student wearing a prohibited headscarf as an expression of her faith, did not violate Article 9 of the European Convention of Human Rights).

119. The First Amendment to the United States Constitution contains both the Establishment Clause and the Free Exercise Clause. It provides that "Congress shall make no law respecting an establishment of religion, or prohibiting the free exercise thereof . . .," US CONST. amend. I. The Establishment Clause "demands religious neutrality government may not exercise a preference for one religious faith over another." Van Orden v. Perry, 545 U.S. 677, 709 (2005). The Free Exercise Clause provides for "the right to believe and profess whatever religious doctrine one desires . . . or the performance of (or abstention from) physical acts" undertaken for religious reasons. Employment Division v. Smith, 494 U.S. 872, 877 (1990).

To the extent that more recent US cases permit greater religious reference or participation in the use of public resources, this fourth category
starts to gravitate toward the third category—that is, inclusionary secularism. As previously mentioned,[120] and as earlier argued, inclusionary

---

The co-existence of both of these clauses implies some measure of neutrality toward
religion, in that "the establishment clause provides a certain limit to the support that
government may give to religion whereas the free exercise clause requires that government give religion a certain measure of support." John H. Mansfield, *Religion Clauses
of the First Amendment and the Philosophy of the Constitution*, 72 CAL. L. REV. 847, 849
(1984). The US Supreme Court, however, has tended to take a restrictive view of these
clauses. "The Establishment and Free Exercise Clause ... together erect a wall of separation between church and state" and "compel ... [g]overnment's obligation to avoid
divisiveness and exclusion in the religious sphere. . . ." Van Orden, 545 U.S. at 677. *See
also*, Cnty. of Allegheny v. Am. Civil Liberties Union, Greater Pittsburgh Chapter,
492 U.S. 573, 593–594 (1989) ("Whether the key word is 'endorsement,' 'favoritism,'
or 'promotion,' the essential principle remains the same. The Establishment Clause,
at the very least, prohibits government from appearing to take a position on questions
of religious belief or from 'making adherence to a religion relevant in any way to a
person's standing in the political community.'") (quoting Lynch v. Donnelly, 465 U.S.
668, 687 (1984) (O'Connor, J., concurring)).

The United States Supreme Court has held, for instance, that various types of state-
sponsored educational activity related to religion are unconstitutional, based on violations of the Establishment Clause of the First Amendment. For example, a state may
neither allow public school students to receive religious instruction on public school
premises, nor allow religious school students to receive state-sponsored education
in their religious schools. *See* State of Illinois *ex rel.* McCollum v. Bd. of Educ., 333
U.S. 203 (1948); School Dist. of City of Grand Rapids v. Ball, 473 U.S. 373 (1985),
overruled by Agostini v. Felton, 521 U.S. 203 (1997). Similarly unconstitutional is
state-sponsored prayer in public schools. *See* Engel v. Vitale, 370 U.S. 421 (1962); Sch.
Dist. of Abington Township, Pennsylvania v. Schempp, 374 U.S. 203 (1963); Wal-
lace v. Jaffree, 472 U.S. 38, 60 (1982). Finally, the content of a public school's curriculum may not promote religious beliefs. *See* Edwards v. Aguillard, 482 U.S. 578
(1987); Epperson v. Arkansas, 393 U.S. 97 (1968). For the same reason, posting the
Ten Commandments on the wall of a public school classroom violates the Establishment Clause. *See* Stone v. Graham, 449 U.S. 39 (1980); *Cnty. of Allegheny*,492 U.S.
at 591.

The Court has also held that the use of federal funds by the City of New York to pay
the salaries of public employees teaching in parochial schools violated the Establishment Clause. Aguilar v. Felton, 473 U.S. 402 (1985), *overruled by* Agostini v. Felton,
521 U.S. 203 (1997).

120. In 2010, for instance, a plurality of the U.S. Supreme Court ordered that the
display of a cross in a California national park be maintained, and that such a display did not necessarily violate the Establishment Clause of the First Amendment.

secularism is more likely to permit both the successful division of public and private spheres that advances the secular interest in civil order as well as the greatest freedom of religious exercise (in addition to correlated freedoms of speech and association).

It is interesting to speculate how one would map Islamic belief in terms of either exclusionary or inclusionary secularism. The very concept of secularism is a Western concept envisioning in its strongest form rationalism displacing spiritual or religious explanation or justification. Yet, we also earlier saw how the doctrine of harmony (understanding reason and revelation to reach similar conclusions over time even if not at the same time) within the Islamic belief suggests a compatibility with democracy, something that the Western mind, out of ignorance of Islamic belief, has difficulty comprehending. The incompatibility that the Western mind usually imputes to Islam is the Western divide between reason and revelation. If Islamic teaching on the doctrine of harmony was better understood this would be seen as a divide not between Islam and the West but between most of the West united with much of Islam and Islamic fundamentalism. When the West pursues exclusionary secularism to address the non-rational aspects of fundamentalism, the West is indulging in undifferentiated or insufficient knowledge of the Islamic tradition and thereby suppressing it where it could bolster and animate democratic values. The mistaken belief that exclusionary secularism is a warranted ideal in governance may actually deprive modern theory and practice of an example of democratic governance more compatible and respectful of the needs of the human person.

By accepting the broader form of exclusionary secularism, or even by the acceptance of the division of public and private spheres of inclusionary secularism, Islamic scholars would argue that the West is

---

Salazar v. Buono, 130 S.Ct. 1803 (2010). To some scholars, this and other recent Supreme Court decisions represent that "America, once the champion of strict separation of Church and state, seems to be moving toward an ever more generous accommodation of its religious traditions and symbols." John Witte, Jr., & Nina-Louisa Arold, *Lift High the Cross? Contrasting the New European and American Cases on Religious Symbols on Government Property*, 25 EMORY INT'L L. REV. 5, 5 (2011).

depriving itself of some unique insights of Muslim belief with respect to human rights.[121] In other words, there is a body of scholarship that argues that Islamic belief is more, not less, compatible with the true purposes of democracy. The Western reader is likely surprised by claims of democratic superiority for Islamic belief, and if it is a surprise, it illustrates the importance of interfaith education to lead to the vocabulary and substantive understanding of faith differences before Western nations again accept the extortionate demands of strongmen like Gaddafi or Mubarak.

5. DEMOCRATICALLY UNACCEPTABLE: COMPELLED ATHEISM
No countries fall into this category.

To summarize, by definition, the first category of compelled theocracy supplies virtually a one-to-one relationship between religion and the law of the state and does not acknowledge that this identity results from imposition as opposed to consensual choice. In this category, one would reasonably place any state that presumed to assign to religious figures or bodies responsibility as the authoritative lawgiver, with little or no freedom for citizens to dissent from religious law as given. At the other end of the spectrum is compelled atheism, which would be democratically unacceptable for similar reasons, even though what is compelled here is more denial than affirmation of God. A denial of God is, to a believer, as repugnant as affirming a belief contrary to one's own religious tradition.

By comparison, a confessional state is one in which there is an established or preferred religion identified in law, but the preference is not binding on individual citizens who are free to believe and act in their own way even if that is somewhat at odds with the orthodoxy of the preferred faith.[122] At the time the United States was founded, established religions existed in a number of states, and this form of confessionalism was not perceived as subtracting from the historical guarantee of

---

121. A. Ezzati, p. 203.
122. Matsuzato & Sawae, *supra* note 113, at 332.

religious freedom that was exercised individually and was unaffected by the corporate choice of the government.[123]

Nevertheless, one of the surprises in examining this area is the extent to which the United States, and not Europe, is more likely to indulge the notion of exclusionary secularism in terms of religious display.[124] Thus,

123. *See, e.g.,* CHRIS BENEKE, BEYOND TOLERATION—THE RELIGIOUS ORIGINS OF AMERICAN PLURALISM 6 (2006) ("Between the 1760s and the 1780s . . . the barriers that had prevented white Americans from practicing their religion freely and speaking their views openly gave way during the revolutionary period. The new state governments either could not or would not maintain the discriminatory policies that continued to characterize European societies.").

124. The inclusion of religious symbols in public holiday displays came before the U.S. Supreme Court in Lynch v. Donnelly, 465 U.S. 668 (1984) and *County of Allegheny,* 492 U.S. 573 (1989). In Lynch, the Court upheld the public display of a crèche, ruling that any benefit to religion was "indirect, remote, and incidental." *Lynch,* 465 U.S. at 683. In County of Allegheny, however, the Court struck down a crèche display, which occupied a prominent position in the county courthouse and bore the words "Gloria in Excelsis Deo!" (Glory to God in the highest), and was the setting for an annual Christmas carol program. *Cnty. of Allegheny,* 492 U.S. at 579–581. The court did uphold a nearby display of a menorah, which appeared along with a Christmas tree and a sign saluting liberty, reasoning that "the combined display of the tree, the sign, and the menorah . . . simply recognizes that Christmas and Hanukkah had become part of the secular winter shopping season." *Id.* at 616. The winter season had "attained a secular status," according to the justices in the majority. *Id.* at 616. *See also* Glassroth v. Moore, 335 F.3d 1282 (11th Cir. 2003), in which famously—or perhaps infamously—Chief Justice Roy Moore of the Alabama Supreme Court was ordered to remove a Ten Commandments monument which he had placed in the central rotunda of the Alabama State Judicial Building. *Id.* at 1288. When he refused to do so, the monument was removed pursuant to federal court order; ultimately, Moore was removed from office as a matter of failing to observe the requirements of judicial ethics and enforcing a court order. Bob Johnson, *Moore's Ten Commandments Fight Is Top Story of Year in Alabama,* ASSOC. PRESS, Dec. 18, 2003.

The closest US decision to that under review by the European Court of Human Rights is Stone v. Graham, 449 U.S. 39 (1980), in which the court addressed the mandated public display, supported by private donations, of the Ten Commandments in Kentucky public school classrooms. *Id.* at 39. The court found an Establishment Clause violation premised upon the absence of a secular purpose. *Id.* at 41. In 2005, the Supreme Court considered two additional cases dealing with the display of the Ten Commandments: Van Orden v. Perry, 545 U.S. 677 (2005) and McCreary County., Ky. v. American Civil Liberties Union of Kentucky, 545 U.S. 844 (2005). The cases were decided 5 to 4, but had different outcomes. In *Van Orden,* the court upheld the Texas display of the Ten Commandments on the Texas State Capitol grounds, surrounded by the large number of other nonreligious statuary and plaques. *Van Orden,* 545 U.S. at 691–692. In McCreary County, on the other hand, the court split

category four represents the United States—which would surprise many European analysts, since this places America behind Europe in terms of its voluntary or consensual reference to religion and its importance. Nonetheless, this exclusionary side of the United States placing it in category four should not be overstated. First, the jurisprudence has subtly but noticeably shifted in favor of including religious entities in government programs on an equal protection theory.[125] Second, the ECHR, while decidedly inclusionary of religious symbol (as in *Lautsi*), is troublingly exclusionary in the treatment of Islam with respect to the protection of faith practice generally.[126] Nonetheless, until recently, the US Supreme Court sought to divide a republic founded on an acknowledgment of the Creator from even any subsequent "tip of the hat" [127] in the direction of religious display on public premises.[128] More recently, Justice Scalia on the Court has made it a point to remind lawyers not to rely on the higher law references in the Declaration of

---

the other way and invalidated a specialized display created for purposes of illustrating a wide variety of documents referencing the divine in American history. *McCreary Cnty.*, 545 U.S. at 872–873.

125. In recent years, "the Court's cases under both the Free Exercise Clause and the Establishment Clause have embraced a norm of equal treatment – a principle that prohibits the government from favoring one religious sect over another." Clifford J. Rosky, *Perry v. Schwarzenegger and the Future of Same-Sex Marriage Law*, ARIZ. L. REV. 913, 958 (2011). *See also* Perry v. Schwarzenegger, 704 F. Supp. 2d 921, 931 (N. D. Cal. 2010) ("The state does not have an interest in enforcing private moral or religious beliefs without an accompanying secular purpose.") (citing Everson v. Bd. of Educ. of Ewing Twp., 330 U.S. 1, 15 (1947) ("The 'establishment of religion' clause of the First Amendment means at least this: neither a state nor the Federal Government can set up a Church. Neither can pass laws which aid one religion, aid all religions, or prefer one religion over another."); Thomas C. Berg, *Can Religious Liberty Be Protected as Equality?*, 85 TEX. L. REV. 1185, 1186 (2007) (book review) ("Many observers see the Court's emphasis changing in the last twenty-five years from church-state separation to equal treatment between religion and nonreligion, with some significant remaining elements of separationism.").

126. *See*, e.g., Şahin v. Turkey, App. No. 44774/98, 2005-XI Eur. C. H. R. (2005) (holding that there had been no violation of Article 9 of the European Convention on Human Rights when a Muslim student had been banned from wearing an Islamic headscarf while a student at a university in Turkey.); Dogru v. France, App. No. 27058/05, 49 Eur. H. R. Rep. 179 (2008).

127. *Everson*, 330 U.S. at 18.

128. *Supra* note 126.

Independence.[129] The Scalian argument has likely more to do with judicial restraint than the significance of the higher law, but the effect is the same: exclusion of a reference that would have ultimately led to a religious root if it had been followed.

The effort to deny the religious origin of the United States, however, has not been totally successful in practical experience.[130] Subsequently, utilizing an equal protection rationale, rather than one referencing the constitutional right to free exercise of religion, the US Supreme Court moderated the impact of excluding public religious displays.[131] In general, there have been modifications of American case law since the mid-1970's that have made it more accommodating and less exclusionary,[132] but it is still more exclusionary than the case law acknowledged by the European Court of Human Rights.

As will be seen in the *Lautsi* decision, Europe's tolerance of the crucifix is similar to American case law, though capable of accommodating far more particularistic display than American law, where equal treatment of religious and non-religious worldviews or practices is said to satisfy the constitutional requirement of not establishing religion.[133] These

129. *See, e.g.,* Antonin Scalia, *Of Democracy, Morality, and the Majority,* 26 Origins 81, 87–90 (1996) ("The Supreme Court of the United States, [nor any] federal court to my knowledge, in 200 years has ever decided a case on the basis of the Declaration of Independence. It is not part of our law."), *quoted in* DOUGLAS W. KMIEC ET AL., INDIVIDUAL RIGHTS AND THE AMERICAN CONSTITUTION 44 (2004).

130. In its Establishment Clause jurisprudence, the Supreme Court has been reluctant, for instance, to find older religious displays and practices (as opposed to more recently installed displays) to be unconstitutional. Witte & Arold, note 120, at 48. "Even if the original inspiration for the old display or practice was religious, its long-standing presence in public life seems to imbue it with a kind of cultural and Constitutional imprimatur. In the Court's view, it has become part of American culture, society, and democracy – and is thus unlikely to be a fateful first step toward an establishment of religion." *Id.*

131. *Supra* note 125.

132. *See, e.g.,* Witte & Arold, *supra* note 120, at 53–54 ("In contrast to earlier case law that] left religion hermetically sealed from political life and public institutions…the Supreme Court has abandoned much of its strict separatism and now allows religious and nonreligious parties alike to engage in peaceable public activities, even in public schools.").

133. *Supra* note 125. The U.S. Supreme Court has embraced "religious neutrality" that is defined as "neutrality not only between and among religions, but also between religion and nonreligion." Daniel O. Conkle, *The Path of American Religious Liberty: From the Original Theology to Formal Neutrality and an Uncertain Future,* 75 IND. L. J. 1, 9 (2000). *But see Engel,* 370 U.S. at 430 (observing that because a state-composed prayer was "denominationally neutral" did not "free it from the limitations of the Establishment Clause.").

cases sit uneasily with others seemingly mandating total separation or exclusion.[134] Moreover, much of the body of case law seems to turn more on the avoidance of content distinction than on the desire to accommodate religion; but the labels matter more to how lawyers reason than to the general population.[135]

As mentioned, the equal treatment cases in the United States turn on a determination of whether competing secular and religious ideas or practices are treated alike. Thus, in one case the Supreme Court held that a student-run Christian magazine could not be excluded from the general fund that supported other exercises of commentary by student organizations.[136] Similarly, a Christian organization has the same right of access as other student organizations to use public school classrooms after hours.[137] This equal protection (or equality) strain in United States church-state litigation softens the exclusionary secularist core of the US Supreme Court's earlier instruction that public entities must be neutral—not just among religions, but also between religion and irreligion.[138]

Exclusionary secularism is the theme of modern American jurisprudence.[139] But as suggested by the recent, lively references to God and faith by all manner of American public officials, it has not captured US culture—yet. Exclusionary secularism dominates law and culture, however, in France.

134. *See,* e.g., Berg, *supra* note 125, at 1185 ("Among the central questions concerning the First Amendment's Religion Clauses is whether their fundamental goal is nondiscrimination or a substantive liberty. Do they primarily require that government not engage in discrimination among religions or between religious and nonreligious ideas? Or do they primarily guarantee for decisions about religious matters and religious life a zone of liberty or autonomy against state restriction, or a degree of separation from state involvement?").

135. *See,* e.g., Rosenberger v. Rector and Visitors of Univ. of Va., 515 U.S. 819, 845 (1995) (holding that a public university's withholding of payments for printing costs for a religiously themed student publication, but not for other student publications, constituted "viewpoint discrimination.").

136. *Id.*

137. Lynch v. Donnelly, 465 U.S. 668 (1984)

138. Conkle, *supra* note 133.

139. *Supra* note 119; *see also* Steven D. Smith, *Separation and the Secular: Reconstructing the Disestablishment Decision,* 67 Tex. L. Rev. 955, 979 (1988–1989) ("The Supreme Court . . . typically present[s] the secularism requirement as . . . [meaning] that institutional separation naturally entails, or simply *means,* a secular state.").

6. THE FRENCH EXCEPTION

Twenty years ago, about 80 percent of French people described themselves as Catholic.[140] Today, it's just over half; and only 10 percent of the population—most of them older—regularly go to church.[141]

In France, religion is widely seen as a source of trouble.[142] *Laïcité*, or secularism, is a principle that is enshrined in the French Constitution and in a 1905 law that instituted the official separation of Church and state.[143] It reflects a national history of confrontation between the Catholic Church and the state, from the French Revolution through the twentieth century.[144] During the twentieth century, *laïcité* has come to be "rigorously enforced . . . in all public spheres" to such an extent that it is referred to as "the alternative religion of France."[145] This history is still extant in lessons taught in French classrooms, movies, and exhibits showing those murdered at the hands of religious believers. In addition, France is the only Western European country without religious instruction in public schools.[146] Instead, in French schools, state-employed teachers may teach religion "only as a sociological phenomenon."[147] Not surprisingly, cathedrals in France (including the famous Notre Dame)

---

140. Henry Samuel, *France "No Longer a Catholic Country,"* THE TELEGRAPH, Jan. 10, 2007, http://www.telegraph.co.uk/news/worldnews/1539093/France-no-longer-a-Catholic-country.html.

141. *Id.*

142. *See*, e.g., MINISTERÈ DES AFFAIRES ÉTRANGERÈS (Fr.), *One Hundred Years of French Secularism*, http://www.diplomatie.gouv.fr/en/article_imprim.php3?id_article=6155 (last visited Oct. 14, 2011) ("From the 1789 Revolution until the beginning of the 20th century, the Catholic Church remained in violent opposition to the Republic."); Stephanie Giry, *France and Its Muslims*, 85 FOREIGN AFF. 87, 89 ("The French model [of secularism] distrusts . . . religious characteristics as divisive.").

143. 1958 CONST. art. I, (Fr.), *available at* http://www.assemblee-nationale.fr/english/8ab. asp ("France shall be an indivisible, secular, democratic and social Republic."); *Loi du 9 decembre 1905 concernant la separation des Eglises et de l'Etat* [Law on the Separation of Churches and State of Dec. 9, 1905], JOURNAL OFFICIEL DE LA RÉPUBLIQUE FRANÇAISE [J.O.][OFFICIAL GAZETTE OF FRANCE], Dec. 11, 1905, p. 7205.

144. *See generally* KURU, *supra* note 18, at 136–158 (2009).

145. Dominique MacNeill, *Religious Education and National Identity*, 47 SOCIAL COMPASS 343, 346 (2000).

146. KURU, *supra* note 18, at 106 n.20.

147. Giry, *supra* note 142; *but see* KURU, *supra* note 18, at 110 ("The popularity of private Catholic schools [in France] and their public funding reveals that French state policies toward religion are not completely exclusionary.").

have been state property for over a century now.[148] While historically marriage was the province of the Church and the Church alone, with marriage being said to have been authored by God himself, today in France the Church wedding counts for nothing beyond ceremony. For a wedding in that country to be acknowledged as legitimate, it must be conducted in a civil office.[149] Finally, a French politician making reference to the divine would subtract from his credibility and legitimacy—which, as we know, is quite the opposite of the situation in the United States.[150]

The exclusionary secularist attitude in France has a significant problem, however, when it comes to that country's Muslim population.[151] France has the largest Muslim population in Europe—according to recent estimates, it is almost five million, twice as large as in the United States.[152] It is a population that is native to France and not merely the

148. Rk Torfs, *Church and State in France, Belgium, and the Netherlands: Unexpected Similarities and Hidden Differences*, 1996 BYU L. Rev. 945, 952 (1996).

149. Dagmar Coester-Waltien & Michael Coester, *Formation of Marriage*, 4 International Encyclopedia of Comparative Law ch. 3, §117, at 74 (2008) (*quoted in* Lynn D. Wardle, *Marriage and Religious Liberty: Comparative Law Problems and Conflict of Laws Solutions*, 12 J. L. & Fam. Stud. 315, 326 (2008)).

150. In 2008, for instance, French president Nicolas Sarkozy received public criticism for "[breaking] traditional presidential reserve about religion" in a speech in which he referenced France's Christian heritage. Tom Heneghan, *Sarkozy Sparks French Debate over God and Religion*, Reuters, Jan. 17, 2008, http://uk.reuters.com/article/2008/01/17/uk-france-religion-idUKL1712352920080117?pageNumber=1&virtualBrandChannel=0. In contrast, American political figures frequently make public reference to the religious heritage of the United States and to their own religious faith, without any apparent serious repercussions from the public. *See*, e.g., Gingrich, *supra* note 4; Obama, Faith and Politics, *supra* note 41.

151. It has been noted that, in general, "no social issue is more pressing for France's center-right government than the integration of that country's Muslims into the fabric of French society." Elaine Sciolino, *Muslim Lycee Opens in Secular France, Raising Eyebrows*, N.Y. Times, Sept. 9, 2003, http://www.nytimes.com/2003/09/09/world/muslim-lycee-opens-in-secular-france-raising-eyebrows.html.

152. Pew Forum on Religion & Pub. Life, *The Future of the Global Muslim Population: Projections for 2010–2030* (Jan. 27, 2011) http://pewforum.org/future-of-the-global-muslim-population-regional-europe.aspx (showing the estimated Muslim population in France in 2010 to number at 4,704,000); Pew Forum on Religion & Pub. Life, *The Global Muslim Population: Projections for 2010–2030: Region: Americas* (Jan. 27, 2011), http://pewforum.org/future-of-the-global-muslim-population-regional-americas.aspx (showing the estimated number of Muslims in the United States in 2010 to be 2,595,000).

product of recent migration. Many are the French-born children and grandchildren of Muslim immigrants from former colonies such as Algeria, who moved to France after these colonies gained independence in the 1960s.[153]

The yearning to express oneself in terms of the divine is especially strong among the Muslim population.[154] For the sake of comity and the need to integrate so as to find employment, immigrant populations of more recent vintage might remain quiet about their faith; not so for native French Muslims and others. For them, the suppression of faith symbols and practices in France is a source of constant aggravation and outrage. For the last seven years, students have not been allowed to wear headscarves, large crosses, or other "conspicuous" religious symbols in public schools.[155] Such bans have not promoted harmony or integration but have resulted in separate schools, some of which are quite angry in instructional tone and direction.[156] (They are attractive, however, since they allow Muslim practice to be overtly undertaken in France.) The 2011 public ban on the full-face veil or *niqab*, worn by very few women,

---

153. *See* BBC News, *Muslims in Europe: Country Guide: France*, Dec. 23, 2005, http://news. bbc.co.uk/2/hi/europe/4385768.stm#france.

154. *See, e.g.*, Qamar-Ul Huda, *Knowledge of Allah and the Islamic View of Other Religions*, 64 THEOLOGICAL STUD. 278, 282 (2003) ("God's existence is self-evident in every aspect of the universe, but those who reflect on the divine will understand that He gives meaning and life to everything . . . .").

155. Law No. 2004–228 of Mar. 15, 2004, Journal Officiel De La Republique Francaise [J.O.] [Official Gazette of France], Mar. 17, 2004, p. 5190.

156. The idea to establish a Muslim high school in the French city of Lille first came to light in 1994, when a local mosque offered classes for nineteen Muslim girls who were not permitted to wear headscarves in the local public school, pursuant to the recent ban on this attire in schools by the French government. Sciolino, *supra* note 151. The mosque eventually opened the first Muslim high school in France, the Lycee Averroes, in 2003. *Id.* This was viewed by some as an "act of defiance against the state" by the Muslim community, especially since the mosque is affiliated with a Muslim organization that "preaches a strict conservative interpretation of Islam. . . ." *Id.* Note, however, that Muslim schools are not widespread in France— as of 2008, there were only four in the entire country, with many Muslim students electing to attend Catholic schools (where girls may also wear headscarves) instead. Katrin Bennhold, *French Muslims Find Haven in Catholic Schools*, N.Y. TIMES, Sept. 29, 2008, http://www.nytimes.com/2008/09/30/world/europe/30schools. html?ref=education.

is also a sore point.[157] The idea of being singled out for disfavor sits quite uneasily among Muslim populations in France. That said, there can be divergent interests within the Muslim population. A husband, brother, or other male in a household may insist on the *niqab* when the female, if given her preference and without family recrimination, would prefer to be free of it. In this way, freedom of religion may actually be a covert means to achieve discriminatory, female submission. These limitations are popular among the general French population, but they also have support from progressive Muslim women.[158] Secularism is seen in France as a necessity to peace, but it also may hold wider educational and employment possibilities for women.[159] Of course, it can be a peace that has shown itself to be quite fragile and unpredictable, especially if the male Muslim population perceives it as an insult to their core faith beliefs. It is a "peace" that makes it impossible to dress in accordance with one's religious tradition; supplies limited spaces for prayer; and fosters attitudes of suspicion and hatred (quite often within the family). The illusory nature of the peace becomes only too obvious when the very high unemployment rate among French Muslims is added in, and helps to explain the rampages of destruction that exploded in the French suburbs just a few years ago.[160]

Exclusionary secularism's French harvest is the pervasive belief—by Muslim and non-Muslim alike—that it is impossible to be both French

---

157. See Loi 2010–1192 du octobre 2010 interdisant la dissimulation du visage dans l'espace public (1) [Law 2010–1192 of October 11, 2010, Prohibiting the Concealment of the Face in Public], Journal Officiel De La Republique Francaise [J.O.] [Official Gazette of France], Oct. 12, 2010, *available at* www.legifrance.gouv.fr/WAspad/UnTexteDeJorf?numjo=JUSX1011390L; *see also* Angelique Chrisafis, *Full-Face Veils Outlawed as France Spells Out Controversial Niqab Ban*, THE GUARDIAN, Mar. 3, 2011, http://www.guardian.co.uk/world/2011/mar/03/niqab-ban-france-muslim-veil (noting that only a few hundred women, out of more than 5 million Muslims in France, wear full niqab.).

158. *The Islamic Veil across Europe: France*, BBC NEWS, Sept. 22, 2011, http://www.bbc.co.uk/news/world-europe-13038095.

159. MINISTERÈ DES AFFAIRES ÉTRANGERÈS, *supra* note 142.

160. Giry, *supra* note 147, at 94 ("Unemployment is believed to affect 30 percent of French citizens of Algerian and Moroccan descent, compared with 10 percent of the population at large, and the jobs [they] do get are more often temporary or beneath their qualifications.").

and Muslim.[161] Just beneath the harms nourished by that doubt is the one suggestion that no religious person can be a good citizen. It is clear that the French legal structure is now aligned to provide its greatest support to atheism.

THE CRUCIFIX CASE—RELIGIOUS DISPLAYS IN EUROPE AND THE UNITED STATES COMPARED

Consider an Italian administrative regulation mandating that the crucifix be on display in every public school classroom. Were this mandate before the US Supreme Court, the US Constitution would prohibit such a display. There is, believes the Court, a "high wall of separation"[162] between church and state. Government has an affirmative obligation to maintain a secular state—that is, not just neutrality between competing religious beliefs but between religion and no religion as well.[163]

From time to time, arguments are made to the Court that distinctly religious symbols may be tolerated in a public setting if they have sufficiently independent cultural significance or are mixed in with other elements of display that already do have such significance. However, this is not a line of argument in which the Court has had particular confidence. Denigrated as the jurisprudence of inferior design, it tends to be quite subjective. *Lynch v. Donnelly* is typical. There, the Court

161. *Id.* at 90 ("Islam was seen [historically] as a barrier to Frenchness – and in one way or another it still is today.").

162. Quite recently, the American Supreme Court has articulated a less exclusionary counterpoint that lowered the wall of separation by occasionally treating the no-establishment principle not as a direction to exclude but rather as an obligation to include on equal terms. While it is not hard to conceive of the no establishment proposition in these terms (and indeed, it may be more historically in keeping with the original understanding of the Establishment Clause), it is not immediately apparent that there is a majority of the Supreme Court concurring. Indeed, under Chief Justice John Roberts, the Court has thus far focused its efforts more on foreclosing Establishment Clause challenges brought by taxpayers, or those with indirect or remote injury, rather than rehearing generations of divisive efforts to agree on a definitive original meaning of the clause. *See* Hein v. Freedom from Religion Found., 551 U.S. 587 (2007) (challenging the constitutionality of Executive Branch Expenditures providing preference to faith-based conferences and initiatives).

163. *Supra* note 126.

accepted public display of a nativity scene only because it was sufficiently neutered by Santa's reindeer and other nonreligious reminders of the season that more and more convey economic, rather than spiritual, significance.[164]

On the issue of displaying religious symbols in the United States, the mandate to draw no distinction between religion and no religion remains. This is apparently not true in Europe.

Lautsi Opinion: The Lower Court of the ECHR

In the case of *Lautsi and Others v. Italy*,[165] after getting no satisfaction from her domestic courts in Italy, Ms. Soile Lautsi, on behalf of her children, challenged the mandate to display a crucifix in public schools under Article 2 of Protocol No. 1 to the Convention for the Protection of Human Rights and Fundamental Freedoms.[166] Article 2 provides: "No person shall be denied the right to education. In the exercise of any functions which it assumes in relation to education and to teaching, the State shall respect the right of parents to ensure such education and teaching in conformity with their own religious and philosophical convictions."[167] Finding this parental right offended in the context of a nonbeliever's challenge, a Chamber of the Second Section of the European

---

164. Lynch v. Donnelly, 465 U.S. 668, 685 (1984) ("Even the traditional, purely secular displays extant at Christmas, with or without a crèche, would inevitably recall the religious nature of the Holiday.").

165. *See* Lautsi and Others v. Italy, App. No. 30814/06, Eur. Ct. H. R. (2011) *available at* http://www.echr.coe.int/echr/resources/hudoc/lautsi_and_others_v__italy.pdf [hereinafter Lautsi]. The Grand Chamber reversed a 2009 decision by the ECHR's Second Section, which had found that the display of the crucifix in Italian public school classrooms "restrict[ed] the right of parents to educate their children in conformity with their convictions and the right of schoolchildren to believe or not believe .... [T]he restrictions are incompatible with the State's duty to respect neutrality in the exercise of public authority, particularly in the field of education." Lautsi v. Italy, App. No. 30814/06, 50 Eur. H. R. Rep. 10,511,064 (2010), para. 57. Lautsi is representative of a change of course toward a more inclusionary posture for the ECHR as compared with Dogru v. France, App. No. 27058/05, 49 Eur. H. R. Rep. 179 (2008).

166. *Lautsi* at para. 1.

167. Convention for the Protection of Human Rights and Fundamental Freedoms, art. 2, Nov. 4, 1950, 213 U.N.T.S. 221.

Court of Human Rights held that Article 2 of Protocol No. 1 had been violated.[168] Its reasoning followed a path consistent more or less with the exclusionary secular side of the American doctrine, although there is no direct reference to American law in the text of the decision (perhaps to avoid the flipside furor of what happens when American jurists employ European precedent). The lower chamber court found "an obligation on the State's part to refrain from imposing beliefs, even indirectly, in places where persons were dependent on it or in places where they were particularly vulnerable, emphasizing that the schooling of children was a particularly sensitive area in that respect."[169] Moreover, the lower tribunal ruled that freedom of religion is not limited to freedom from publicly conducted liturgical practice; the freedom also extends to practices and symbols.[170]

The Irony

The decision of the lower court of the ECHR was not received well in the general European population.[171] In a matter of months, in fact, it would be roundly reversed by the ECHR's Grand Chamber in 2011. Ironic? On its face, it would seem so. The jurisprudence of the United States demands stricter separation between church and state, even though its founding charter traces inalienable rights to a divine Creator. By contrast, the existing European Union was constructed upon a charter notably leaving out all reference to the Divine.[172] In contrast to the repeated general affirmation of belief in God in the United States, *Time* magazine reported that "a 2008 Gallup poll registered a continued decline in Christian faith across Europe. More than two-thirds of respondents in countries such as Britain, France, the Czech Republic and all of Scandinavia responded 'No' to the question of whether religion was important

---

168. *Lautsi* at para. 30.
169. *Lautsi* at para. 31.
170. *Id.*
171. Dominick McGoldrick, *Religion in the European Public Square and in European Public Life—Crucifixes in the Classroom?*, 11 HUM. RTS. L. REV. 451, 470 (2011).
172. *See generally* Charter of Fundamental Rights of the European Union, 2000 O.J. (C 364) 1, *available at* http://www.europarl.europa.eu/charter/pdf/text_en.pdf.

to them."[173] For this reason, Europe was the focal point of Pope Benedict XVI's efforts against secularism. So what then explains the swift, and largely negative, reaction to a judicial ruling imposing a fine for display of what is surely the most familiar symbol of Christianity?

Possible Explanations for ECHR's Inclusionary Stance on Religious Displays

LOCAL DEFERENCE: "MARGIN OF APPRECIATION" COMPARED TO US FEDERALISM

The Grand Chamber reversed the lower court's decision by 15–2. The court accepted the Italian government's argument that the crucifix formed part of that nation's identity, and to that extent was not solely a religious symbol.[174] Even as a symbol, it was "passive" in that it involved no coerced liturgical exercise.[175] Finally, the Grand Chamber was not so much endorsing a crucifix display mandate as reflecting that there is not one uniform answer regarding this issue among the forty-seven member nations ("the High Contracting Parties") under the Convention of Human Rights.[176] In reversing the lower court or chamber tribunal, the Grand Chamber would make note of this variation, writing that there was "no common approach in Europe in these fields," and therefore "each of the member states had a particularly wide margin of appreciation."[177] The jurisprudence of the United States would find the first two rationales as insufficient to uphold the mandate under the facts as given. The third factor warrants a closer look.

The concept of "margin of appreciation" is one akin to the American federalism that supports "laboratories of experimentation" (across the fifty sovereign states), but in reality, the European concept is more permissive of variation and subsidiarity. Today, US federalism is an enigmatic feature of American constitutional practice. It is given regular lip

---

173. Jeff Israely, *Will Crucifixes Be Banned in Italian Schools?*, Time, Nov. 5, 2009, *available at* http://www.time.com/time/world/article/0,8599,1934859,00.html.
174. *Lautsi*.at para 36.
175. *Id.* at para. 72 ("A crucifix on a wall . . . cannot be deemed to have an influence on pupils comparable to that of didactic speech or participation in religious activities.").
176. *Id.* at para. 68.
177. *Id.* at para. 34.

service in political campaigns by local candidates excoriating national counterparts for imposing unfunded mandates. National candidates join that chorus just long enough to be elected before indulging in the "pass the no bucks [back to the states]" practice themselves. Doctrinally, conservatives have bemoaned for decades an ever-enlarging national commerce power which, with an occasional assist from the Necessary and Proper clause, sweeps all significant regulatory authority into what Madison perhaps disingenuously described as the "few and defined"[178] powers of the federal government.[179] Authority

178. THE FEDERALIST No. 45, at 241 (James Madison) (George W. Carey & James Mc-Clellan ed., 2001).

179. The Commerce Clause in Article 1 of the US Constitution allows Congress "to regulate Commerce with foreign nations, and among the several states, and with the Indian tribes." US CONST, art. I, § 8, cl. 3. The Necessary and Proper Clause states that Congress has the power "To make all Laws which shall be necessary and proper for carrying into Execution the foregoing Powers, and all other Powers vested by this Constitution in the Government of the United States, or in any Department or Officer thereof." US CONST. art. I, § 8, cl. 18. To determine whether Congress has power to regulate an activity under the Commerce Clause, a court must look at "whether a regulated activity 'substantially affects' interstate commerce." U.S. v. Lopez, 514 U.S. 549, 559 (1995).

The US Supreme Court has noted that "limitations on the commerce power are inherent in the very language of the Commerce Clause." Id. at 553 (citing Gibbons v. Ogden, 9 Wheat. 1, 194–195 (1824)). During the twentieth century, however, beginning with the New Deal, "an era of Commerce Clause jurisprudence greatly expanded the previously defined authority of Congress under that Clause ... reflect[ing] a view that earlier Commerce Clause cases artificially had constrained the authority of Congress to regulate interstate commerce." Id. at 556.

To many conservatives, Congress has repeatedly overstepped its Commerce Clause authority over the years, recently "pass[ing] laws about a variety of modern issues that the Founders didn't mention" (such as abortion) and claiming authority to do so under both the Commerce Clause and the Necessary and Proper Clause. David A. Fahrenthold, In House, GOP Invokes Constitution, WASH. POST, Sept. 17, 2011, at A3. This perspective has gained new ground in the recent battles over national healthcare reform; the recently enacted 2010 Patient Protection and Affordable Healthcare Act requires citizens to purchase a minimum level of health insurance coverage. Many conservatives believe that the law's requirements impose an "individual mandate" that constitutes a severe overreaching of federal authority under the Commerce Clause. See, e.g., Edmund Haislmaier and Brian Blase, Obamacare: Impact on States, THE HERITAGE FOUNDATION, July 1, 2010, available at http://www.heritage.org/research/reports/2010/07/obamacare-impact-on-states ("The federal [healthcare law] ... constitutes a significant usurpation by the federal government of long-standing state authority over health insurance regulation."); Adam Liptak, Some Common Ground for Legal Adversaries on Health Care, N.Y. TIMES, Sept. 29, 2011, http://www.nytimes.com/2011/09/30/us/health-care-adversaries-have-common-ground.html.

reserved to the states was briefly given constitutional protection by the Court in the 1990s,[180] but today what state and local authority remains depends almost entirely upon the self-imposed restraint of Congress or the national legislature.[181]

While the absence of local control of economic and regulatory policy generally is grist for endless political debate and campaign, there is little or no sentiment in the United States for locally controlled definitions of human right.

This is certainly true since the twentieth century given the advent of "judicial incorporation" of basic rights by the Supreme Court on the several states—with the corollary proposition that the federal articulation of any right so incorporated is to be uniformly enforced, or at least understood as a minimum or floor. There is little or no leeway for the states to be *less* generous in the interpretation of freedom of religion, freedom of speech, and a whole variety of criminal adjudication rights (such as the mandated right to be given Miranda warnings).[182]

---

180. In 1995, the U.S. Supreme Court, under Justice William Rehnquist, limited congressional power under the Commerce Clause to regulating only intrastate economic activity. *See Lopez*, 514 U.S. at 567 (holding that possessing a gun in a school zone did not constitute an economic activity that "substantially affect[ed] . . . interstate commerce," and therefore Congress had no authorization to regulate the carrying of handguns near schools.) *See also* City of Boerne v. Flores, 521 U.S. 507 (1997) (holding that the federal Religious Freedom Restoration Act exceeded Congress's enforcement powers, and failed to maintain "separation of powers and the federal balance."). *But see* Gonzales v. Reich, 545 U.S. 1 (2005) (holding that federal law regulating controlled substances such as marijuana did not infringe upon state authority under the Commerce Clause, even where a state had already passed legislation authorizing the use of marijuana for medicinal purposes.).

181. States can, however, sue the federal government if they believe that federal legislation oversteps congressional authority. No fewer than twenty-six states have challenged Obama's healthcare reform law in court. *See* Liptak, *supra* note 179.

182. Per the doctrine of "selective incorporation," "only those provisions of the Bill of Rights that the [US Supreme] Court considers fundamental to the American system of law are applied to the states through the due process clause of the Fourteenth Amendment." RONALD D. ROTUNDA & JOHN E NOWAK, 2 TREATISE ON CONSTITUTIONAL LAW—SUBSTANCE AND PROCEDURE §14.2(a) (4th ed.) (2011). To date, the Court has incorporated the First Amendment's guarantees against establishment of religion and freedom of speech, as well as the Fifth Amendment's privilege against self-incrimination, against the states (among other constitutional protections located in the Bill of Rights). *Id.*

A NON-JUDICIAL FACTOR: IRREGULAR MIGRATION TO EUROPE

To a greater extent than the United States, Europe is witnessing large-scale irregular migration, especially with regard to an influx of Muslim believers.[183] Invariably, this brings to local communities the desire for minarets, burqas, and the accommodation of other Islamic practices and holidays not familiar to the typical European citizen. It is also blamed for rioting when social changes have not kept pace with migrant need, or when migrant need is perceived to worsen the opportunities of native citizens.[184] Regardless of whether such dislike is the product of uninformed fear of the stranger, the fully informed violent disorders in migrant enclaves in European capitals, or the more contested loss of low-wage jobs to immigrant laborers willing to work for less than prevailing wage, some disaffected citizens saw the crucifix as a symbolic means to draw an exclusionary line in the sand. There clearly is something serious going on.

Predictably, American commentators accustomed to understanding the freedom *of* religion as the freedom *from* it in the strongest, exclusionary secular sense saw the reversal of the ECHR Second Chamber's decision as a "contortion that would be the envy of Houdini."[185] Certainly, from the vantage point of an American litigant, it would be quite unusual to find the government on the side of religious display. By comparison, the Italian government was tasked with defense of its own administrative choice in *Lautsi.*

Could it be that the reasoning favoring the crucifix display simply overwhelmed the counter-arguments? The answer is "no," at least according to the eminent American linguist and student of interpretation, Stanley Fish.[186] Dr. Fish is distinctly unimpressed by the Italian government's defense of its regulatory permission. For example, he sees little merit in the government's contention that the lower court confused an

---

183. *See* TONI JOHNSON, COUNCIL ON FOREIGN RELATIONS, *Europe: Integrating Islam,* July 25, 2011, http://www.cfr.org/religion/europe-integrating-islam/p8252.

184. *Id.*

185. Stanley Fish, *Crucifixes and Diversity: The Odd Couple,* N.Y. TIMES, Mar. 28, 2011, http://opinionator.blogs.nytimes.com/2011/03/28/crucifixes-and-diversity-the-odd-couple/?hp.

186. *Id.*

obligation to be neutral with a mandate for secularity, calling the assertion "a union of bad argument and bad theology."[187]

From Dr. Fish's perspective, the factual assumptions behind the argument were also "bad" as he disputes the assertion that the crucifix has been or could be anything other than a religious symbol. To think of it as a mere linkage to national or cultural identity is not "plausible," he concludes, thus rejecting the ECHR rationale.[188]

The Italian government's argument, however, was more nuanced than Dr. Fish concedes. Its claim was not that the crucifix could be shorn of religious meaning but that its symbolism is far more than religious; specifically, that it is a matter of cultural identity.[189] It is on this wider cultural understanding that the true difference between the applicant and the government emerges: apart from giving deference on a matter of education traditionally handled locally, the government believed its obligation was not to excise or exclude religious display from culture (a.k.a. "exclusionary secularism"), but to allow a thousand flowers of faith belief to keep blooming perceptibly, and to be nourished by the diverse religious practices and traditions of the individual rights-bearers in its ethnically diverse cultural soil (a.k.a. "inclusionary secularism"). The Italian regulation requires not irreligion or exclusion, but a conception of neutrality that allows or invites inclusiveness. Government has an obligation to take into account the sensitivities of all religions and not to end or break off relations with religious aspects of our lives.

What Dr. Fish believes is "bad theology" is the notion that the symbol of Christ crucified could be an unencumbered symbol of love or charity, with tolerance of opposing views derived therefrom. The Christian religion, argues Dr. Fish, subscribes to a transcendent God first, and love thereafter; he also notes that "it has always been a matter of debate

---

187. *Id.*
188. *Id.*
189. *Lautsi* at para. 36 ("The [Italian] Government . . . argue[d] that it was necessary to take account of the fact that a single symbol could be interpreted differently from one person to another. That applied in particular to the sign of the cross, which could be perceived not only as a religious symbol, but also as a cultural and identity-linked symbol, the symbol of the principles and values which formed the basis of democracy and western civilization.").

in Christian theology" whether a man can be saved who has not been born again.[190] Therefore, "generous though it may be in many respects, Christianity is hard-edged at its doctrinal center and it is to that center to which the crucifix speaks."[191]

Whether or not Fish is right on his theology—and the Catholic and Protestant understandings may differ—this is a most uncomfortable basis upon which to critique the outcome of a court. Readers are likely to see Fish's own theological statement as arguable and that he has issued an invitation to take sides. Fish is likely to respond that his wandering into theology illustrates the virtues of exclusionary secularism and a high wall of separation. In some ways, Fish would be correct, but the cost of preventing his trespass and others like it is all borne by believers. Why is it not preferable to adopt a posture of non-interfering equal treatment, rather than wholesale exclusion?[192]

A SPECULATION: SYMBOLIC FAITH AS THE TROJAN HORSE OF SECULARISM

This explanation posits that the greater tolerance for religious symbols in Europe may be a stratagem on the way toward reducing religion's significance. In this argument, tolerating *symbol* avoids Huntington's predicted clash of civilizations[193] over *substance*. The allowance of religious symbols in this sense would be like ordinary wall displays—a matter of taste but not much else. No prayers would ever be directed at the crucifix nor would any part of the school day be taken up with scriptural study, let alone the significance and meaning of Christ's death on the cross. The fact that the schoolday would be conducted without any knowledge of the symbol would be to demean it by the subtlety of silence. The very liberality of allowing the display will ultimately dilute

190. Fish, *supra* note 185.
191. *Id.*
192. *See*, e.g., Zelman v. Simmons-Harris, 536 U.S. 639, 680 (2002) (Thomas, J. concurring) ("I cannot accept [the] use [of the Fourteenth Amendment] to oppose neutral programs of school choice through the incorporation of the Establishment Clause. There would be a tragic irony in converting the Fourteenth Amendment's guarantee of individual liberty into a prohibition on the exercise of educational choice.").
193. *See* SAMUEL HUNTINGTON, THE CLASH OF CIVILIZATIONS AND THE REMAKING OF WORLD ORDER (1996).

any specific message and slowly deaden the spirit of religious belief. A subsequent generation will see the public display of religious symbol as a meaningless—or inconsequential—gesture, stirring little interest, let alone passion; and in due time, these successors to empty display will come to believe this about faith in its entirety as well.[194]

By contrast, American jurisprudence on religious displays indulges an exclusionary view; unless the public property is a public forum (such as a public park) that by tradition has been open to every idea, religious or not, religious displays are unacceptable on public property in the United States without some kind of subterfuge that preserves a religious display for non-religious or cultural reasons.[195] To ascertain whether this secular motivation for keeping a religious object in a public space exists, the court will look for evidence that the religious symbol is intermixed with nonreligious symbols.[196]

The Holy Father, thinking the United States to be more inclusionary toward the display of religious symbols (perhaps based on the recitals in our founding documents), openly worried about the consequence of hiding anti-religious sentiment in the cloak of rationalized toleration of religious display. Here is the Holy Father's observation in response to a question put to him by the American bishops during his visit to the United States in 2008:

> [The United States] allows for professing belief in God, and respects the public role of religion and the churches, but at the same time it can subtly reduce religious belief to a lowest common denominator. Faith becomes a passive acceptance that certain things 'out there' are true, but without practical relevance for everyday life. The result is a growing separation of faith from

194. McGoldrick, *supra* note 171, at 479–480 ("One technique for securing a role for religious symbols in the public sphere is to de-religionise them, that is, to transform the sacred to secular, or to trivialize them. . . . If the crucifix loses its specific religious value and become[s] a general symbol of civilization and culture this arguably blurs the line between secularism and religion. . . . It erodes any clear cut distinction between the realm of faith and that of reason, and any possibility of ruling the public sphere according to the dictates of reason.").
195. *See, e.g., Cnty. of Allegheny*, 492 U.S. at 598–599.
196. *Id.*

life: living 'as if God did not exist.' This is aggravated by an individualistic and eclectic approach to faith and religion: far from a Catholic approach to 'thinking with the Church,' each person believes he or she has a right to pick and choose, maintaining external social bonds but without an integral, interior conversion to the law of Christ. Consequently, rather than being transformed and renewed in mind, Christians are easily tempted to conform themselves to the spirit of this age.[197]

The Holy Father's observation or concern—as it turns out, surprisingly, to this observer—is more applicable to Europe. The ECHR decision in *Lautsi* has accepted religious display on an inclusionary, or more accepting, basis than the United States; however, as discussed, the ECHR is less likely to accommodate non-Christian (in particular, Islamic) claims for exemptions from generally applicable laws that are said to substantially burden religious practice. Here, then, is an irony within an irony. Earlier we noted the irony that Europe, supposed to be more secular than the United States, was, after *Lautsi* at least, more tolerant of religious display. It turns out, however, that inclusionary Europe is so only in a discriminatory sense—that is, it is protective of religious tradition, so long as it is Christian. Were Europe to adopt the position of non-discrimination observed in the United States under the Establishment clause, would this advance or inhibit the Holy Father's objectives? It would promote civil peace among religion, but as it happens, it would

197. Pope Benedict XVI, Responses of His Holiness Benedict XVI to the Questions Posed by the Bishops (Apr. 16, 2008), http://www.vatican.va/holy_father/benedict_xvi/ speeches/2008/april/documents/hf_ben-xvi_spe_20080416_response-bishops_ en.html. The Holy Father was indeed excited by the challenge posed by secularism in America, concluding: "Much more, of course, could be said on this subject: let me conclude, though, by saying that I believe that the Church in America, at this point in her history, is faced with the challenge of recapturing the Catholic vision of reality and presenting it, in an engaging and imaginative way, to a society which markets any number of recipes for human fulfillment. I think in particular of our need to speak to the hearts of young people, who, despite their constant exposure to messages contrary to the Gospel, continue to thirst for authenticity, goodness and truth. Much remains to be done, particularly on the level of preaching and catechesis in parishes and schools, if the new evangelization is to bear fruit for the renewal of ecclesial life in America." *Id.*

also deprive Catholicism and/or Christianity in general of its favored advantage under ECHR precedent. The pope explained his objective in working against secularism in this way:

> Secularism challenges the Church to reaffirm and to pursue more actively her mission in and to the world. As the Council made clear, the lay faithful have a particular responsibility in this regard. What is needed, I am convinced, is a greater sense of the intrinsic relationship between the Gospel and the natural law on the one hand, and, on the other, the pursuit of authentic human good, as embodied in civil law and in personal moral decisions. In a society that rightly values personal liberty, the Church needs to promote at every level of her teaching—in catechesis, preaching, seminary and university instruction—an apologetics aimed at affirming the truth of Christian revelation, the harmony of faith and reason, and a sound understanding of freedom, seen in positive terms as a liberation both *from* the limitations of sin and *for* an authentic and fulfilling life. In a word, the Gospel has to be preached and taught as an integral way of life, offering an attractive and true answer, intellectually and practically, to real human problems. The "dictatorship of relativism," in the end, is nothing less than a threat to genuine human freedom, which only matures in generosity and fidelity to the truth.[198]

The papal commentary suggests that Dr. Fish's critique of *Lautsi* is misplaced: being open to a pluralism of religious symbols being displayed in public places should promote tolerance, not division. Toleration of display of passive religious symbol for the secularist may also facilitate a re-linkage of natural and civil law in the country. Whether this is a good thing from the perspective of a particular faith adherent will require an assessment of the authority divided between public and private spheres. It is conceivable that a believer would still prefer living in a confessional state where he or she is in the majority and part of the established religion. The papal view might ultimately realize that what

198. *Id.*

is really to be preferred is some form of democratic confessionalism, as in the Republic of Malta. After all it would take a good deal of hard work to achieve interfaith understanding and then to arrange governing institutions in a manner that shared moral authority based on different moral conceptions. Malta's success may be traceable, of course, to its modest geographic size and Catholic homogeneity,[199] which leaves the small number of non-Catholic-Christian, Islamic, and Jewish believers in Malta free to worship as they desire, but does not nourish among their ranks aspirations to occupy the leadership positions in the country's government.

The Islamic populations that dominate the "Arab Spring" nations in North Africa, however, have arguably greater expectation that their reformed governments will favor Islam and leadership positions will be well populated with Muslims. Thus, the notion that a strong conception of secularism can keep Islam from being part of the governing structures in the "Arab Spring" nations where they are a majority presence seems unrealistic as well as democratically unfair. Yet, it is not uncommon to hear discussion in Europe stating, much as in the *Refah* opinion, that the highest aspiration is to remake the Libyan, Tunisian, and Egyptian governments in the mold of enforced secularism observed by the government of Turkey.[200] Assuming that it is possible for Europe, the United States, or NATO to have some influence on the choices to be made (and the president has said that will not be our role), it is likely that the influence would be at its zenith now in the early organizational period, but not thereafter. As for the prospects for exclusionary secularism in particular, the Muslim majority in Libya would be no happier consigned to the sidelines of power than Catholics would be in Malta. Were that consignment attempted, the resentments would be great and quite likely to abet violence.

199. Ninety-eight percent of the population in the Republic of Malta is Roman Catholic. US DEPARTMENT OF STATE, *Background Note: Malta*, Aug. 24, 3011, http://www.state.gov/r/pa/ei/bgn/5382.htm.

200. *See*, e.g., Thomas E. Leonard, *Qaddafi's Death and Tunisian Elections Interest European Leaders*, ACROSS THE POND BLOG (Oct. 26, 2011), http://iuwest.wordpress.com/2011/10/26/2703/.

THE ISLAMIC VIEW OF SECULARISM (*ALAMANIYAH*)

For many Muslims, secularism, especially in its exclusionary guise, is practically the equivalent of atheism.[201] As described earlier, secularism cannot mean the same thing for Muslims that it does for Europeans, or even more broadly for Americans, since there is no equivalent of rendering unto Caesar what is Caesar's in Muslim theology.[202] In the writings of Vladimir Lenin and of Mustafa Kemal Atatürk, one of the founding fathers of modern Turkey, Muslims came to understand secularism as the distraction of their faith.[203] There was little opportunity for Arab Muslims to try to steer a middle course of inclusionary secularism.

There was a brief attempt for five years following the fall of the Ottoman Empire to reestablish theocratic leadership in Arab lands, in accordance with Islamic belief. This effort is most encapsulated in the history of the Muslim Brotherhood, which is largely unknown in the West but is prefiguring largely in the Arab Spring, especially in Egypt.[204]

---

201. John Keane, *Secularism?*, 71 POL. Q. 5, 15 (2002) ("For [Muslims] . . . the division between the temporal and the spiritual is literally unthinkable.").

202. *Cf.* Keddie, *supra* note 74, at 30 ("The relative weakness of secular trends in the Arab world is related to Arab identification with original Islam, and is also due to efforts in areas once ruled by the West to assert local, non-Western, cultural values. . . . The fatal association of secularism with autocracy and Western influence helps account for the anti-secular trend in the Muslim world.")

203. *See, e.g.*, Dave Crouch, *The Bolsheviks and Islam*, 110 INT'L SOCIALISM (April 6, 2006), *available at* http://www.isj.org.uk/index.php4?id=181 ("Socialists [including Lenin] expect people to hold religious ideas when they first come into contact with socialist organisations, and to lose their religious convictions only insofar as they become convinced of their power to change the world."); Keddie, *supra* note 74, at 28–29 (noting that Atatürk, following his rise to power in Turkey after World War I, rejected an Islamic basis for law and institutions, instituting numerous secularizing measures such as outlawing the use of Arabic and abolishing religious education and Sharia law. Following World War II, public backlash arose to his aggressively secular policies.).

204. *See* James A. Montgomery, *Arabia To-Day: An Essay in Contemporary History*, 47 J. AM. ORIENTAL SOC. 97 (1927) (providing an extensive historical account of attempts to create a pan-Islamic or pan-Arabic empire in the early twentieth century). This idea persisted even after the end of World War I, although geographic remoteness, as well as cultural, racial, and religious differences among the Arab nations

Should we expect the Arab Spring to bring a new flowering of con-
fessionalist Islamic states? From a solely geo-political perspective,
absent a military takeover, it is hard to know why this would not be the
case. However, it would be somewhat inconsistent with the words of the
prophet Mohammed (praise be unto him), who anticipated that such
a resurgence of faith greater than his own time would not occur until
the end times. But then, perhaps, it is later than we think. A number of
passages in the *hadith,* or the tradition of the prophet, corroborate this
supposition.[205] Perhaps the prophet's foretold future can be linked to
the present by an effort at interfaith power sharing. This would be easier
if the ECHR had not already proclaimed Islam to be fundamentally at
odds with democracy.

As recounted in the ECHR's *Refah* opinion earlier referenced, Islam
is a faith of great stability.[206] The court found that this stability makes

---

encouraged attempts to create a confederation of individual Arab states instead. *See*
Philip K. Hitti, *The Possibility of Union among Arab States,* 48 AM. HIST. REV. 722
(July 1943). Throughout this period, some Muslim leaders expressed a strong interest
in creating a pan-Islamic state or empire, governed by Islamic theocracy and led by a
caliph, or "necessary religious and political head of [the] community." Majid Fakhry,
The Theocratic Idea of the Islamic State in Recent Controversies, 30 INT'L AFF. 450, 451
(Oct. 1954). This aligns with the ideals of the Muslim Brotherhood, "who stand for the
restoration of Islamic institutions and the total regeneration of Islam in all spheres."
Id. at 456.

It can be argued that the defeat of the Ottoman Empire and the subsequent attempt
to establish a pan-Islamic movement is just one factor contributing to the development of Islamic modernism in countries like Egypt. Events such as the initial invasion of Egypt by Napoleon, the colonization of Islamic countries by Western nations,
and post-Ottoman movements to reassert Islamic cultural and political dominance
have impacted the development of modern Islamic ideas about law, politics, culture,
society, and government authority. *See* Mansoor Moaddel, *Discursive Pluralism and
Islamic Modernism in Egypt,* 24 ARAB STUD. Q. 29 (Winter 2002); *see also* Francis
Robinson, *Islam and the West: Clash of Civilizations?,* 33 ASIAN AFF. 307 (Oct. 2002)
(discussing the transformation of the Muslim position in the world in the nineteenth
and twentieth centuries, and how this influences pan-Islamism and the formation of
current Islamic groups like Al Qaeda).

205. Mishaal Al Gergawi, *What Secularism Means to Us,* GULF NEWS, June 26, 2011,
http://gulfnews.com/mobile/opinions/columnists/what-secularism-means-to-us-
1.827374.

206. Refah Partisi, 35 Eur. H. R. Rep. 56, 87 (2001).

it incompatible with democratic principle and practice. Nevertheless, there are references to suggest that Islamic belief allows for change with respect to matters that are not at the core of religious belief. Again, the *hadith* suggests that if a question relates to purely day-to-day business or other affairs, that these matters would not be for the prophet but for others more directly experienced.[207] There is the possibility in these writings, therefore, that one could find some compatibility between Islam and a legal system that would govern these other mundane, operational matters. Far more study of this would be needed, since even this statement seems in tension with the aforementioned notion that all of life is to be governed under Sharia.

Yet beyond the possible instrumental separation of function, which could accord Islamic belief to fully govern a sphere, say family, leaving economic regulation to be handled by wholly secular law, there are other deeper possibilities that turn on the Islamic conception of natural law, and in particular the aforementioned doctrine of harmony. Known as *Farabi-Avicenna*, this doctrine of harmony seeks to explain religious judgment in the vocabulary of philosophy and intellectual thought. This is the opposite of *al-Kindi* which attempts to fit religion into the secular.

Beginning in the middle of the fourth century, the so-called sincere brethren or brethren of purity sought a harmony of philosophy and faith. In this, it was assumed that the rulings of Sharia could be in complete harmony with the dictates of reason and philosophy. It is said that one of the great Muslim philosophers, Avicenna, likely read their books and extended their influence. Avicenna suggested that the human intellect is best regarded as a type of inter-process with the prophet. This process might follow one of two competing paths—the interpretation of religious principles and religious texts in a philosophical or rational way or, alternatively, to understand human reasoning through religion and its principles.

With reference to the relationship of church and state from an Islamic perspective that may be best informed by the work of noted

207. Al Gergawi, *supra* note 205.

medieval Islamic scholar Ibn Rushd, or Averroes as he is better known in European literature. Averroes's philosophy, as expressed in works such as *The Decisive Treatise*, does provide some groundwork for the justification of separate church and state.[208]

Arrived at in this way, it is possible for a Muslim to accept secularism provided it is not hostile to religion. In other words, if the secularist direction is reflective of the mind of Allah (praise be unto him), secularism has a chance to be found compatible (harmonized) with Islamic practice. This harmony is manifest when secularist philosophy creates or safeguards the pure part of one's life that is reserved for religious matters.[209] In other words, secularism can be seen as an instrument of the Divine ensuring that the righteous Muslim would be wise in matters affecting them on earth in the same way as the Qur'an ensures his correct path with respect to matters eternal.

Comparable to the Holy Father's argument that reason and faith are compatible, Rushd outlines a case for the compatibility of secularism and religion that in terms of the models outlined earlier would be closest to inclusionary secularism.[210]

208. Elements of Averroes's philosophy have been used to "generate religious, intellectual, political and social reform" in the Arab world. Fauzi M. Majjar, *Ibn Rushd (Averroes) and the Egyptian Enlightenment Movement*, 31 BRIT. J. MIDDLE EASTERN STUD. 195, 203 (2004). For instance, the Lebanese intellectual Farah Antun advocated the separation of "temporal and spiritual authorities" on the basis of Averroes's teachings, in order "to promote the establishment of a secular state and the Western scientific culture." *Id.* Similarly, "Averroism" has been perceived as holding "the possibility of reaching the same conclusion in Islam that Europe had reached in Christianity, namely separation of church and state." *Id.* at 204.

209. Some of the writings of Averroes considered the "compatibility" of philosophy and Islam; he "claimed that the Qur'an cannot teach anything that is false, since it is a divinely revealed text and God is a source of truth. Nor does the text forbid the study of philosophy, for God is the source of human reason." Seymour Feldman, *Philosophy: Averroes, Maimonides, and Aquinas*, in RELIGIOUS FOUNDATIONS OF WESTERN CIVILIZATION: JUDAISM CHRISTIANITY AND ISLAM 209, 211–212 (Jacob Neusner, ed., 2006).

210. To Averroes, "religion has a political purpose: it teaches all the members of a polity a common set of beliefs and regulations, so that an orderly and peaceful society results. That some of these beliefs are in fact literally not true need not worry the philosopher as long as they have desirable practical consequences." *Id.* at 213.

THE CATHOLIC VIEW

Moving from Individual Freedom to Influencing Public Decision

The importance of consent in a democratic regime is self-evident for purposes of transparency and accountability, as well as stability. Moreover, from the Catholic perspective, since the 1965 publication of *Dignitatis Humanae*, freedom from coercion in matters of religious belief has been denominated an intrinsic right of the human person.[211] The right does not depend upon proof of the "correctness" of the faith; and ideally, individual religious freedom should be enshrined in the basic charter or constitution of a government.[212] The Catholic position does not endorse the separation of church and state, but instead argues that a faithful citizen will make an effort to apply the principles of faith to the policy decision making of his home country.[213]

The Catholic position as stated in *Dignitatis* is thus fully compatible with the dual provisions of the First Amendment in the American Constitution protecting religious belief and practice, by precluding a prohibition of free exercise and admonishing the government not to pass laws respecting the establishment of religion. Free exercise protection guarantees not only an unmolested or undisturbed liturgy, but also the right of the Church to articulate its point of view within the political process using religious arguments.[214]

---

211. *See* Second Vatican Council, *Declaration on Religious Freedom* (*Dignitatis Humanae*) (Dec. 7, 1965), para. 2, available *at* http://www.vatican.va/archive/hist_councils/ii_ vatican_council/documents/vat-ii_decl_19651207_dignitatis-humanae_en.html [hereinafter *Dignitatis Humanae*] ("The Vatican Council declares that the human person has a right to religious freedom.").

212. *Id.*

213. *Id.*

214. The First Amendment guarantees "the full and free right to entertain any religious belief, to practice any religious principle, and to teach any religious doctrine which does not violate the laws of morality and property, and which does not infringe on personal rights." Watson v. Jones, 80 U.S. 679, 728 (1871). In general, churches are not prohibited by the First Amendment from engaging in the political process. *See generally* Keith S. Blair, *Praying for a Tax Break: Churches, Political Speech, and the Loss of Section 501(c)(3) Tax Exempt Status*, 86 DENV. U.L. REV. 405 (2009). However, churches, as religious organizations, are exempt from paying federal income taxes

Faith as Proposition versus Faith as Legal Imposition

In modern times, some of the hierarchy of the American Catholic Church have sought more than *Dignitatis* prescribes. The "more" consists of insistence either that the Church view prevail in enactment pertaining to non-negotiable intrinsic evils, or that it be exempt from laws that depart from the Church view on these subjects.[215]

This all or nothing view seems contrary to the allocation Christ conceded in his instruction to give to Caesar what his Caesar's, the reform explicit in *Dignitatis* and simply what would be modernly

---

under Section 501(c)(3) of the Internal Revenue Code, which impacts their political speech rights. *Id.* at 414. What this means in a practical sense is that a church may engage in various aspects of the political process, such as non-partisan voter education, sponsoring candidate speaking appearances under certain conditions, and taking positions on political issues that do not favor a certain candidate. *See Id.* at 415–419. However, a church can lose its tax-exempt status by engaging in activities that attempt to influence political campaigns, despite any First Amendment protections it otherwise enjoys. *Id.* at 414.

215. In June 2011, Archbishop Timothy Dolan of New York implored that state not to legalize gay marriages. *See* Archbishop Timothy Dolan, *The True Meaning of Marriage*, THE GOSPEL IN THE DIGITAL AGE (June 14, 2011, 9:26 A.M.), http://blog.archny.org/?p=1247. His chief complaint was that it violated natural law to define marriage as any union other than one man and one woman. *Id.* However, he also noted that this redefinition eliminated children's rights to be raised by a father and a mother, and would force Catholics to obey laws to which they fundamentally and morally objected. *Id.* In addition to communicating his views through his blog, he also discussed them in the media, characterizing the passage of a law legalizing gay marriage as "unjust and immoral," as well as "detrimental for the common good." Michael Paulson, *Archbishop Calls Gay Marriage Bill an "Ominous Threat,"* CITY ROOM, N.Y. TIMES (June 17, 2011, 12:49 P.M.), http://cityroom.blogs.nytimes.com/2011/06/17/archbishop-calls-gay-marriage-bill-an-ominous-threat/. Archbishop Dolan's pleas were, in the end, unsuccessful, as the law was passed in New York on June 24, 2011. Nicholas Confessore & Michael Barbaro, *New York Allows Same-Sex Marriage, Becoming Largest State to Pass Law*, N.Y. TIMES, June 24, 2011, http://www.nytimes.com/2011/06/25/nyregion/gay-marriage-approved-by-new-york-senate.html?_r=1&ref=nyregion.
    When it cannot prevent enactment of laws to which it objects, the Church has sought exemptions from them. In England, citing its opposition to facilitating adoptions by gay couples, the Church tried unsuccessfully to be excluded from a legal ban of discrimination against homosexuals. *See* George Jones, *Falconer Refuses to Exempt Catholics from New Gay Laws*, THE TELEGRAPH, Jan. 22, 2007, http://www.telegraph.co.uk/news/uknews/1540172/Falconer-refuses-to-exempt-Catholics-from-new-gay-laws.html. In the United States, courts in both New York and California rejected

expressed as religious pluralism. Should public law mandate the personal performance of actions that Catholic magisterium would view as intrinsically evil (e.g., the performance of an abortion by a Catholic doctor who is the only doctor on staff in a hospital setting without sufficient staff or planning to allow conscientious objection). This is deeply troubling, but inescapable where the evil action is mandated by law. Yet such direct mandates are thankfully rare, although for reasons of political advantage, the public discussion has been flooded with overstated claims of clash between law and religion (e.g., a Catholic doctor is exempt from abortion practice but must facilitate a substitute; the act of finding a substitute is then claimed to be formal cooperation with evil). No one of us can presume either to have government enforce the Catholic view on others or that Catholics will be exempted from a generally applicable law. The notion that one is morally complicit in actions performed by others, however, unravels the democratic system.

To illustrate how the resulting cultural strain can be too great, an additional example can help clarify. Assume that a generally applicable nondiscrimination law provides that a landlord may not discriminate on the basis of the usual categories of race, gender, or national origin. Observing these strictures of civil rights which are commonplace in statutes will not be a problem for a Catholic landlord. But the situation changes if discrimination is also prohibited on the basis of marital status or sexual orientation. What of the Catholic landlord who takes the teaching of the Church seriously with respect to the avoidance of premarital intimacy or the Church's hesitation with respect to homosexual orientation and its disapproval of homosexual conduct? Focusing on the unmarried couple, the landlord believes that renting to an unmarried couple would implicate him in a moral wrong. If the legislature chooses to give him an exemption, the legislature may do so. Under the current thinking of the Supreme Court, the Constitution permits, but does not

---

the Church's request to not have to comply with laws requiring it to provide health insurance to its employees that covered the costs of contraception. *See* Thomas J. Lueck, *State Court Rules against Catholic Church on Insurance*, N.Y. TIMES, Oct. 20, 2006, http://query.nytimes.com/gst/fullpage.html?res=9A00E5DD163FF933A15753C1 A9609C8B63.

require, exemption—an outcome traced to a 5–4 opinion authored by Antonin Scalia.[216]

Religion writers have harshly criticized this aspect of Justice Scalia's often admired exposition regardless of whether one subscribes to its invariably conservative ideology.[217] Indeed, the recently retired Justices O'Connor and Souter had targeted this body of case opinion for reversal, but their service to the Court concluded before the matter returned to the Court's docket, as it did in 2011 in the context of a lawsuit by a Lutheran school seeking a "ministerial" exemption from the federal law against discrimination against those with disabilities.[218] In oral argument, the justices had a great deal of difficulty ascertaining how they were to evaluate who did and did not fit within the ministerial exemption.[219] Some probed the doctrinal theology, and while that proved awkward, the lawyer for the school posited that who was a minister should be thought of as a legal rather than a religious question.[220] Justice Scalia defended his prior position, articulating the view that the relationship between a teacher and her religious school was not the Court's business.[221] Justice Alito, as a lower court judge, construed this aspect of Scalia's work narrowly;[222] Chief Justice Roberts often agrees with Alito,

216. See Emp't Div., Dep't of Human Res. of Or. v. Smith, 494 U.S. 872, 879 (1990), *superseded by statute*, Religious Freedom Restoration Act of 1993 (RFRA), 107 Stat. 1488, 42 U.S.C. § 2000 et seq. *as recognized in* Cutter v. Wilkinson, 544 U.S. 709 (2005) ("An individual's religious beliefs [do not] relieve an individual of the obligation to comply with a 'valid and neutral law of general applicability on the ground that the law proscribes (or prescribes) conduct that his religion prescribes (or proscribes),'" (quoting United States v. Lee, 455 U.S. 252, 263 n.3 (1982) (Stevens, J. concurring)).

217. See, e.g., David L. Gregory and Charles J. Russo, *Let Us Pray (But Not "Them"!): The Troubled Jurisprudence of Religious Liberty*, 65 ST. JOHN'S L. REV. 273, 274 (1991) (opining that Justice Scalia's opinion in Employment Division v. Smith "severely debilitated . . . the fundamental right of free exercise of religion.").

218. Hosanna-Tabor Evangelical Lutheran Church and Sch. v. EEOC.

219. Lyle Denniston, *Argument Recap: Blurry Line between Church and State*, SCOTUS BLOG (Oct. 5, 2011, 3:41 P.M.), http://www.scotusblog.com/?p=129054.

220. *Id.*

221. *Id.*

222. See Fraternal Order of Police v. City of Newark, 170 F.3d 359, 365 (3d Cir. 1999) (holding that a police department policy forbidding officers from wearing facial hair for religious reasons, but not for medical reasons, constitutes "differential treatment of medical exemptions and religious exemptions."). Prior to his confirmation to the

his one-time Reagan Justice Department colleague. Newly minted Justices Sotomayor and Kagan are more of a question mark, but one would expect these progressive voices to show some empathy for religious minorities often in need of exemption from general laws.

Scalia's reasoning, construing constitutional religious freedom claims narrowly, is not without its own logic, and it largely depends on not having judges second-guess the legislature—in part because that is beyond the judicial role, but also because it invites judges to favor their own faiths. That is especially problematic, as can be seen in our hypothetical case, since protecting the freedom of the landlord limits the freedom of the couple. The consequence of a law permitting such exemption from a generally imposed duty to rent is an indirectly authorized private "coercion" (e.g., the disapproval and exclusion of the unmarried couple by the landlord).

The hypothetical landlord claim for exemption from a nondiscrimination law seems qualitatively weaker than the case of the school dismissing even a handicapped teacher who is found by the religious school not to meet the religious requirements for teaching. It is likely that many landlords would not perceive a conscience problem associated with renting to an un-married couple. Landlords generally have no intent to know about, let alone authorize, improper intimacy outside marriage, and of course, an unmarried couple can rent without any intent to undertake immoral conduct. Even if a landlord adopted the policy against unmarried couples, few would know. Landlords have property doctrines that affirm a common law right to exclude, and it would be unusual for such exclusion to become known as an expression of faith. This suggests that the theology underlying the landlord's free exercise claim for exemption may be overbroad.

By comparison, a religious school often manifests its religious commitment in the selection of faculty and students. This is arguably the unavoidable consequence of allowing the formation of any association

---

US Supreme Court, Alito had been dubbed "Scalito" or "Scalia-lite" due to his prior opinions "mirroring" those written by Scalia. *Alito Has Hefty Resume and Record That Recalls Scalia's*, N.Y. TIMES, Oct. 31, 2005, http://www.nytimes.com/2005/10/31/world/americas/31iht-profile.html.

with specialized beliefs, like the Catholic Church or a religiously affiliated college, to exist—which a government must do if it observes the
"free exercise" rights that the Church holds is a matter of the intrinsic
dignity of the human person (*Dignitatis Humanae*).[223]

Intuitively, the matter becomes more difficult when the issue is
dismissal rather than hiring of a teacher, and particularly so when the
teacher is alleging that faith has merely been used as a pretext to con-
ceal handicap discrimination. But why is the matter more difficult in
this context? A denial of admission only appears easier to sustain since
it does not take away a tangible position already granted. This is a matter
of common sense. A student or faculty member not yet admitted or
hired will have less motivation to file suit than a student expelled or a
faculty member dismissed on religious grounds. The free exercise and
free speech interest of a school seeking to shape or maintain its class
composition in a distinctly religious way is the same.

This social harm of accepting the type of overstated landlord claim
comes into sharper relief when the unmarried couple is not Catholic,
and under their faith or belief system there is no interdiction of cohabitation. Under those circumstances, how can the landlord exert coercive force under the general public law in aid of his particular Catholic
beliefs? In other words, since accommodation is intended to lift burdens imposed by the government—not to empower one religious
believer to impose his faith view on others—why isn't the landlord's
exclusion of the couple then seen as an impermissible establishment
of religion?

Not All Claims of Conscience Are Created Equal

The importance of working through these analytical wrinkles in a fair-
minded way is revealed in the number of places these wrinkles turn up.
The competition between faith and other public policy is not isolated
to pious landlords and the employment practice of religious schools; it
is also found in such high-profile topics as same-sex marriage litigation
and the administration of the death penalty. Some Islamic taxi drivers in

223. *Dignitatis Humanae, supra* note 211, at para. 2.

Minneapolis argue that they can deny service to members of the public whom they suspect of carrying liquor. Pharmacists claim the right to refuse to fulfill prescriptions they believe are immoral, even if they are the only pharmacist available.

Not every one of these cases of religious objection can be accommodated by the larger culture, even where governing structures are already well established. It would be unrealistic to expect the nascent democracies of North Africa to accomplish more. Presently, as a constitutional matter in the United States, the Court's rule of general applicability in *Employment Division v. Smith* means that contrary religious practice is not constitutionality entitled to an exemption unless the law in question specifically targets religion. Nevertheless, there is nothing precluding the democratic legislature from granting an exemption if as a matter of prudence it would seem warranted to avoid a religious clash. Beyond the formal teaching of Justice Scalia in the *Smith* decision, then, context matters. Such a prudential exemption seems quite tenable if it allows a Catholic or religious college to have a free hand in employment and admissions. Harder to justify is allowing a pharmacist with religious objection to the use of artificial contraception to be excused from the law that mandates competence and service in this area. What is the difference? Unlike the college where faculty and staff could choose to sign up or not in light of the college's published description, the pharmacist occupies a place of public accommodation (as the law uses that term); he or she is a pivotal player in the delivery of health services, and obviously, neither medical ethics nor licensing as a pharmacist confers an agreement to offer limited pharmaceutical service. Moreover, US Supreme Court precedent does not credit every faith-based claim of conscience when it is weighed against other public policy. For example, Bob Jones University was told by the Supreme Court that scripturally based racism was still racism, and that the university and its donors could be denied tax benefits if they pursued a course of such racism.[224]

How does one weigh these matters? One can hope with a high level of civility, if not empathy. To those who have faith-related, ethical

---

224. *See* Bob Jones Univ. v. United States, 461 U.S. 574 (1983).

concerns, there presumably must be a distinction between the uncompromising commitments that religion calls us to make and the public policy that we can realistically expect. This is a dose of political pragmatism and arguably quite reasonable regarding virtually any issue not involving a grave moral evil. It's not an easy answer. As a Senator, Obama once said:

> I may be opposed to abortion for religious reasons, but if I seek to pass a law banning the practice, I cannot simply point to the teachings of my church or evoke God's will. I have to explain why abortion violates some principle that is accessible to people of all faiths, including those with no faith at all.[225]

The ECHR's Surprisingly Unequal Treatment of Islam

Having surveyed the treatment of claims for religious exemption under US law, we need to make greater examination of the remarkably unsympathetic treatment of Islam by the ECHR. In Europe, the protection for freedom of religion is found in Article 9 of the European Convention on Human Rights:

1. Everyone has the right to freedom of thought, conscience and religion; this right includes freedom to change his religion or belief and freedom, either alone or in community with others and in public or private, to manifest his religion or belief, in worship, teaching, practice and observance.
2. Freedom to manifest one's religion or beliefs shall be subject only to such limitations as are prescribed by law and are necessary in a democratic society in the interests of public safety, for the protection of public order, health or morals, or for the protection of the rights and freedoms of others.[226]

---

225. Obama, Call to Renewal, *supra* note 41.
226. Convention for the Protection of Human Rights and Fundamental Freedoms, art. 9, Nov. 4, 1950, 213 U.N.T.S. 221.

In addition, Article 14 of the Convention protects against discrimination on the basis of religion:

The enjoyment of rights and freedoms set forth in this Convention shall be secured without discrimination on any ground such as sex, race, color, language, religion, political or other opinion, national or social origin, association with a national minority, property, birth or other status.[227]

Over two decades ago, in *Choudhury v. United Kingdom*, a British citizen sought to prosecute author Salman Rushdie on the grounds that Rushdie's book, *The Satanic Verses*, constituted blasphemous attack against Islam.[228] British anti-blasphemy law was determined by the British courts to be applicable only to Christianity.[229] Relying on both the protection for freedom of religion in Article 9 and the general protection against discrimination in Article 14 of the European Convention on Human Rights, the applicant eventually appealed to the European Commission of Human Rights.[230] Prior precedent suggested that the Commission would be sympathetic to the applicant's claim.[231] It was not. The Commission rejected the notion that the English law protecting

---

227. *Id.*
228. Choudhury v. United Kingdom, App. No. 17439/90, 12 Hum. Rts. L.J. 172, 172 (1991). The applicant also sought the same prosecution against the publisher of The Satanic Verses, the Viking Penguin Publishing Co. *Id.*
229. *Id.*
230. The European Commission on Human Rights, which operated from 1953 to 1999, was set up alongside the European Court of Human Rights in order to act as a protective "barrier" shielding the Court from frivolous lawsuits as well as to "facilitate suits against states by private parties." MARK JANIS ET AL., EUROPEAN HUMAN RIGHTS LAW: TEXT AND MATERIALS 27 (2d. ed. 2000). The Commission and the Court were merged in 1998. *Id.* at 26.
231. In 1982, for instance, the Commission "had upheld the successful prosecution of a British magazine for publishing a poem found to be blasphemous to Christians partly on the basis that the 'main purpose' of the English common law offense of blasphemous libel is 'to protect the rights of citizens not to be offended in their religious feelings by publications.'" Peter G. Danchin, *Islam in the Secular Nomos of the European Court of Human Rights*, 32 MICH. J. INT'L. L. 663, 665 (2011) (quoting Gay News Ltd. v. United Kingdom, App. No. 8710/79, 5. Eur. H. R. Rep. 123, 130, P. 11 (1982)).

only Christianity against blasphemy was a form of discrimination precluded by Article 14.[232] In addition, it found that there was no "link between freedom from interference with the freedoms of Article 9 para. 1 of the Convention and the applicant's complaints."[233] Remarkably (to an American constitutional practitioner), the Commission found no positive obligation on the part of states under the ECHR to protect all religions equally.[234]

Future cases also gave favorable treatment to Christianity,[235] in ways that would easily transgress American constitutional doctrine. (Indeed, as we have already seen, under established doctrine in the United States, such disparate treatment would be unconstitutional as an infringement upon free exercise, an improper establishment of religion, a violation of equal protection, or all of the above.) As one scholar has noted, "these early cases in the [ECHR]'s Article 9 jurisprudence provide evidence of a disparity in the treatment of the claims of majority and minority religious groups"[236] resulting in substantial damage to the cause of interfaith understanding.[237] The tragic unprovoked mass murder of terrorist attacks on September 11, 2001, further eroded the possibility of harmony between Islam and Christianity and prompted a number of discriminatory forms of legislation throughout Europe, from bans on wearing "conspicuous" religious attire at school in France to prohibitions on the construction of minarets in Switzerland.[238]

---

232. *Choudhury*12 Hum. Rts. L.J. at 172.

233. *Id.*

234. Danchin, *supra* note 231.

235. *See id.* For instance, in 1994, the ECHR upheld the Austrian government's seizure of a film on the basis that the film's content was deemed blasphemous against Christianity. Otto-Preminger-Institut v. Austria, 295 Eur. Ct. H. R. (ser. A) at 1, 17–18 (1994). Two years later, the ECHR upheld a decision by the British government to refuse to circulate a film, noting that the government had the responsibility to "protect 'against seriously offensive attacks on matters regarded as sacred by Christians.'" *Id.* (quoting Wingrove v. United Kingdom, 23 Eur. Ct. H. R. 1937, 1957 (1996)).

236. Danchin, *supra* note 231, at 666; *see also* Sandy Ghandhi & Jennifer James, The English Law of Blasphemy and the European Convention on Human Rights, 4 EUR. HUM. RTS. L. REV. 430, 450 (1998) (*cited in* Danchin, *supra*).

237. *Id.*

238. *Id.* at 666–667.

Secularism is unpalatable to the Muslim; discrimination is an outrage—as it would be to Christians were the situation reversed. These cases suggest that secularism as practiced throughout Europe is one-sided and framed from a Christian perspective only. Given the disparity, it is not surprising that more subtle distinctions between Christianity and Islam are virtually ignored. For example, cases such as *Choudhury* fail to take into account how Islamic claims for freedom of religion and belief differ from those occurring within Christianity.

This is not dissimilar to what Catholics endured when they arrived in large numbers in the United States in the late eighteenth and nineteenth centuries, only to find a quite hostile culture. When large numbers of Catholics emigrated from Poland, Ireland, and Germany, the majority Protestant population could not grasp why Catholics would object to the Protestant majority running the school systems complete with Protestant prayers and textbooks. Catholics were free upon arrival in the United States to practice their faith so long as it was Christianity understood on Protestant terms.[239]

Legal doctrine that treats Christianity and Islam with inequality reflects the larger culture's unfamiliarity with non-Christian religions. This unfamiliarity leads to an inability to understand or appreciate how the two religious traditions could have different conceptions of religious freedom. The lack of that understanding precludes altogether an assessment of whether claims like those raised by the landlord or the pharmacist, if raised in relation to Islamic teaching, should be considered overstated and undeserving of exemption from the general laws. The last point is taken up in some detail in the next section. The admonition, of course, to "Give unto Caesar" is from the Christian Bible, but the considerable work that has been done by popes, emperors, and scholars over the millennia is a study unto itself. My supposition is that Islamic scholars could supply the same for the Muslim faith, but to my knowledge this has not been requested and accomplished, even though it is essential

---

239. *See, e.g.,* CHESTER GILLIS, ROMAN CATHOLICISM IN AMERICA 52–58 (1999) (describing anti-Catholic sentiment during the American colonial period); WILLIAM R. HUTCHISON, RELIGIOUS PLURALISM IN AMERICA: THE CONTENTIOUS HISTORY OF A FOUNDING IDEAL 59–60 (2003) (describing a dominant "Protestant hegemony" that had developed in American by the nineteenth century).

if we are to salvage any of the hope that at one point blossomed with the Arab Spring. There are a great many forces and interests beneath that once hope-filled banner of the movement for democracy in North Africa. Some forces are well intentioned; others are not. Those who seek to provoke anger and anarchy will employ any available grievance, especially those perceived to have a religious origin. We are nonetheless nowhere close to an equivalent analysis for Islam as that sketched later for Catholicism. Is it not the source of some apprehension to be so unprepared for this moment in history? The relentless push to substitute a form of secular government is more a sign of the world's ignorance of competing values than a necessity borne out of irreconcilable difference.

GIVE UNTO CAESAR

Prior to the 2008 election, the US Conference of Catholic Bishops published *Forming Consciences for Faithful Citizenship: A Call to Political Responsibility from the Catholic Bishops of the United States*, a document that thoughtfully attempted to resolve the extent to which Catholics as candidates, voters, or scholars could participate in the public discussion.[240] This is indeed a very old question. One might say that it begins with the division between Church and state which originates with Christ himself. "Give to Caesar what is Caesar's and to God what is God's."[241]

The Gelasian Thesis

The problem has always been separating the two, as well as determining who has the ultimate authority for resolving a conflict. In the fifth century, the Gelasian thesis gave us the narrative frame we still use today. Church and state have separate authority over the same human subject,

---

240. US Conference of Catholic Bishops, *Forming Consciences for Faithful Citizenship: A Call to Political Responsibility from the Catholic Bishops of the United States* 11 (2007), http://www.usccb.org/issues-and-action/faithful-citizenship/upload/forming-consciences-for-faithful-citizenship.pdf [hereinafter *Faithful Citizenship*].

241. *Luke* 20:25.

with the authority of the Church directed at salvation and the authority of civil government directed at a peaceable civil order that makes all freedom possible.[242]

Pope Gelasius in A.D. 494 wrote to Emperor Anastasius I that "there are two powers by which this world is chiefly ruled: the sacred authority of the Popes and the royal power. Of these, the priestly power is the weightier, because it has to render account for the Kings of men themselves at the divine tribunal."[243]

So who has the authority to resolve disputes? Pope Gelasius is clear; it is the Church. It is said that the Gelasian thesis is "to this day the most succinct expression of the Church's mind on the subject [of church-state relations]."[244] While it has been examined by others extensively, let me merely note the following features of the thesis:

- There are two powers (Church and state).
- God's authority is more important.
- The Divine law is therefore binding on the state.
- The salvation of the state's own leader is dependent upon the divine law and its observance.
- The Church should generally be obedient to the state, knowing that it has been empowered by God with respect to purely temporal and material affairs.
- The Church must govern its own discipline in relation to the Divine; if the state interferes in that discipline, it shows disrespect to the Divine which is the very source of the state's own authority.[245]

As helpful as that listing is, it hardly supplies a discernible path for avoiding head-on clash over some weighty and consequential matters. For example, note how the Gelasian thesis does not resolve without substantial conflict some troubling present controversies. When a state

242. *See* JOHN A. HARDON, THE CATHOLIC CATECHISM 246 (1975).
243. *Id.* at 245.
244. *Id.*
245. *Id.* at 244–245 (quoting Gelasius I, *De Duplici Supreme Potestate in Terris*)

authorizes same-sex marriage, must the Church perform that marriage ceremony, or at least not discriminate against same-sex couples in the operation of its schools or other charitable auxiliaries? The Gelasian thesis presents the guidance that the Church should be generally obedient to the state, but of course also that Divine law is binding upon the state. When clergy are accused of committing sexual crimes against minors, should the bishop have the clergy arrested and civilly investigated and prosecuted, or should the matter be investigated and disciplined only within the Church? The Church must govern its own discipline, but of course, the Church should generally obey the state. Admittedly, this is an easier question to answer in light of the magnitude of the recent sex abuse scandal involving Catholic priests in the United States, but would it have been so easy, say, in 1970, when the scope of the problem and the causal factors of the abuse were less understood by, or at least less known to, individual bishops? When the Church proclaims the protection of unborn life non-negotiable but the state refuses to enact unqualified protection of unborn life so as to not offend multiple and variant faith beliefs, what role should the Church play in seeking to change the perspective of the state? Through these examples, it can be seen that unless the state is generally prepared to yield its position, the Gelasian thesis does little to resolve the conflict of the "two powers."

Alfred Smith

The claim of authority for the Church to resolve church-state disputes has over time posed real difficulty for Catholics running for public office. In 1927, Governor Alfred E. Smith, the first Catholic to run for the presidency from a major political party, was challenged to defend the Gelasian thesis in an open letter published in the *Atlantic* by Charles C. Marshall. As Marshall wrote, "The doctrine of the Two Powers, in effect and theory, inevitably makes the Roman Catholic Church at times sovereign and paramount over the state."[246] Moreover, Marshall

---

246. Charles C. Marshall, *An Open Letter to the Honorable Alfred E. Smith*, ATLANTIC MAG. (April 1927), *available at* http://www.theatlantic.com/magazine/archive/1927/04/an-open-letter-to-the-honorable-alfred-e-smith/6523/?single_page=true.

complained, it is Roman Catholic teaching that there is not a lawful equality of other religions with that of the Roman Catholic Church, and that other religions are merely tolerated for politic reasons.[247]

Smith responded to Marshall by essentially denying the Gelasian thesis: "These convictions are held neither by me nor by any other American Catholic, as far as I know," wrote Smith.[248] To the extent that Smith made a substantive response that was not at odds with his faith, it was the claim that

> the essence of my faith is built upon the Commandments of God. The law of the land is built upon the Commandments of God. There can be no conflict between them. Instead of quarreling among ourselves over dogmatic principles, it would be infinitely better if we join together in inculcating obedience to these Commandments in the hearts and minds of the youth of the country as the surest and best road to happiness on this earth and to peace in the world community.[249]

When challenged further to defend statements and encyclical writing that gave preference to the Catholic Church over all others, Smith responded by asking:

> By what right do you ask me to assume responsibility for every statement that may be made in any encyclical letter? As you will find in the *Catholic Encyclopedia* (citation omitted), these encyclicals are not articles of our faith. . . . So little are these matters of the essence of my faith that I, a devout Catholic since childhood, never heard of them until I read your letter. . . . You may find some dream of an ideal of the Catholic state, having no relation whatsoever to actuality, somewhere described. But, voicing the best Catholic thought on the subject, Dr. John A. Ryan, Professor

247. *Id.*
248. Alfred E. Smith, *Catholic and Patriot*, ATLANTIC MAG. (May 1927), *available at* http://www.theatlantic.com/magazine/archive/1927/05/catholic-and-patriot/6522/.
249. *Id.*

of Moral Theology at the Catholic University of America . . ."[t] he propositions of Pope Pius IX condemning the toleration of non-Catholic sects do not now . . . apply even to Spain or to the South American republics, to say nothing of countries possessing a greatly mixed population."[250]

Pope Leo XIII

Smith's understanding of his faith was more practical and instrumental than theological. He admitted as much himself. It certainly was not subtle enough to capture Leo XIII's somewhat earlier amendment of the Gelasian thesis that the Holy Father was refining in light of the American experiment. Leo began to recognize something that John Courtney Murray would later exploit: namely, that the human person is both a child of God and not just a citizen of the state, but a member of a community.[251] The concept of community reminded us that state and society were different, with society being the amalgam of family,[252] Church,[253]

---

250. *Id.*
251. "As to the duties of each one toward his fellow men, mutual forbearance, kindliness, generosity are placed in the ascendant; the man who is at once a citizen and a Christian is not drawn aside by conflicting obligations; and, lastly, the abundant benefits with which the Christian religion, of its very nature, endows even the mortal life of man are acquired for the community and civil society." Pope Leo XIII, *Immortale Dei: Encyclical on the Christian Constitution of the States* para. 19 (1885), *available at* http://www.vatican.va/holy_father/leo_xiii/encyclicals/documents/hf_l-xiii_ enc_01111885_immortale-dei_en.html [hereinafter *Immortale Dei*].
252. "Each family is a part of the commonwealth." Pope Leo XIII, *Rerum Novarum: Encyclical on Capital and Labor* para. 14 (1891), *available at* http://www.vatican.va/ holy_father/leo_xiii/encyclicals/documents/hf_l-xiii_enc_15051891_rerum-novarum_en.html [hereinafter *Rerum Novarum*].
253. Pope Leo XIII often discussed the multitude of necessary services the Catholic Church provides to society. He cites the Church's historical role as a protector against unchecked power and tyranny: "In truth, whatever in the State is of chief avail for the common welfare; whatever has been usefully established to curb the license of rulers who are opposed to the true interests of the people, or to keep in check the leading authorities from unwarrantably interfering in municipal or family affairs; whatever tends to uphold the honour, manhood, and equal rights of individual citizens—of all these things, as the monuments of past ages bear witness, the Catholic Church has always been the originator, the promoter, or the guardian." *Immortale Dei, supra* note 251, at para. 38. As a moral guardian, "[the Church] holds it as her

school,[254] and workplace.[255] The complaint against Smith leveled by Marshall was that his church wanted to be the established church and therefore to impose itself under the coercion of law upon the state.[256] The American Constitution, of course, denies any faith an established or favored position.[257] While this seemingly denied one of the main precepts of the Gelasian thesis—that in a jurisdictional dispute over what is God's or what is Caesar's, the Church should be the arbiter—Leo began to perceive a way to resolve the constitutional difficulty posed by that claim; namely, that the Church might not ask for a favored established position in America, but instead ask merely sufficient freedom of action to have an indirect teaching effect upon society and its subcomponents.[258]

---

sacred duty to admonish every one of what the law of God enjoins, to unite the rich and the poor in the bonds of fraternal charity, and to lift up and strengthen men's souls in the times when adversity presses heavily upon them." Pope Leo XIII, *Graves de Communi Re: Encyclical on Christian Democracy*, para. 27 (1901), *available at* http://www.vatican.va/holy_father/leo_xiii/encyclicals/documents/hf_l-xiii_enc_18011901_graves-de-communi-re_en.html.

254. Pope Leo XIII was a strong believer in the societal necessity of a sound Christian education, as provided by Catholic schools, "for there is no better citizen than the man who has believed and practiced the Christian faith from his childhood." Pope Leo XIII, *Spectata Fides: Encyclical on Christian Education* (1885), *available at* http://www.vatican.va/holy_father/leo_xiii/encyclicals/documents/hf_l-xiii_enc_27111885_spectata-fides_en.html.

255. Pope Leo XIII, in recognition of the working man's role in creating a prosperous and morally upstanding society, repeatedly called for the just and equitable treatment of workers, not only through the charitable auspices of the Church, but also in the workplace itself. For example, he implored wealthy business owners to maintain a workplace free of "corrupting influence and dangerous occasions," and to not force workers to perform tasks "beyond their strength" or "unsuited to their sex and age." *Rerum Novarum, supra* note 252, at para. 20.

256. Marshall, *supra* note 246.

257. This is per the Establishment Clause in the First Amendment to the US Constitution, which provides that "Congress shall make no law respecting an establishment of religion, or prohibiting the free exercise thereof." US CONST. amend. I.

258. The theme of Catholic Church as societal instructor is common throughout Pope Leo XIII's writings. In the *Diuturnum*, he spoke of the Catholic Church's responsibility to guide society's secular leaders toward morally righteous exercise of the powers of their offices: "Being, by the favor of God, entrusted with the government of the Catholic Church, and made guardian and interpreter of the doctrines of Christ, [w]e judge that it belongs to [o]ur jurisdiction ... publicly to set forth what Catholic truth demands of every one in this sphere of duty." Pope Leo XIII, *Diuturnum: Encyclical on the Origin of*

This restatement of the Gelasian thesis might avoid the extreme of either imposed faith or banished faith. It made sense of the notion of indirect power by recognizing a difference between state and society and giving freedom of the Church a wide berth to influence society, and indirectly, the direction of the state.

One can see the importance of this subtlety in the same-sex marriage debate. Prior to this refinement by Leo, it might be thought that the only way for the Church to be heard would be by something akin to the passage of Proposition 8[259] (overturning by initiative a California Supreme Court decision in favor of same-sex marriage)[260]—that is, using the force of law to define marriage consistent with the authorship of marriage by God himself. Leo's Gelasian refinement, however, allows at least for the possibility that the state would not sanction either heterosexual or homosexual marriage but leave the entire usage of marital terminology and practice to the Church as the most relevant component

---

Civil Power para. 3 (1881), *available at* http://www.vatican.va/holy_father/leo_xiii/encyclicals/documents/hf_l-xiii_enc_29061881_diuturnum_en.html. The Church had engaged in this practice in the past by being "the mediator for peace[, r]ecalling all to their duty" to show "equity, mercy, and kindness." *Id.* at para. 22. The *Diuturnum* concludes by imploring both the leaders and the citizens in modern society to adhere to the Church's teachings on "government and the duty of obedience[,]" including the instillation of "gentleness to the minds of men, kindness to their manners, and justice to their laws." *Id.* at para. 26, 27.

In 1895, Pope Leo XIII took up this theme as it shaped Catholic life and practice in the United States. He implores the American government to "let those of the clergy . . . who are occupied with the instruction of the multitude treat plainly th[e] topic of the duties of citizens[, and] . . . the priests be persistent in keeping before the minds of the people the enactments of the Third Council of Baltimore, particularly those which inculcate the virtue of temperance, the frequent use of sacraments and the observance of the just laws and institutions of the republic." Pope Leo XIII, *Longinqua: Encyclical on Catholicism in the United States* para. 15 (1895), *available at* http://www.vatican.va/holy_father/leo_xiii/encyclicals/documents/hf_l-xiii_enc_06011895_longinqua_en.html.

259. Proposition 8 added the following language to the California Constitution: "Only marriage between a man and a woman is valid or recognized in California." CA. CONST. art. 1 § 7.5 (enacted through Prop. 8, § 2, approved Nov. 4, 2008, eff. Nov. 5, 2008), *held unconstitutional by* Perry v. Schwarzenegger, 704 F.Supp.2d 921 (N.D.Cal. 2010).

260. In re Marriage Cases, 183 P.3d 384 (Cal. 2008) (holding that sexual orientation was a suspect classification for the purposes of equal protection under the California Constitution, and that the California Family Code's language restricting marriage to between one man and one woman was unconstitutional).

of society.[261] Under this rubric, the state would civilly license a union for purposes of assuring itself that prospective fathers were readily correlated with their mothers and their offspring, that the population would be properly counted, and that community health would be preserved, but it would leave it up to churches to define and apply their own doctrinal standards to the question of who may marry within its tradition and what marriages will be acknowledged by its tradition.[262] Perhaps there is a source for compromise there for Californians to pursue.

John F. Kennedy

But even this indirect power to influence the state through the Church's influence on society has been held suspect by some. It was for this reason that prior to *Dignitatis Humanae*, recognizing religious freedom as an intrinsic aspect of the human personality not dependent on the truth of the particular religion, John Kennedy would be aggressively pressed by skeptical Protestant ministers to make a personal assurance that his Catholic faith would indeed allow different faith conceptions of the common good.[263] Kennedy was pressed in this manner not, as

---

261. In one of his earlier writings, Pope Leo XIII's strongly condemns the introduction of civil laws that treat marriage merely as a civil contract, thereby "setting at naught the sanctity of this great sacrament." Pope Leo XIII, *Inscrutabili Dei Consilio: Encyclical on the Evils of Society* para. 14 (1878), *available at* http://www.vatican.va/holy_father/leo_xiii/encyclicals/documents/hf_l-xiii_enc_21041878_inscrutabili-dei-consilio_en.html. However, in a later writing, he leaves open the possibility that a marriage, "contracted in accordance with the laws of the State," but not entered into as a sacrament in accordance with the doctrine of the Catholic Church, can be a valid quasi-marital partnership, established under the "rite and custom introduced by civil law." Pope Leo XIII, *Arcanum: Encyclical on Christian Marriage* para. 40 (1880), *available at* http://www.vatican.va/holy_father/leo_xiii/encyclicals/documents/hf_l-xiii_enc_10021880_arcanum_en.html. Perhaps one justification for this change of heart was the recognition that for the protection of children, "the effects of marriage [should] be guarded in all possible ways." *Id.*

262. *See id.*

263. During Kennedy's presidential campaign, some Protestant ministers argued that "clerical pressure to align his decisions with the Holy See's religious dogma would prevent a Catholic president from governing independently and objectively in pursuit of the ideals and security of diverse U.S. citizens." THOMAS CARTY, A CATHOLIC IN THE WHITE HOUSE? RELIGION, POLITICS, AND JOHN F. KENNEDY'S PRESIDENTIAL CAMPAIGN 6 (2004).

is commonly thought, because Protestants feared formal Catholic instruction would be imposed upon them by law. As noted by Al Smith, the Catholic Church in America had never assumed it could impose its will on the non-Catholic public.[264] Protestants weren't going to disappear merely because JFK was elected. Rather, it was because the Catholic Church of the 1940s and '50s in America was a distinctively strong family-based community that powerfully influenced the direction of the law in ways that the solitary nature of Protestantism could not.[265]

The Catholic situation at the time of Kennedy's 1960 speech to the Greater Houston Ministerial Association was a situation of religious distinctiveness that included publicly noticeable religious expression, such as May crownings, Corpus Christi processions, and Friday fish fries. Catholics were professionally in the larger world but residentially often in their own parish neighborhoods. This made the Protestant culture suspicious. Catholics had their own system of schools and hospitals, both of which observed unique religious services, such as the distribution of ashes on the beginning of Lent.[266] And of course there was the fundamental Protestant-Catholic divide, with Catholics looking to the magisterium of the Church for guidance as to life's most difficult and perplexing questions, especially those related to the marital estate

264. Smith, *supra* note 248 ("Under our system of government the electorate entrusts to its officers of every faith the solemn duty of action according to the dictates of conscience. I may fairly refer once more to my own record to support these truths. No man, cleric or lay, has ever directly or indirectly attempted to exercise Church influence on my administration of any office I have ever held, or asked me to show special favor to Catholics or exercise discrimination against non-Catholics.... In my public life I have exemplified that separation of Church from State which is the faith of American Catholics today.").

265. To American Protestant liberals in the mid-twentieth century, "Catholic families seemed distant from the democratic ... ideal"; one study framed them as a "'united religious front'" where there was unquestioned acceptance of religion as an "'external authority.'" John T. McGreevy, *Thinking on One's Own: Catholicism in the American Intellectual Imagination, 1928–1960*, 84 J. Am. Hist. 97, 117 (1997) (quoting Theodor W. Adorno et al., The Authoritarian Personality 221, 310, 218 (1950)). The perceived "overly restrictive" nature of Catholic families even reminded some of "the authoritarian German model [of families]," which was characterized by a "rigid obedience" that "served as the underpinning of fascism." *Id.*

266. *See id.* at 125 ("Not only did Catholic schools isolate students from their non-Catholic peers, but they also shielded young Catholics from what became termed the 'democratic way of life.'").

in the direction and upbringing of children.[267] Catholics had survived by relying on a closely knit religious subculture for shelter, support, and a sense of belonging.

Kennedy would make a promise that he did not intend to consult with Rome in his presidential decision making, but he really couldn't dissociate himself from his own Catholic upbringing. Catholic practice in the 1940s and '50s clearly situated Catholics—even Catholics in wealthy families like the Kennedys—in the realm of dual citizenship at the very time when the individual conscience of Protestant America was being overcome by 1960s individualism and secularity.[268] The Catholic mind was therefore far more ready than the Protestant or nonbelieving mind to achieve consensus on moral questions that could be incorporated into public law.[269] Since that was the case, Protestant ministers wanted to know if the Catholic senator from Massachusetts intended to import the Catholic consensus into national policy if given the opportunity to serve in the presidency. Kennedy tried to answer these questions in his landmark 1960 address to the Greater Houston Ministerial Association.[270] JFK's speech, and a later address by Catholic New York Governor Mario Cuomo at Notre Dame in 1984 that applied Kennedy's arguments to the abortion debate, sought to reassure the Protestant community that Catholic thinking would guide the private, but not the public, man.[271] Both of these addresses essentially sought to immunize

267. "The Catholic prohibition against remarriage within the church after divorce seemed a considerable limitation on human freedom, as did the demand that non-Catholic spouses agree to raise their children as Catholics." *Id.* at 118–119.
268. To Protestants, their own religion "molded the national traits of independence and individualism," whereas Catholic practices, such as those related to the family and marriage, appeared to stand against such traditional US values. CARTY, *supra* note 263, at 50.
269. *Id.* (noting the perception that Catholics could not resist clerical authority on fear of banishment from the religious community, and thus could not truly act as independent decision makers.).
270. Kennedy, *supra* note 9.
271. Cuomo noted in his speech that "Catholic public officials take an oath to preserve the Constitution that guarantees freedom . . . because they realize that in guaranteeing freedom for all, they guarantee our right to be Catholics [which includes] our right . . . to reject abortion." Mario Cuomo, Address at the University of Notre Dame: Religious Belief and Public Morality: A Catholic Governor's Perspective (Sept. 13, 1984), transcript *available at* http://archives.nd.edu/research/texts/cuomo.htm.

the public debate from religious influence through the privatization of faith belief.

The result of Kennedy's speech was the beginning of the forfeiture of the unique value of the Catholic community, and with it the fuller freedom of the Church to form the conscience of the people of God. The political race in 1960 was extremely close. Kennedy chose quite logically to write in an uncharacteristically blunt manner drawing an absolute line to the effect that his faith was a private matter. A more nuanced presentation removed from the glare of political gamesmanship would have illustrated that Kennedy had no need to run from his faith since the Catholicism of the 1960s was not relying upon political success so much as the pervasive Catholic culture in the neighborhoods and parishes and social organizations that seemingly shaped the worldview of Catholics at that time. Of course, the Kennedy speech can't be blamed entirely for the decline in the strength and influence of these Catholic modalities; the 1960s and the age of skepticism and challenge would not leave any source of authority unexamined or deconstructed.

As a matter of law, Article VI of the Constitution provides: "No religious Test shall ever be required as a Qualification to any Office or public Trust under the United States."[272] Al Smith and John Kennedy were treated differently based on their religion. Smith lost the presidency; Kennedy won, but that victory is probably more explainable by the ingenuity of the mayor of Chicago than by the refinements of Catholic theology.[273]

But this history has a curious progeny: With the law subsuming so much of what had previously been allocated to the private components of society—such as family and church—the Church either had to succeed in convincing the state as a whole to incorporate its religious instruction into the law, or to learn to live within a polity where Catholic teaching would always be imperfectly incorporated into the legal order.

---

272. U.S. CONST, art. VI.

273. It is popularly believed that the "Chicago democratic machine" of then-mayor Richard J. Daley stole the 1960 presidential election in Kennedy's favor. Peter Carlson, *Another Race to the Finish: 1960's Election Was Close but Nixon Didn't Haggle*, WASH. POST., Nov. 17, 2000, at A1, http://www.washingtonpost.com/ac2/wp-dyn/A36425-2000Nov16?.

The Church could not simply insist, Gelasian-style, that the law and religion coincide; this would be contrary to the Establishment Clause. For the most part, the Church was willing, within the spirit of *Dignitatis Humanae*, to live and let live, making its best case for its own point of view but accepting others when it did not prevail to have its view incorporated into the law.[274]

IS CONFESSIONALISM THE ANSWER?

The unease with the limited material focus of the exclusionary secular state has provoked questions that have been simmering in the schools of theology and philosophy for generations in the United States and abroad. Recently, however, there has been a scholarly flowering and defense of both the realism of the dissatisfaction with, and thus unsteadiness, of an exclusionary secularist republic and a growing defense of confessionalism.[275] This realism might prompt Dr. Fish to articulate an intellectual "I told you so" justifying his skepticism toward allowing the public display of religious symbols. The confessional proposition could signal a loss of human freedom of belief if it arrived in the form of mandated or compelled confessionalism. One supposes that Dr. Fish shares in the view of the exclusionary secularist voices in Europe that are constantly warning against—not without reason—the imposition of Sharia law on peoples of diverse belief. It is less clear whether Dr. Fish and others would be equally alarmed by a non-compelled confessional state, such as the Republic of Malta where I was in residence for the last several years.

Malta takes seriously both faith and the political freedom necessary for vibrant discussion of faith-based public policy, and in my view,

---

274. *See,* e.g., McGreevy, *supra* note 265, at 128 (noting that by the 1950s, "the public posture of American Catholicism . . . became less combative," with "the gradual assimilation of Catholics into American intellectual circles [due to a postwar increase of Catholic students attending non-Catholic universities] allow[ing] Catholic liberals to begin echoing criticisms of conformity originating outside the church.").
275. THADDEUS J. KOZINSKI, THE POLITICAL PROBLEM OF RELIGIOUS PLURALISM AND WHY PHILOSOPHERS CAN'T SOLVE IT, xiii (2010).

it balances these considerations so well that it arguably refutes the claim of Dr. Fish and other exclusionary secularists that a confessional state—that is, one with an established church—denies full human flourishing. Obviously, any claim in polite intellectual company that a confessional state is compatible (maybe necessary) for the full advancement of human dignity and capabilities is extremely provocative. Moreover, Malta's compact size, with scarcely more than 400,000 people living in a geographic area with a size akin to that of the District of Columbia, may be a pre-condition to its success.[276]

Nevertheless, contemporary philosophy is paying considerable attention to the argument for confessionalism. One of the most explicit proponents of this argument is Thaddeus Kozinski. In his 2010 publication *The Political Problem of Religious Pluralism and Why Philosophers Can't Solve It*, Kozinski dismisses the efforts by John Rawls, Jacques Maritain, and Alasdair MacIntyre to defend either the exclusionary secular model (Rawls) or inclusionary secularism (MacIntyre). However, Kozinski finds that MacIntyre is not much of a defender of this proposition either.[277] Inclusionary secularism is insufficient, according to Kozinski, because it fails to recognize that all political systems are ultimately dependent upon a religious tradition of some sort.[278] MacIntyre demonstrates, according to Kozinski, that a nation-state cannot on that scale produce a "morally robust" political order—in the context of pervasive pluralism.[279] Kozinski finds Rawls's suggestion for a "freestanding, purely political and overlapping consensus" to borrow heavily from theological premises.[280] So, too, Maritain's model for a

---

276. The estimated population of Malta as of July 2011 is 408, 333. CIA WORLD FACT-BOOK, *Malta, supra* note 104. In addition, the country is just slightly less than twice the size of Washington, DC. CIA WORLD FACTBOOK, *Area—Comparative*, https://www.cia.gov/library/publications/the-world-factbook/fields/2023.html (last visited Oct. 14, 2011).

277. THADDEUS J. KOZINSKI, THE POLITICAL PROBLEM OF RELIGIOUS PLURALISM AND WHY PHILOSOPHERS CAN'T SOLVE IT, 240 (2010) ("MacIntyre has made it clear that the ultimate reason for the superior strength of Thomistic philosophy is precisely its theological underpinnings.").

278. *Id.* at xiii.

279. *Id.*

280. *Id.*

democratic charter is directed by the work of Thomas Aquinas even as it speaks of neutrality.[281]

Kozinski's work draws out MacIntyre's suggestion that "political deliberation in . . . pluralism" should have as its aim "the creation of the best social, cultural, and political conditions for the communal discovery and political establishment of that intellectual tradition" which best advances human nature.[282] For the pluralist inclusionary state to be successful, there must be conscious effort directed at finding the minimal consensus that will assure our living together. However, currently, such conscious effort is not to be found; and even if a unifying vision is identified, it seldom has involved any real commitment to transcendent propositions, or any real commitment to what Thomas Jefferson denoted as self-evident truth.

Kozinski's project argues that the public good requires serious public effort to resolve diverse and often conflicting truth claims.[283] It is not enough for the modern state to tolerate the presence of diverse traditions and religions while making no serious effort to discern truth. The closest one finds in the modern state for reconciliation is a commitment to mutual toleration and dialogue. However, if the toleration and dialogue are for their own sake and not aimed at some consensus about truth, what is the point?

The point for Dr. Kozinski is that Roman Catholicism is the confessional state; but there is little given to explain how that would come about without the suppression of other faith claims and competing traditions.[284] Nonetheless, the Roman Catholic Church has described an ideal form of the Catholic confessional state. Such a state is described as the outcome of a living faith.[285] *Gaudium et spes* invites the laity to make matters of conscience front and center.[286] The Divine law should be impressed on the affairs of the earthly city.[287] If this is done

281. *Id.*
282. *Id.*
283. *Id.* at xxiv.
284. *Id.* at 204.
285. Peter Kwasniewski, Basic Notes on the Catholic State (April 2006) (unpublished lecture notes) (*cited in* KOZINSKI, *supra* note 275 at 204 n.27).
286. *Id.*
287. *Id.*

consistently, a Catholic culture will become a Catholic state.[288] For the majority of citizens in such a confessional state, Church teaching will be the point of reference for understanding that they are for interpreting the world order, for perceiving the nature of public and private responsibilities on a day-to-day basis, and for evaluating arts and letters.[289] It is contemplated that the transcendent focus of the confessional state will draw it to all that is uplifting and truly important. Pius XII put it this way in 1955:

> While the Church and State have known hours and years of conflict, there were also from the time of Constantine the Great until the contemporary era and even recently, tranquil periods, often quite long ones, during which they collaborated with full understanding in the education of the same people. The Church . . . considers such collaboration normal, and . . . she regards the unity of the people in the true religion and the unanimity of action between herself and the State as ideal.[290]

Kozinski's final recommendation for reaching this confessional "ideal" is this:

> If the ultimate moral and political good for man can be fully intelligible and attainable only from within the particular tradition of rationality, and if a tradition of rationality can be rationally evaluated according to the degree to which it allows its adherence to know and practice the good, then any just political order must not only be open to, but also specifically and deliberately ordered to public discussion and debate about the truth and goodness of diverse traditions. The political good requires above all the discovery of that moral and intellectual tradition most conducive to

288. *Id.*

289. *Id.*

290. Pio XII, *Vous avez Voulu: Discurso Sobre La Iglesia Y La Intelligencia de la Historia* (Sept. 7, 1955), http://www.vatican.va/holy_father/pius_xii/speeches/1955/documents/ hf_p-xii_spe_19550907_vous-avez-voulu_sp.html, *translated in* Kwasniewski, *supra* note 285.

human flourishing, which is to say, the true one, for only upon and through it can one ground and secure political justice. The 'fact of reasonable pluralism' can be interpreted in no other way. In sum, *the purpose of any overlapping consensus or democratic charter is to create the conditions for the communal discovery of the true tradition.* Only in the event of such a discovery could there be any real possibility of morally based political unity. Large-scale political unity and the truth is a good that must be sought, in spite of the great difficulty in attaining it.... And, *pace* Rawls and Maritain, it is not an impossible goal.[291]

Is this hubristic academic philosophy run riot? Why would it not be understood as discomfiting to the religious freedom interests of an Islamic believer, or for that matter, a non-Catholic? Has Kozinski unintentionally succeeded in making the most persuasive case for church-state separation? For exclusionary secularism?

Is the case for exclusionary secularism made stronger when there is a papal pronouncement that speaks of a politics opening itself up and ordering itself to the transcendent? Is this nothing else but the confessional state? Isn't connecting the dots all that is left to do?

Maybe Kozinski means something less dramatic and arguably more salutary to the human circumstance. Assuming, however, Kozinski wishes to do more than separate us from the diminishment of humanity to its materialistic desires, is there any realistic way in which we can imagine Kozinski's aspiration to come about short of religious war? At a minimum, one would need some mechanism for prompting departure from the old, secular order. The first step would be allowing small-scale political secession from the larger political order from the liberal confessional nation-state—meaning not to war against it, but only to have some level of political autonomy, perhaps just enough to ban abortion in a particular locality. Of course, to be really practical, one would then have to have some mechanism for resolving conflict with people of other religious traditions who pre-settled that nation-state and would be seeking to undertake the same effort or to resist all such efforts at that same

291. KOZINSKI, *supra* note 275, at 239–240.

place. Given the Tea Party hatred on the political right in the United States, and the anxiety and animus from the left that already exist in our political system, is it realistic to suppose that the political arrangement proposed by Kozinski would not further undermine love of neighbor?

But there's a more fundamental problem. Is the transition from unfocused inclusionary secularism to exclusionary secularism to a form of confessionalism actually transforming the society in the image of Christ, or running from that responsibility? Isn't it akin to the Amish living separate, but without grounding in the scriptural lineage of either the Amish or Mennonite traditions? In this regard, it is something of a concession that those who hold political power are beyond the message of Christ. Of course, if one wants to keep the thought experiment alive, one has to speculate what happens when the confessional state gets under way, how big it should become, and so forth. Size is problematic, since history suggests that, operationally, there is a tendency for favored churches—like other corruptible human institutions—to care about the pursuit of authority and to lose sight of the transcendent aim.[292] In brief, confessional states on a large scale may look promising only because the rudderless materialism of the large-scale non-confessional state looks comparatively dismal, especially if as a result of exclusionary secularism there is less of an oasis of religious reference to sustain the spirit. Several hundred years ago, vast sections of the globe were confessional states, with not very good results.[293]

Even putting these instrumental or practical considerations aside, there is no particular reason to believe that the Holy Spirit is aimed at the construction of the ideal political system on earth. The clericalism of the past and associated abuses suggests that we would be trading

292. In France, for instance, secularism arose so aggressively as a response to the "temporal grip of the clergy in the spheres of political, academic, creative and private life." MINISTERÈ DES AFFAIRES ÉTRANGERÈS, *supra* note 142.

293. In some confessional states, "those who resisted inclusion in the established church were excluded from society and subjected to numerous indignities and punishments, as overcame the Roman Catholics in the Russian Empire and Swedish Kingdom, and Jews and Muslims in Spain." Hans Knippenberg, *The Political Geography of Religion: Historical State-Church Relations in Europe and Recent Challenges*, 67 GEOJOURNAL 253, 260 (2006).

one set of problems for another. To paraphrase G. K. Chesterton, this sounds like an idea that was tried and found wanting, and not one that was found wanting and never tried. On that score, a few people might remember that the United States itself owes part of its founding to those escaping from confessional states.

CONCLUDING OBSERVATIONS

To conclude this inquiry into secularism, it is fair to say that examining whether the display of a crucifix in an Italian public school classroom was permissible is not just a question dealing with a well-known symbol; it is a fundamental question regarding the organization of society. Those who argue for exclusionary secularism or atheism to be the basis of that organization have a burden of explanation. This is not an atheist or exclusionary secular world (apart from France). Most of the nations of the world are moderate, confessional states that attempt to preserve their democratic acceptability by at least theoretically remaining open in political debate to the diversity of religious thinking within their polity, even if there are preferences for a given one. These democratically acceptable states recognize that for men and women to know their purpose and to act well in respect to it, faith is a prerequisite. Arguably, Dr. Fish is right: the ECHR failed to appreciate the continuing importance of symbol. To the believer, the crucifix is hardly passive in the way described by the Grand Chamber's decision in *Lautsi*. There would be strong agreement between democratically acceptable confession lists and Dr. Fish that, for the believing Christian, the crucifix is too consequential to be a mere artifact of culture, or some splendid bauble bringing back warm reminiscence of national or cultural identity.

The proponents of exclusionary secularism are rightly concerned about divisions that provoke violence or war, and the modern pluralism of religious belief can be a source of division. If we assume from history that faith will continue to play a large role in the structuring of new governments and the sustenance of existing ones, then a good place to begin might be to discern some sustaining principles of harmony—to pick the Islamic natural law term.

No Indoctrination or Prostelyzation

While divisiveness might be lessened through either of the extremes—coerced confessionalism or the expedient of exclusionary secularism—religious tolerance cannot include public (or various forms of private) compulsion. The ECHR's lower Second Chamber court had found in its 2009 decision in *Lautsi* that insofar as Catholicism was Italy's majority religion, the mandated display of the crucifix could be construed as an attempt to indoctrinate by suppressing minority religions.[294] The Grand Chamber denied this implication, and it is important that it found no evidence of majority indoctrination or prostelyzation.[295] The presence of the crucifix invited all children to understand that they were part of the national community that had its own multifaceted traditions.[296] The right of parents to educate their children must be construed in light of these diverse beliefs. Exhibition of the crucifix no more undermines parental direction than does the accommodation of Islamic headscarves in apparel, or observances noting the beginning and end of Ramadan. Italy allowed all this and more, including—in direct contrast to practice in the United States—religious instruction in public school of all recognized creeds; and the different Sabbaths of children of minority faiths were taken into account by not having the affected children sit for examinations with conflicting times.[297]

No Suppression of Religious Argument

Modern democracies need to openly address the effort by parts of the polity to enact religiously grounded perspectives into law. The Church is an advocate of confessionalism when it insists on any of the following: tax law changes favoring working families; responsible stewardship of the environment; limits on the death penalty; restrictions on the power of the president to enter into ethically ill-considered military campaigns; freedom to assist illegal migrants without legal consequence;

294. *Lautsi* at para. 37.
295. *Id.* at para. 52.
296. *See id.*
297. *Id.* at para. 39.

the denial of same-sex marriage, abortion, healthcare expenditures indirectly expanding reproductive choices, embryonic stem cell research, in vitro fertilization, artificial contraception, divorce, cohabitation; or exemption from nondiscrimination laws for religious preference to be anchored not only in Scripture and Magisterium, but also in statute. The Church then seeks not just to persuade and guide its own voluntary flock but to direct by the coercive means of the law citizens who dissent or are members of other flocks, or of none at all.

Is there anything wrong with this? No, and indeed, the transformation of the world in which we live is very much a part of the Catholic faith and many others. Where the line is crossed is when the Church loses its argument and the law is written contrary to its own doctrine or teaching. Rather too quickly, any and all divergence between faith perspective and the public choice is said to pose a moral dilemma for the person of faith, akin to that faced by Thomas More. More, himself, worked assiduously to avoid the direct clash between church and state. More appreciated the value of the rule of law even if that law was imperfect. In short, he would have taken the oath had there been enough ambiguity in the words to permit its accommodation. This was not weakness on More's part, but a sincere respect that all government originates with God and its inability to reach a proper destination is man's failure, not God's. For More, there is only one way to correct such failing—that is, pun intended, not to rush to lose one's head over the matter.

Various public intellectuals, including John Rawls, have suggested that religious argument is inappropriate with respect to these public questions in the context of public debate.[298] With due respect, efforts to draw a content line based on what is and is not a religious argument is fraught with the empowerment of government to censor speech and ideas quite contrary to democracy itself. It would also prove to be quite unworkable insofar as we do not—or at least we should not—categorize our lives into religious and nonreligious boxes.

But isn't exclusionary secularism exactly the effort to muffle religious voices? Isn't American jurisprudence that upholds the exclusion of religious displays and other disqualification of religious interaction with civil institutions—for example, applying generally applicable laws to religious

298. RAWLS, *supra* note 88, at 155.

bodies even as such application may burden belief or practice—effectively requiring religious believers to choose between faith and public job or benefit, and thereby making believers into second class citizens?

Is there a way to even up the sides without taking one side out of the process? Maybe. This, of course, is part of the impetus for a more inclusionary form of secularism; but is there not more that should be done to bring greater balance to the role of faith in public life?

Not Everything Needs to Be a Law—at Least, Not Immediately

There are some issues that could, and arguably should, be kept out of public decision making. Whenever it is clear that an attempt to legislate on a particular issue would deepen religious divisions in society, arguably a discussion waiting period should be triggered, deferring the public process of decision making. These issues would be placed off limits to public decision making for a responsible period to explore the possibility of greater consensus; and if consensus is impossible, to improve the accommodation of religious diversity.

This idea of a waiting period to avoid religiously divisive public decision is novel, but not entirely foreign to the underlying structure of human rights jurisprudence in Europe or America. For example, American and European human rights litigation already elevates some individual rights over others by providing these favored rights more sensitive treatment usually through the expedient of greater judicial scrutiny.[299]

299. Case law involving the right to federal protection against discrimination by a government actor clearly demonstrates varying levels of judicial scrutiny in the United States. According to the Supreme Court, the Equal Protection Clause of the United States Constitution prohibits discrimination on the basis of race. *See* Strauder v. West Virginia, 100 U.S. 303, 307 (1879), *abrogated by* Taylor v. Louisiana, 419 U.S. 522 (1975) ("The amendment . . . declare[s] that the law in the States shall be the same for the black as for the white; that all persons, whether colored or white, shall stand equal before the laws of the States.") Therefore, the Court has established that any racial classification by a government actor that results in unequal treatment must be subjected to "the strictest of judicial scrutiny[,]" which means that "such classifications are constitutional only if they are narrowly tailored measures that further compelling government interests." Adarand Constructors, Inc. v. Pena, 515 U.S. 200, 227 (1995). Discrimination on the basis of gender, however, is not expressly prohibited

The proposal merely adds religious subject matter to the list and contemplates, as does strict judicial scrutiny, leaving an area unrestricted by this public mechanism. (This thereby enhances individual religious freedom and the abilities of churches to guide this human behavior through religious sanction, which by definition would be coterminous with the consenting congregation.)

These reservations of religious authority to religious believers alone already exist in the Christian, Judaic, and Islamic worlds. If doing so would promote greater religious pluralism and cultural peace, more scope could be given, and resolved, in these religious tribunals. For example, it is the tradition of the Shia Ismaili Muslims to resolve disputes

---

in the United States Constitution. Therefore, classifications based on gender are not subject to the same strict scrutiny as racial classifications. However, the Supreme Court has established that gender-based classification are still suspect; accordingly, they are subject to a heightened level of scrutiny: "Parties who seek to defend gender-based government action must demonstrate an 'exceedingly persuasive justification' for that action." U.S. v. Virginia, 518 U.S. 515, 531 (1996) (quoting J.E.B. v. Alabama *ex. rel.* T.B., 511 U.S. 127, 136–137 (1994); Miss. Univ. for Women v. Hogan, 458 U.S. 718, 724 (1982)). Other types of classifications, such as age, are not considered to be suspect, regardless of their discriminatory effect. Accordingly, these classifications are only subject to a "rational basis" level of scrutiny, and courts will only overturn the law if it does not "rationally further the purpose identified by the State." Mass. Bd. of Ret. v. Murgia, 427 U.S. 307, 315 (1976).

The doctrine of proportionality shapes the nature of permitted judicial scrutiny in European human rights litigation. Under this doctrine, a European court can assess an action or measure by a member state to ensure that it meets three requirements: it must be "suitable to achieve a legitimate purpose," as well as being "necessary to achieve that purpose," and it must not "impose burdens . . . that outweigh the objectives achieved by the measure." Aaron Baker, *Controlling Racial and Religious Profiling: Article 14 ECHR Protection v. U.S. Equal Protection Clause Prosecution*, 13 Tex. Wesleyan L. Rev. 285, 295 (2007). Under the European Convention of Human Rights (ECHR), signatory nations are prohibited from preventing "the enjoyment of rights and freedoms" defined in the ECHR by means of discrimination based on "sex, race, colour, language, religion, political or other opinion, national or social origin, association with a national minority, property, birth or other status." Convention for the Protection of Human Rights and Fundamental Freedoms art. 14, Nov. 4, 1950, 213 U.N.T.S. 221. Armed with the ECHR language and the doctrine of proportionality, European courts such as the European Court of Human Rights can scrutinize any member state action that is necessary to achieve a legitimate purpose and results in discrimination under Article 14, "whatever the motive behind the action[,]" to determine whether its discriminatory burdens outweigh the achievement of its objectives. *See* Baker, *supra* at 293–295.

amicably through the intervention of elders in the community. Over time the imams established institutions to take on this role. These institutions are worldwide and exist in the United States. For example, Ismaili Muslims have seven regional boards throughout the United States to help resolve disputes if at least one of the parties is an Ismaili Muslim and the other consents to submit the matter to the board. Since 1986 the boards have handled several thousand cases, most of which relate to matrimonial issues or commercial disputes involving businesses owned and operated by members of the Islamic community. This greater scope for diverse religious decision making would be reinforced by the signals it would send not just to public officials but also to the participating counsel. Lawyers prevail by making their side seem to be uneventful or the natural extension of what already exists. Thus, the Italian government opened its advocacy in *Lautsi* with the claim that the lower court had basically failed to perceive a long-standing inclusive understanding of secularism that would permit public display of the crucifix.[300] The government did not insist upon the democratically acceptable confessionalism that exists in Malta, and the other party did not contend for the extreme of exclusionary secularism. Instead, both sides claimed their respective positions to be familiar, and here is the key for the winning, pro-crucifix display side: it allows for nominal equal treatment. From the Grand Chamber's perspective, the crucifix is let in to compete side by side with the idea of the secular republic.[301]

The Truth of the Human Person, Mutual Understanding, and Mutual Respect

Advocacy for freedom and democracy must always be tempered by the insight of John Paul II that, as earlier mentioned, a democracy unattached from moral truth is a "thinly disguised totalitarianism."[302] Part

---

300. *Lautsi* at para. 34.

301. *See id.* at para. 70 ("The Court concludes in the present case that the decision whether crucifixes should be present in State-school classrooms is, in principle, a matter falling within the margin of appreciation of the respondent State. Moreover, the fact that there is no European consensus on the question of the presence of religious symbols in State schools . . . speaks in favor of that approach.").

302. Veritatis Splendor, *supra* note 42.

of that truth can only be revealed by the recognition that in a religiously pluralistic world, there is a duty to search for common ground. That search may lead to a claim of conscience warranting exemption from the laws applying to all others, but those claims ought not be made or granted casually, lest they undermine the democratic aspiration altogether. A proper understanding of secularism, as reserving to the private sphere of faith and family those topics that have no present consensus, should again take hold to reduce the number of public fracases over faith.

As presented through the *Lautsi* case, Europe and the United States are in somewhat different postures: Europe is liberal toward religious display but not in favor of Islamic belief and practice. The United States excludes the religious displays Europe allows but treats with equality all faith beliefs before the law.

Exclusionary secularism does not honor the histories of either the United States or Europe. More important, it is along the path of respect and inclusion that civil peace is to be found. New governments need not make our mistakes of exclusion, and we have much of value to share in constitutional structure and the protection of human rights. President Obama has a great sensitivity to the importance of faith in America and internationally. His Cairo speech calling for "mutual interest and mutual respect"[303] is premised upon a simple prayer he once told me and others that he said for the United States every day—that, despite our profound disagreements, "we can live with one another in a way that reconciles the beliefs of each with the good of all."

Both the United States and the European Union have been fortunate in modern time to have this prayer answered in the affirmative. It is a prayer that needs to be said, and heard, in the countries of North Africa and the Middle East. If democracy is to survive in these venues, interfaith understanding must infuse diplomatic initiative.

While history has shown that no constitution is fully transferable from one nation to another, the insights and mechanisms for avoiding religious clash, some of which have been discussed here, reveal that the need to reconcile church and state, religion and law, morality and

303. Obama, Remarks on a New Beginning, *supra* note 40.

cultural practice have similarity whether one is in Jerusalem, Valletta, or Cairo. However, because of their nuanced differences, specific study of each is a necessity. Understanding what makes a faith tradition unique is a matter of respect; grasping the similarity of mechanisms potentially available for resolution of dispute within a particular faith and between that faith and the larger culture is a matter of common sense.

Huntington's *Clash of Civilizations* has been found by most not to be inevitable. But to avoid the potential cataclysm of conflict between religion and government one certainly does not have to tear from the world the source of transcendent hope by an imposed, exclusionary secularism.

As presented here, secularism can be crucified and a peaceful world resurrected.

PART TWO

RELATIONS BETWEEN CHURCH AND STATE

Chapter 2

Proposal for a Theoretical Linchpin for Church-State Relations

MICHAEL ANDERHEIDEN

The late Winfried Brugger (1950–2010) was a leading constitutional comparativist; called to the prestigious chair for Constitutional Law, Constitutional Theory and Philosophy of Law at Heidelberg University in 1992, Brugger concentrated on the German and US American legal systems, writing extensively on constitutional and, to a lesser degree, administrative law, as well as some aspects of European and public international law. He focused, however, on the basic rights of the German Grundgesetz (GG) and the First Amendments to the US Constitution. His major concerns were free speech, freedom of religion, and "Menschenwürde," human dignity, which form the basis of the German GG. Trained in both the United States and Germany, Brugger's constitutional comparisons were based on both grand theory and extended case studies. He never aspired to a political career nor held a position in politics; and he never served as a judge, let alone an ambassador. His research can be characterized by a bottom-up approach leaning toward inductive methods, dating back as far as his legal and sociological training at the University of California–Berkeley with the late Philip Selznick. When he arrived at Berkeley, Brugger had already studied some of Germany's greatest theorists—Max Weber and Immanuel Kant in particular. Thus he merged characteristically bottom-up and top-down approaches in most of his writing, and consequently had something to say to both practitioners of the law and legal scholars on both sides of the Atlantic.

Accordingly, Brugger traveled frequently for studies and lectures in the US, and was finally hospitalized the day after his return from his last visit to the Georgetown Law Center, his "second home base."

A fine example of Brugger's style and teaching is his posthumously published article titled "Separation, Equality, Nearness: Three Church-State Models."[1] Here Brugger first argues for a general measure to order arguments in discussions on state-church relationships, and then assesses whether this measure works by trying to fix constitutional arguments with his method. If successful, the yardstick may be seen as useful, but it is by no means exhaustive or exclusionary of other means of constitutional comparison. Brugger's approach starts with a very broad picture of "modern constitutions," which all operate on a "separation of or distinction between the spheres of state and religion, respectively, church," and Brugger notes that "church" comprises every religious organization in general regardless of its standard of organization or legal recognition. Since this is so, Brugger discards from the outset all church-state models that form a strong identification or union of spiritual and secular authority, like the Vatican, some Islamic states, or, with some qualifications, the late medieval Christian Holy Roman Empire in Europe.[2] Modern constitutions respond somehow to the ideas of freedom of religion, equality of religion, and the possibility of a rapprochement between the state and religion/church.

Obviously there are different ways to map the field of political constitutions and arrangements on state-church relations. Two of them are Kmiec's and Brugger's versions. In effect, none of Kmiec's categories fits one to one with Brugger's. To me, this seems to be the result of their different starting points. Kmiec's starting point is a public-private divide which is of no concern to Brugger.[3] In Kmiec's view, the public life is etched out of the private sphere,[4] religion belongs to the private sector, and every attempt at policies designed to leave little to be resolved in the private sphere is of great concern to him (and to the Holy Father). Accordingly, he maps state-church relations by the quantity to which they leave religion in the private field. Brugger's idea, however, is based on the groundings of democracy and thus links the question of state-church relations even more than Kmiec to the democratic form of government. "Liberty" as freedom from state intervention and "equality" are seen as the basis of democracy, enshrined, for example, in the Bill of Rights of the US Constitution and especially in its "equal concern and respect" clause. They come never alone but are accompanied by a third element that is sometimes taken to be communitarian and sometimes republican. Both center on the idea of an active life as a citizen—in the communitarian version as a member of the group of equals, in the republican one as the single citizen conscious of his political and social responsibilities.[5] Accordingly, Brugger maps state-church relationships around these three basic ideas of democracy that correspond to three models of church-state relations.

A first model of responding to these ideas concentrates on the freedom of religion: By creating a "wall of separation" between the state and all religions, the state is kept from infringing religious liberties. The distance towards all religions comprises equal treatment of all these religions by the state. The distance may be ameliorated only if religious beliefs serve as a reason to attack (and bodily harm) somebody, be it a member of the religious creed or an outsider, or some other religion or church. Only in these cases should the state keep its position as guardian of and judge over individual and group rights. Even mere factual interference with religious liberty suffices for a violation of this right. In addition, no public subsidies are given to religious communities—for example, no schoolbuses are subsidized for moving students to or from private and religious schools. States are to avoid any interaction with religion at all. Thus, no Christmas trees are allowed on public property, no religious signs are in schools or courts, and no prayer is offered at public ceremonies. Brugger takes France and Turkey (up to the Millennium) as exemplar cases.

Though the model seems to be straightforward, problems arise if public and private morals clash. Those clashes are likely since state and religion/church are portrayed as separate, isolated sources of orienting life. In effect, it is up to the individual citizen to resolve these problems. State and religious belief or community alike ask for superiority. So the individual must decide whether to behave as citizen or as believer. The model externalizes the cost of reconciliation between belief and common sense towards the citizenry. However it renders impossible any reconciliation of state and church and at least interferes with the development of socially integrative orientations. This model, concludes Brugger, may have value in times of "serious and potentially dangerous religious contentions" or when the state might be "overtaken by religion." In these situations, fiction or not, maximal distance between church and state makes sense.

Another challenge to this first model is not mentioned by Brugger in his posthumously published text but was addressed by him earlier. It results if harm to others is close to the core of a religion. Thus, a lively debate in Germany started earlier this year with a State Court decision that punished certain people for participating in the circumcision of a thirteen-year-old boy. Though circumstances of the case may be special, the Court held that circumcisions performed on minors were unjustified, with no excuse possible. Religious reasons were overridden by those of the bodily integrity of the boy. Thus, it did not matter to the Court which religion was at stake or what role male circumcision played in that religion. Little wonder that Muslim and Jewish authorities were quick to renounce the verdict as unacceptable, and most Christian authorities of different denominations joined them, all predicting that full religious life is now made impossible for Jews and Muslims (and some Christian denominations) within Germany, and that their true believers now have to leave Germany to have the circumcision done abroad. But others, for example, psychoanalysts and public educators of rank, applauded the Court for its bravery to act against a religious tradition that inflicts permanent harm on the boys far beyond the actual cut. This is not the place to discuss the case in depth or to side with the Court or its critics. Rather, our concern is the problem the verdict poses for the first model of state-church relations: How should states behave if religions of quite some standing among the citizenry urge their members to perform an action that is seen outside the religious context as a crime? The first model can only recommend that the believers abstain from their religious beliefs in certain respects. But if religious people have to leave their country to live a full life according to the rules of their denomination, the state is dependent on other communities with another model of state-church relationship in place. So the first model of state-church relationship may be self-effacing, claiming respect for religious adherence (though from a distance) but render a life according to these religions impossible within its territory. At the same time it provides no means to ameliorate the clash between state and religion.

As much as the first model of state-church relations according to Brugger was based on liberty; his second model is dominated by the idea of equal treatment of all religions. Again no material union between church and state exists. But also, the idea of equality does not prescribe any proximity between the two. Thus, even the first model of utmost distance between church and state can be restructured around the idea of formal equality between religions. However, the focus on equality opens up much more complex relations between state and religions. Typical for this model are state prescriptions that all religions should have a fair chance to gain support. Even radical churches and creeds are to be protected, sometimes more than established religions and churches. Brugger had no prime examples for this view but he was convinced that some decisions of the German Constitutional Court (e.g., on displaying a cross in classrooms) and some decisions of the US Supreme Court (e.g., on school busing)[6] could be read as supporting this model. Since I trust that most readers will know the US decisions in detail, let me briefly summarize the decision of the German Constitutional Court.[7] Its main ideas are these:

The state should be neutral toward all religions; it is not allowed to have a religious position. At the same time, the state is to foster mutual tolerance between religions. Since there is no possibility for giving all religions equal weight in classrooms, no religious symbol is allowed in public schools. Observe, however, that this position is not sterile toward religious affiliations. State officials including teachers in public schools can observe their religious duties. Again, the different religions are to be treated equal. Thus it is up to the legislators to decide how much display of personal religious affiliation is allowed to an individual while fulfilling a public function.[8]

Religious symbols may be displayed in public places as long as all religions and creeds that want such a display are taken into consideration and given the same amount of space and publicity. The same holds true even for symbols of an aggressively secular nature. Financial support for religious groups and churches falls under the same idea of equality. So schoolbuses may be subsidized for pupils of all beliefs equally.

To prevent any interference of the state with the core of a religion, or even to undermine the other core idea that some distance between religion and state is a defining element for modern constitutions, ritual, and avowal of faith remain beyond the limits of state action. The proper place for public subsidies for religious groups is rather the care for the elderly and for the youth, for the poor and the hopeless, the weak and sick.

The major problem of this equality approach to state-church relationship lies at the level of implementation. Religious communities are diverse, some small, others large, some loosely organized, others strictly hierarchical, some moderate, others (more) fundamentalist, some poor, few rich. What, then, exactly is required by equality of treatment? Are smaller religions to be preferred to give them an equal chance to win as much support as bigger, more established churches? (Brugger is a skeptic on this point.) Should the state promote education in the study of religion to introduce pupils to a variety of religions so they can make a reasonable choice for affiliation between religious "offers"? What if it is practically impossible for a state to support all religions alike? In actuality, equal treatment of all religions would be impossible. The challenges to this model may concentrate around the question of what the aim of equality is. Thus, a state may spend an equal amount for all religious communities for schoolbuses or an equal amount per student or even the same number of buses for all religions, with quite different effects in practice, and adverse effects to religious communities promoting home schooling. Even the state's choice between individual and community as a benchmark for monetary support is not innocent from the point of view of different religions, since some of them see themselves based on their doctrine as a closely knit community (e.g., Islam, Mormons); others center around the individual and his or her life (at least some of the Lutheran Churches). If both kinds of groups are present in a modern state, then no neutral procedure exists to support all religions alike. Under these circumstances states are always biased.

Finally, this second model has basically the same externalization problem as the first: Since the state tries to treat all religions alike it cannot rely in its arguments and decisions on one or the other religion substantively. In consequence, the state cannot respond to the needs of a single religion. Treating all religions alike may also contradict religious self-understanding to be the only way to answer the deepest questions there are. In general, public and religious reasoning may conflict, with both sides demanding supremacy and no procedure available to solve the disagreements or even to exchange arguments. Equal consideration for all religions does not (necessarily) imply a serious debate between state and religious communities. Consequently, every argumentative difference between state and religion is still to be answered by the individual: If the state asks to go to war and the religion forbids doing so, it is the individual's decision to act as citizen or as believer. Some difference with the first model lies in the role of the religious community, which is now recognized as a possible player molding and shaping individuals' ideas and decisions.

The third and final model is designed to answer the request for responsiveness. A complementary relationship of public and religious morality requires, first and foremost, that the two complement each other. So the backbone of this model is a complementary relationship of public and religious morality. Since citizens in their vast majority are shaped and molded not only by public institutions but also by their families, religions, and communities of faith, there is most likely no such thing as a citizenry that relies on purely public values only. It rather is likely but by no means necessary that centuries-old social, including religious, values form the background of the political community. The open question is how much political debate is to rely on this background. Some suggest a close tie between the social (including the religious) past of a community; others are skeptical and note that convincing arguments towards members of other traditions have either to take their views into account or try to give reasons which nobody can reasonably deny.[9]

To be sure, even if public argument relies heavily on religious reasoning, public and religious morals and ideals of upbringing are not identical and neither are state and church. Even the third model is based on the actual difference between state and church(es). The two spheres remain at least partially autonomous. And the same holds true for the values of private life. Hence, as Brugger points out, from the point of view of family values one may criticize religious ideals or political goals—and vice versa. All three orders are based on a synthesis between individual and community life, individualism and holism. For their own common good, however, all rely upon the others.

However, the complementary connection of state and religion, and of political and social life, is a contingent one. It is also possible that fractious and destructive powers dominate in one or all of the "core communities," or between them. Brugger is convinced that the ideal of the common good will then be missed. Thus, for him there may be historical circumstances when this model of state-church relations is unsatisfactory for a peaceful community life or one of the other models is superior to restore peace and the flourishing of the public.

One likely, though not necessary, feature of this third model of church-state relations follows from the historical weight certain religions have had in a certain area. For a long time up to now a meaningful part of the community's shared morals may have been heavily formed by a majority religious tradition. In turn, lawmakers have enacted laws that at least lean toward this tradition. This (part of the) law is valid even today. In that sense, legitimacy and genealogy of the law coincide in these legal systems. For Brugger, an example in case is the first paragraph of the first article of the German "Basic Law": "The dignity of man shall be inviolable. To respect it and protect it shall be the duty of all state authority." This clause is more than just another constitutional phrase. It is the expression of the belief in our country that every person is indispensable and irreplaceable, that it is forbidden to exploit or instrumentalize them. The ideas of the phrase have strong Christian but also strong philosophical connotations going back to the philosophy of Immanuel Kant. But they converge on the point of human dignity. Even more, the idea behind this clause is habitualized and institutionalized in German public life. It forms the center of what can be called Germany's civil religion. Other countries in Brugger's view rely on other core ideas taken from their religious and philosophical traditions.

This third model is therefore often characterized by a "civil religion," which combines two elements: Religious values that have made their way into the legal system, and its public value system. Furthermore, the depth and normative strength of genuine religious commands are borrowed by the legal system as well. Both aspects work together so that the legal system cannot be changed easily. If all this holds true, Brugger elaborates, then it would be counterproductive for the legal system to ignore the "common fountain of virtue which began as a religious value, and, over the course of time, morphed into a partially universal, 'secularized' value called civil religion."

This last point of course raises the question of neutrality and religious freedom, especially for religious minorities. The goal of integration may also be unrealistic if the majority religion is not itself moderate enough to allow for other religious views and services. But this problem seems to be a common problem of all three models of state-church relations. It seems likely that it is a direct consequence of the separation of religion and state in the first place: Whoever allows a state to have a life of its own independent of the religious order must also give way for views that are not those of that particular religious belief. All three models of church-state relations in democracies therefore ask for a minimum of religious tolerance for political reasoning. All three models are contingent upon such tolerance. If this tolerance is present, as it is for Brugger, a question of historical circumstance whether the advantages of one or the other of the models he outlined outweigh the disadvantages. This leaves a lot to politics, a lot to decide, and a lot to take responsibility for. In any case, Brugger's classification can serve as a counterpart from the point of view of democracy to Professor Kmiec's elaborated view on the current state of the church-state relations in the United States.

NOTES

1. Winfried Brugger, "Separation, Equality, Nearness: Three Church-State Models," *International Journal of Semiotics and Law* (2011).
2. Compare Kmiec's models 1 and 5, which he takes to be irreconcilable with modern democratic states. We should observe, however, that France from 1791 until 1794 can be seen as attempting to bring together a radical atheist doctrine with at least the aim of democratic procedures. The result was terror.
3. Presumably Brugger would point to European history to tell quite a different story: that "the private" was etched out of "the public" or social sphere, with the "private sphere" denoting a room where individuals can seek reclusion and separation from social duties, and be alone or together with one other person, sometimes a small family. He would point to the development

of private homes and private rooms within homes, notably private bedrooms, which were uncommon up to the twentieth century; and he would insist that the small or core family we know today was virtually unknown up to the eighteenth century. At the same time, politics became more and more open to everybody, especially in democracies. This in turn may have triggered the differentiation of the "social" and the "political" sphere. As a consequence, religion, churches, and creeds can now be seen as part of the "social," and hence neither the "political" nor the "private" sphere (notwithstanding the fact that a prayer may be one of the most private actions possible). For this view see Georges Duby, ed., *History of Private Life* (Cambridge, MA: Belknap Press, 1987–1998), esp. volumes 3 and 4.

4. Kmiec, "Secularism Crucified?," see section "Secularism in Relation to Public/Private Spheres of Decision Making".

5. Brugger was a communitarian; the author leans much more toward republicanism; for this chapter the differences among us are put aside.

6. *Everson v. Board of Education*, 330 U.S. 1 (1947).

7. Bundesverfassungsgericht (German Constitutional Court) Decision of May 16, 1995, case 1 BvR 1087/91, published in the official records vol. 93, pp. 1 ff. Brugger was a leading German critic of this decision; see Winfried Brugger and Stefan Huster, eds., Der Streit un das *Kreuz in der Schule* (Baden-Baden: Nomos, 1997).

8. Compare The "Headscarf Decision" of the German Constitutional Court of September 24, 2003, case 2 BvR 1436/02, published in vol. 108, pp. 282 ff.

9. Observe, however, that his last position can be held by authors as diverse as, say Thomas Aquinas in his *Summa contra Gentiles*, and Tim Scanlon in his "Contractualism and Utilitarianism," first published in 1982, republished in T. M. Scanlon, *The Difficulty of Tolerance: Essays in Political Philosophy* (New York: Cambridge University Press, 2009), 124–150.

Chapter 3

Secularism Resurrected? The European Court of Human Rights after *Lautsi*

GEOFFREY R. WATSON

Has Europe crucified secularism? Douglas Kmiec raises this possibility in the chapter that opens this book.[1] He points to *Lautsi v. Italy*,[2] in which the Grand Chamber of the European Court of Human Rights (ECHR) rejected a challenge to the public display of crucifixes in the classrooms of a state-run school. But recent developments—the ECHR's headscarf cases, other changes in European law, and even *Lautsi* itself— all suggest that European secularism is more alive than dead.

Unlike the US Constitution, the European Convention on Human Rights[3] contains no Establishment Clause. Article 9 of the Convention protects Free Exercise but it has little to say about state sponsorship of religion. It provides the following:

1. Everyone has the right to freedom of thought, conscience and religion; this right includes freedom to change his religion or belief, and freedom, either alone or in community with others and in public or private, to manifest his religion or belief, in worship, teaching, practice and observance.
2. Freedom to manifest one's religion or beliefs shall be subject only to such limitations as are prescribed by law and are

necessary in a democratic society in the interests of public safety, for the protection of public order, health or morals, or the protection of the rights and freedoms of others.

Likewise, Article 14 of the Convention provides for non-discrimination with respect to religion, but it does not purport to prohibit state establishment or sponsorship of religion. It says only this:

The enjoyment of the rights and freedoms set forth in this Convention shall be secured without discrimination on any ground such as sex, race, colour, language, religion, political or other opinion, national or social origin, association with a national minority, property, birth or other status.

Finally, Article 2 of Protocol 1 to the ECHR provides the following:

No person shall be denied the right to education. In the exercise of any functions which it assumes in relation to education and to teaching, the State shall respect the right of parents to ensure such education and teaching in conformity with their own religious and philosophical convictions.

It's hardly astonishing that there is no pan-European Establishment Clause. After all, some European states, such as Great Britain, have established state religions. Other European states give special treatment to one or more faiths, even if they are not formally established. The recently adopted Charter of Fundamental Rights of the European Union, the EU's companion document to the Council of Europe's human rights regime, stresses free exercise rather than non-establishment.[4]

Moreover, before the initial chamber decision in *Lautsi*, a number of European states permitted public displays of the crucifix in state-run classrooms, and a few even required such a display. Practice was not uniform, of course. Some European courts had invalidated laws permitting or requiring religious displays in the classroom. But these were decisions of state constitutional law, not European law, and in any case they represented only a minority of European states. In the "great majority" of states of the Council of Europe, "no specific regulation" on the matter governed.[5]

Against this backdrop, then, the first decision in *Lautsi v. Italy*[6]—the lower chamber decision of 2009—came as a surprise. The seven-judge chamber unanimously ruled that the public display of the crucifix in state schools violated Article 2 of Protocol 1, the provision safeguarding the right of parents to "ensure such education and teaching in conformity with their own religious and philosophical convictions." There was nary a dissent. The chamber found

> an obligation on the State's part to refrain from imposing beliefs, even indirectly, in places where persons are dependent on it or in places where they are particularly vulnerable. The schooling of children is a particularly sensitive area in which the compelling power of the State is imposed on minds which still lack (depending on the child's level of maturity) the critical capacity which would enable them to keep their distance from the message derived from a preference manifested by the State in religious matters.[7]

And the Court concluded:

> The presence of the crucifix may easily be interpreted by pupils of all ages as a religious sign, and they will feel that they have been brought up in a school environment marked by a particular religion. . . . Negative freedom of religion is not restricted to the absence of religious services or religious education. It extends to practices and symbols expressing, in particular or in general, a belief, a religion or atheism. That negative right deserves special protection if it is the State which expresses a belief and dissenters are placed in a situation from which they cannot extract themselves if not by making disproportionate efforts and acts of sacrifice.[8]

The decision prompted an outcry in Italy and elsewhere, especially in Central and Eastern Europe. In the appeal to the Grand Chamber— a super-chamber of seventeen judges, none of whom participated in the lower chamber decision—a number of European states, including several from Central and Eastern Europe, filed statements supporting Italy's position. It is probably no coincidence that some of the loudest objections to the chamber decision came from states in the eastern half of Europe, where communist governments had not long ago suppressed many forms of religious observance. Although some European non-governmental organizations filed statements in support of applicant Soile Lautsi, no European state sided with her. Even so, some court-watchers expected the Grand Chamber to affirm.[9]

The Grand Chamber reversed by a lopsided vote of 15–2. Even allowing for the fact that different judges decided this phase of the case, the difference in vote between the lower chamber and the Grand Chamber is striking. Some critics suggested that the court had bowed to popular pressure. But that doesn't necessarily mean the Grand Chamber got the case wrong.

The Grand Chamber acknowledged that the primary significance of the crucifix is religious, but it also took note of the Italian government's arguments that the crucifix has important non-religious connotations:

> The Government, for their part, explained that the presence of crucifixes in State-school classrooms, being the result of Italy's historical development, a fact which gave it not only a religious connotation but also an identity-linked one, now corresponded to a tradition which they considered it important to perpetuate. They added that, beyond its religious meaning, the crucifix symbolised the principles and values which formed the foundation of democracy and western civilisation, and that its presence in classrooms was justifiable on that account.[10]

The Grand Chamber did not explicitly adopt the government's characterization of the crucifix as embodying democratic values, but neither did the court reject it. The opinion emphasized that the crucifix was merely a "passive symbol" that "cannot be deemed to have an influence on pupils comparable to that of didactic speech or participation in religious activities."[11] The Grand Chamber observed that different European states had different views on the meaning of the symbol, and thus it was appropriate to grant states a "margin of appreciation" in respect of its use.

The Court takes the view that the decision whether or not to perpetuate a tradition falls in principle within the margin of appreciation of the respondent State. The Court must moreover take into account the fact that Europe is marked by a great diversity between the States of which it is composed, particularly in the sphere of cultural and historical development. [12]

What, then, are American readers to make of *Lautsi*? Was it rightly decided? Does it support Kmiec's assertion that the United States is generally more oriented toward free exercise and non-establishment, whereas in Europe things are reversed? Is Kmiec right that the ECHR tends to disfavor Islam, in contrast to US law on religion? Whose approach is preferable: The American or the European? Finally, does *Lautsi* signal that European secularism has been "crucified," as the title of Kmiec's chapter suggests? The remainder of this chapter takes up these questions.

First, was *Lautsi* rightly decided? The outcome would be unlikely, to say the least, in American courts. But in the European context, it's a much closer question. On a formal level, as we have already seen, there is no strong anti-Establishment norm in the positive law of the Council of Europe or the European Union. Moreover, the long-standing practice of public display of the crucifix in classrooms in Italy (and elsewhere) creates a sort of "constitutional gloss"[13] that's hard to ignore.

Some might dismiss *Lautsi* as a judicial evasion. On this view, the ECHR was doing what it usually does: Repeating the "margin of appreciation" mantra when it wants the state to win, and disregarding it when it wants the state to lose. Or, as Grant Gilmore said in a different context, the "margin of appreciation" is "simply a way of saying that, for reasons which the court does not care to discuss, there must be judgment" for the state.[14]

Less cynically, though, one might see *Lautsi*'s recourse to the "margin of appreciation" as a reasonable application of subsidiarity. On this view, *Lautsi* reaffirmed the ECHR's traditional commitment to state autonomy, a type of judicial restraint that has helped the court build legitimacy in the eyes of the member states of the Council of Europe. The decision's recourse to the "margin of appreciation" might also be regarded as a welcome reaffirmation of subsidiarity, of respect for differing local customs and traditions. A reasonable jurist might disagree with Italy's policy choice but be reluctant to overturn it, and all similar policy choices by other European states, without a clear mandate in the text of the European Convention.

In some ways, this "subsidiarity" explanation of the case might resonate with American jurists. The notion that judicial restraint might promote judicial legitimacy is a familiar one in the United States. Moreover, as Kmiec notes, US constitutional law has its own version of subsidiarity—federalism. Some things in American law are left to the states and local governments.

That said, the "subsidiary" justification is less familiar to Americans in the context of human rights. In fact, the "margin of appreciation" doctrine does not really have a counterpart in American human rights jurisprudence. As Kmiec observes, the American version of subsidiarity is generally applied only to governmental powers, not human rights.[15] He overstates the case only a little when he writes:

> there is no sentiment in the United States for locally controlled definitions of human right. . . . [T]here is little or no leeway for the states to be less generous in the interpretation of freedom of religion, freedom of speech, and a whole variety of criminal adjudication rights (such as the mandated right to be given Miranda warnings).[16]

The US Supreme Court has occasionally allowed for some local control of individual rights, as in its obscenity doctrine, which purports to rely partly on "contemporary community standards,"[17] but that prong of the doctrine may be fading into desuetude in the Internet era. And of course the several states are, theoretically, free to *enlarge* upon human rights, by providing greater protections for individual rights in their state constitutions. But by and large Kmiec is right: Human rights law in the United States is not generally subject to a "margin of appreciation."

Nonetheless, there is a difference between a national human rights court (the US Supreme Court) and a super-national court like the ECHR. If legitimacy is an ongoing concern for the US Supreme Court, it is a far greater concern for an international tribunal like the ECHR. The position of the ECHR, like that of the euro, would be stronger if it were part of a unitary central government with true federal powers. Unless and until that day arrives, however, the ECHR is well advised to maintain its "margin of appreciation."

So for a variety of reasons, the Grand Chamber's decision in *Lautsi* seems defensible. It's grounded in positive law and "constitutional gloss," and, most important, it's sensible as a matter of subsidiarity. The decision leaves it open for individual member states to decide whether the benefits of displaying a crucifix in a public classroom outweigh the possibility of alienating young, impressionable students who are not Christian.

But the decision would be more palatable if it were not coupled with a series of cases on Muslim headscarves that almost seem to evince a preference for Christianity over Islam. The *Lautsi* majority labored to distinguish the European Court's holding in *Dahlab v. Switzerland*,[18] in which the court held inadmissible a Muslim teacher's complaint that she was not permitted to teach while wearing a headscarf. In that case, the court noted that teachers were "important role models" for young students, and that

> the Court accepts that it is very difficult to assess the impact that a powerful external symbol such as the wearing of a headscarf may have on the freedom of conscience and religion of very young children. The applicant's pupils were aged between four and eight, an age at which children wonder about many things and are also more easily influenced than older pupils. In those circumstances, it cannot be denied outright that the wearing of a headscarf might have some kind of proselytising effect, seeing that it appears to be imposed on women by a precept which is laid down in the Koran and which, as the Federal Court noted, is hard to square with the principle of gender equality. It therefore appears difficult to reconcile the wearing of an Islamic headscarf with the message of tolerance, respect for others and, above all, equality and non-discrimination that all teachers in a democratic society must convey to their pupils.

Accordingly, weighing the right of a teacher to manifest her religion against the need to protect pupils by preserving religious harmony, the court considers that in the circumstances of the case and having regard, above all, for the tender age of the children for whom the applicant was responsible as a representative of the state, the Geneva authorities did not exceed their margin of appreciation and that the measure they took was therefore not unreasonable.

Lautsi explicitly contrasted the "passive symbol" of the crucifix with the "powerful external symbol" of the headscarf at issue in *Dahlab.* That's a distinction that might leave a person of any faith uncomfortable. Surely it would have been preferable for the ECHR to reconsider its holding in *Dahlab,* but that would have required the court to overcome its traditional reluctance to overrule its own decisions.

Formally, *Lautsi* and *Dahlab* can be reconciled. They are similar in that the court deferred to the state in both cases, invoking the "margin of appreciation." Taken together, they add up to a rule that the state has the discretion to decide whether to expose young children to religious symbols in state schools. The state is not required to provide religious displays, but it may do so at its option.

But *Dahlab* is hardly the only case that sets up an uncomfortable contrast with *Lautsi.* In a series of headscarf cases, the court has sided with state restrictions on headwear with remarkable consistency.[19] A Muslim citizen of Europe could be forgiven for wondering why it is acceptable to display a crucifix in a classroom but not a Muslim headscarf. In *Hassan and Eylem Znegin v. Turkey,* moreover, the court found that Turkey violated the Convention by requiring a student to take a course in religious culture and ethics at a state school in Istanbul.[20]

The juxtaposition of these cases leads to the next question: Is Kmiec right that the ECHR is disfavoring Islam in religion cases, in contrast to the US approach?[21] There certainly is a difference between the American and European approaches, but one must be careful not to overstate it. For example, the ECHR has been skeptical of state efforts to insert religious teaching in public school curricula even when the religion in question is Christianity. In 2007, a 9–8 majority of the Grand Chamber found that Norway had violated Article 2 of Protocol 1 by requiring students to take a course in "Christianity, Religion and Philosophy."[22] Similarly, in 2010, the Court held that Poland violated the Convention by withholding a certification for "religion/ethics" from an agnostic student who refused to take a course in religion and was unable to take an alternative course in ethics.[23]

Outside the context of state schools, the ECHR's jurisprudence on Establishment is not so terribly far removed from the American model. Admittedly, many of these cases partake as much of Free Exercise as Establishment, but in some of them there is a question of state support for religion as well as protection of individual religious belief (or non-belief). For example, the European Court has struck down obligations to swear a religious oath to take a seat in parliament[24] or to practice law.[25] Jehovah's Witnesses have successfully asserted a right of conscientious objection to military service.[26] Indeed, many of the violations identified by the European Court have involved state support for Christianity, not Islam. The Jehovah's Witnesses successfully pressed conscientious objection claims not just against Turkey but also against Armenia and Greece.[27] The oath cases involved Christianity, as do most of the curriculum cases.[28] The leading ECHR case on proselytism, *Kokkinakis v. Greece*,[29] found a violation for a criminal conviction of a Jehovah's Witness. It's true that the European Commission on Human Rights held in 1990 that an Established state religion is not necessarily incompatible with the Convention,[30] but the court's case law makes plain that it is willing to limit Established religions, including Christianity, if Establishment conflicts unduly with Free Exercise or other human rights norms.

Moreover, some of the ECHR's "Free Exercise" cases on headscarves might have gone the same way in American courts. For example, the ECHR found no violation when France denied an entry visa to a Moroccan woman who refused to remove her headscarf temporarily for a momentary identity check at the French consulate general in Marrakesh.[31] A US court might likewise find that such a requirement, being so limited in time, might be justified by a state interest in security. And a US court probably would have reached the same result in *Ahmet Arslan and Others v. Turkey*,[32] in which the court found that Turkey violated the Convention by convicting members of a religious group for wearing religious garments in public areas open to all, as opposed to schools.

Just as European law is neither uniformly pro-Establishment nor implacably anti-Free Exercise, American law is neither implacably anti-Establishment nor uniformly pro-Free Exercise. American courts have occasionally sustained public displays of religious symbols that also have secular significance.[33] (This rationale resembles that of the Italian courts in *Lautsi,* which emphasized the non-religious "educational" attributes of the crucifix.) Likewise, in American Free Exercise cases, the state does occasionally win, though not as often as in Europe.[34] In sum, there is a difference between American and European approaches to religion cases, but it is not as sharp as Kmiec suggests.

Still, it remains true that European judicial institutions have generally been more receptive to public displays of religious symbols than have their American counterparts. It is unlikely that this pattern will change in the short term, even if the US Supreme Court throws caution to the winds and decides to cite the ECHR in every American decision on religious liberty.[35] Kmiec is also right that Islamic claims to Free Exercise have not fared as well in Europe as they might in the United States, but that is mostly because Free Exercise claims in Europe generally do not fare as well as they might in the United States.

So the next question is: Which side of the pond has the better side of the argument? (Another interesting question is: Why did these differences arise in the first place? That is a complex historical and political inquiry, well beyond the scope of this chapter, and the subject of a voluminous amount of literature.[36]) Kmiec gets at this question by constructing a useful typology of state approaches to religion, ranging from "Compelled Theocracy" to "Democratically Acceptable Confessionalism" to "Democratically Acceptable Inclusionary Secularism (Europe) to "Democratically Acceptable Exclusionary Secularism" (the United States) to Compelled Atheism (no state). These are sensible divisions, and they imply a sort of one-dimensional spectrum of approaches, from most theocratic to most atheistic.

Alternatively, one might construct a matrix in two dimensions, juxtaposing Free Exercise along the x-axis and Establishment along the *y*-axis. One configuration—the first "cell" of the matrix—might favor both Free Exercise and Establishment: Something like the British or Israeli models. A second might favor Free Exercise but disfavor Establishment: The American model. A third might disfavor Free Exercise but favor Establishment: A theocracy, perhaps. A fourth might disfavor both Free Exercise and Establishment: An atheist state, say, or perhaps some form of totalitarian government.[37] One might even imagine gradations within each "cell" of the matrix, like a scatter diagram. Thus the United States might be high along the "*x*-axis" of Free Exercise but not far down the "negative *y*-axis" of Establishment, whereas Britain might be not quite so high along the "positive *x*-axis" of Free Exercise, but quite high on the "positive *y*-axis" of Establishment. One advantage of this methodology is that it might permit regression analysis. Such analysis could explore whether a high Free Exercise "score" tends to correlate with a low Establishment score.[38] A rigorous empirical investigation of such questions might be enlightening.

Whether the optimal constitutional geometry is linear (the Kmiec model) or on a Cartesian plane (as suggested here), there's no disputing Kmiec's assertion that more than one configuration is democratically acceptable. Free countries can have varying mixes of Free Exercise and Establishment. More than one cell of the matrix is workable. But which is preferable?

No legal math can answer that question. The answer depends, of course, on the cultural and religious heritage of the peoples involved. What makes sense for Israelis, Saudis, or Britons might not make sense for Americans, Chinese, or the French. If, as Kmiec implies, democratic values should inform the choice, then perhaps one should consider how people would "vote" in the abstract. Is it possible for us to step behind a Rawlsean veil of ignorance and choose the optimal cell of the matrix for a hypothetical new state?[39] If we could not know whether we would start life as Americans or Europeans or Africans or Asians, or whether we would be born and reared in a household that was Christian, Muslim, Jewish, Buddhist, or atheist, would we have any reason to prefer one religion jurisprudence to another, a priori?

It is, of course, difficult to imagine ourselves as something different from what we are, and thus difficult to guess what option we might prefer if we really did not know how we would enter the world.[40] Still, it seems safe to assume that most people would, a priori, opt for a system that offers strong protection for Free Exercise. It seems less safe to assume, however, that a clear majority of people would have a strong preference for either Establishment or non-Establishment. The existing legal landscape reflects these assumptions: Free Exercise is firmly endorsed in virtually every instrument on international human rights law and most state constitutions, whereas Establishment and non-Establishment norms are less universal. If these assumptions have any merit, they might suggest that the United States has the better part of the argument on Free Exercise, but they might not lead to a strong conclusion one way or the other on Establishment.

The final question, raised by the title of Kmiec's chapter is empirical: Has European secularism been "crucified"? The tempting answer is that *Lautsi* is a serious blow to secularism. European states may now display a crucifix in state schools without violating the European Convention on Human Rights. But it's also possible to read *Lautsi* as a partial, backdoor victory for secularism.

Recall that the Grand Chamber downplayed the power of the crucifix, labeling it a mere "passive symbol," as opposed to the supposedly more "powerful" and active "external symbol" of the headscarf in *Dahlab*. The idea of a "passive symbol" almost seems a contradiction in terms, like "jumbo shrimp." Are not all symbols to some extent "active"? Is it not their point to communicate to others actively, rather than to receive inputs passively?[41] Ironically, the seven-judge lower chamber in *Lautsi*, which unanimously held the public display of the crucifix to be a violation of the Convention, accorded the symbol much deeper significance. In its view, crucifixes were "powerful external symbols," not just "passive symbols."[42] The two dissenting judges from the Grand Chamber judgment echoed these comments.[43] In other words, the Grand Chamber downplayed the religious significance of the crucifix in order to save it.[44] If this is true, then the holding might not be much of a repudiation of secularism at all. It might instead indicate a sort of cultural devaluation of the religious significance of the crucifix, as a mere "passive symbol."

Judge Power's concurrence dealt with secularism more thoughtfully than the majority opinion. As noted earlier, the European Convention does not contain an Establishment Clause, and it does not enshrine secularism as a core human right. Judge Power elaborated on these themes:

> A preference for secularism over alternative world views—whether religious, philosophical or otherwise—is not a neutral option. The Convention requires that respect be given to the first applicant's convictions insofar as the education and teaching of her children was concerned. It does not require a preferential option for and endorsement of those convictions over and above all others.[45]

But even this more forthright discussion of secularism hardly means it is dead. Judge Power puts it on the same plane as other worldviews. Secularism is one of many people at the dinner table; it is not sitting outside in the cold.

Moreover, the evidence beyond *Lautsi* is that secularism is alive and well in Europe and in European law. Beginning in 1996, Sweden took a series of steps to de-Establish Lutheranism as its state Church,[46] a process that was largely completed by 2000. Despite intense lobbying by various Christian leaders that the 2007 Treaty of Lisbon makes some mention of Christianity, the Treaty amended the Treaty on European Union to include only a brief reference to the "cultural, religious and humanist inheritance" of Europe.[47] The EU itself remains a decidedly secular institution, dedicated to separation of church and state—prompting the Vatican to complain repeatedly about its "militant secularism."[48] Religious observance has been on the decline in Europe for years.[49] Some observers have asserted that environmentalism is *the* "mainstream religion" in parts of northern Europe, such as Denmark and Sweden.[50] Others even perceive a gradual "weakening" of ties between the Church of England and the British government,[51] though many would surely disagree.

"The past is never dead. It's not even past."[52] Quoting Faulkner, Judge Bonello's concurrence emphasized the "age-old presence of crucifixes in Italian schools" and the relatively recent involvement of the Italian state in schooling.[53] But Judge Bonello might as well have been referring to Europe's not-so-distant secular past. It hasn't been crucified, and it isn't dead. It's not even past.

NOTES

1. See Douglas W. Kmiec, "Secularism Crucified?," this volume.
2. No. 30814/06 (Grand Chamber Judgment March 18, 2011).
3. *Convention for the Protection of Human Rights and Fundamental Freedoms,* 213 UNTS 221, (1950).
4. See European Union, "Charter of Fundamental Rights of the European Union, Dec. 7, 2000," in *Official Journal of the European Communities,* Dec. 18, 2000 (2000/C, 364/01), Art. 10.
5. *Lautsi,* Grand Chamber Judgment, paras. 26–28 at 13–14.
6. Chamber Judgment, No. 30814/06 (Nov. 3, 2009).
7. Chamber Judgement, para. 48 at 11.
8. Chamber Judgement, para. 55 at 12–13.
9. See Gabriel Andreescu and Liviu Andreescu, "The European Court of Human Rights' Lautsi Decision: Context, Contents, Consequences," *Journal for the Study of Religions and Ideologies* 9, no. 26 (Summer 2010): 65. ("We believe it unlikely for the Grand Chamber to change the initial decision. This impression is shared by other experts working on the European Convention.") (citation omitted).
10. *Lautsi,* Grand Chamber Judgment, para. 67 at 28.
11. Ibid., para. 72 at 29.
12. Ibid., para. 68 at 28.
13. See *Youngstown Sheet & Tube Co. v. Sawyer,* 343 U.S. 579, 610–611 (1952) (Frankfurter, J., concurring) ("In short, a systematic, unbroken, executive practice, long pursued to the knowledge of the Congress and never before questioned, engaged in by Presidents who have also sworn to uphold the Constitution, making as it were such exercise of power part of the structure of our government, may be treated as a gloss on 'executive Power' vested in the President by § 1 of Art. II.").
14. Grant Gilmore, *The Death of Contract* (Columbus: Ohio State University Press, 1974), 64.
15. Kmiec, "Secularism Crucified?," See section "Possible Explanations for ECHR's Inclusionary Stance of Religious Displays."
16. Ibid.
17. *Miller v. California,* 413 U.S. 15, 37 (1973).
18. No. 42393/98 (Chamber Judgment of Feb. 15, 2001).
19. See *Aktas v. France,* No. 43563/08, *Bayrak v. France,* No. 14308/08, *Gamaleddyn v. France,* No. 18527/08, *Ghazal v. France,* No. 29134/08, *J. Singh v. France,* No. 25463/08, *R. Singh v. France,* No. 27561/08 (application declared inadmissible on June 30, 2009) (finding no violation in a school's ban on headwear); *Dogru v. France,* No. 27058/05, and *Kervanci v. France,* No. 31645/04 (Chamber judgment of Dec. 4, 2008) (holding that a

requirement to remove headscarves in a physical education class did not violate the Convention); *Leyla Sahin v. Turkey*, No. 44774/98 (Grand Chamber Judgment of Nov. 10, 2005) (finding no violation in Turkey's rule prohibiting medical students from wearing a headscarf during class or exams).

20. No. 1448/04, Judgment (Oct. 9, 2007).
21. Kmiec, "Secularism Crucified?." See sections "A Preliminary Inquiry into Islam's Compatibility with Democracy" and "A Speculation: Symbolic Faith as the Trojan Horse of Secularism."
22. *Case of Folgero and Others v. Norway*, App. No. 15472/02, Judgment (June 29, 2007).
23. *Grzelak v. Poland*, No. 7710/02, Judgment (June 15, 2010).
24. *Buscarini and Others v. San Marino*, No. 24645/94 (Grand Chamber Judgment of Feb. 18, 1999).
25. *Alexandridis v. Greece*, No. 19516/06 (Chamber Judgment of Feb. 21, 2008).
26. See *Ercep v. Turkey* (Judgment of Nov. 22, 2011); *Bayatyan v. Armenia*, No. 23459/03 (Grand Chamber Judgment of July 7, 2011); *Thlimmenos v. Greece*, No. 34369/97 (Grand Chamber Judgment of April 6, 2000).
27. See *supra* note 6.
28. See *supra* note 4.
29. No. 14307/88 (Chamber Judgment of May 25, 1993).
30. *Darby v. Sweden*, 187 Eur. Ct. H.R. (ser. A) (1990). Protocol 11 of the European Convention, which entered into force in 2008, abolished the commission as part of a restructuring of the court.
31. *El Morsli v. France*, No. 15585/06 (declared inadmissible, Mar. 4, 2008).
32. No. 41135/98 (Chamber Judgment of Feb. 23, 2010).
33. See *Lynch v. Donnelly*, 465 U.S. 668 (1994) (upholding public display of a Christmas crèche); *Allegheny College v. ACLU*, 492 U.S. 573 (1989) (invalidating public display of a Christmas crèche, but upholding public display of a menorah).
34. See *Employment Decision v. Smith*, 494 U.S. 872 (1990) (upholding a state's ban on unemployment benefits to a former state employee fired for using peyote, even though the drug use was for religious purposes).
35. American jurists disagree about whether it is appropriate to cite international law in judicial opinions on constitutional law. See "The Relevance of Foreign Legal Materials in U.S. Constitutional Cases: A Conversation between Justice Antonin Scalia and Justice Stephen Breyer," *International Journal of Constitutional Law* 3 (2005): 521–531.
36. Donald L. Drakeman, *Church, State, and Original Intent* (Cambridge: Cambridge University Press, 2009); John C. Jeffries, Jr., and James E. Ryan, "A Political History of the Establishment Clause," *Michigan Law Review* 100 (2001): 279; Michael W. McConnell, "The Origins and Historical Understanding of Free Exercise of Religion," *Harvard Law Review* 103 (1990): 1437; Sydney E. Ahlstrom, *A Religious History of the American People*

(New Haven, CT: Yale University Press, 1972). Other related questions include the influence of religion on the development of Western law and public international law. See Harold J. Berman, *Law and Revolution, II: The Impact of the Protestant Reformations on the Western Legal Tradition* (Cambridge, MA: Belknap Press, 2003).

37. David S. Law and Mila Versteeg, "The Evolution and Ideology of Global Constitutionalism," *California Law Review* 99 (2011): 1208–1210 (mapping competing constitutional norms onto a two-dimensional space).

38. Ibid., 1213–1217.

39. John Rawls, *A Theory of Justice* (Cambridge, MA: Belknap Press, 1971); John Rawls, *A Brief Inquiry into the Meaning of Sin and Faith* (Cambridge, MA: Harvard University Press, 2009) (posthumous publication of undergraduate thesis).

40. Indeed, there is a sort of variation on Heisenberg's Uncertainty Principle at work here. To offer a vulgar précis of Heisenberg: Studying particles changes their behavior, since one must bombard them with photons to observe them, and yet that bombardment itself excites the particles, making them move differently. Laurence H. Tribe, "The Curvature of Constitutional Space: What Lawyers Can Learn from Modern Physics," *Harvard Law Review* 103 (1989): 19 (the "observer is never really separate from the system being studied."). By analogy, imagining ourselves in a Rawlsian state of ignorance requires that we sprinkle ourselves with magic dust, changing who we are, and thus tainting the results of any inquiry into our choices made during that state of ignorance.

41. See Lorenzo Zucca, "A Comment on Lautsi," *EJIL Talk!* (blog), http://www.ejiltalk.org/a-comment-on-lautsi/ (pondering the distinction between "active" and "passive" symbols).

42. Ibid., para. 73, p. 30, quoting *Chamber Judgment*, No. 30814/06 (Nov. 3, 2009), paras. 54 and 55.

43. See "Dissenting Opinion of Judge Malinverni Joined by Judge Kalaydjieva," para. 5 at 51.

44. The text echoes the military officer who supposedly said "We had to destroy this village to save it." One commentator calls the remark an "urban legend." Colin Warbrick, "The European Response to Terrorism in an Age of Human Rights," *European Journal of International Law* 15 (2004): 1016.

45. "Concurring Opinion of Judge Power," 45.

46. See "Swedes End Long Union of Church and State," *New York Times*, Dec. 31, 1995. See Claudia E. Haupt, "Transnational Nonestablishment," *George Washington Law Review* 80 (2012): 993.

47. The Treaty of Lisbon amended the Treaty on European Union to include this recital: "DRAWING INSPIRATION from the cultural, religious and humanist inheritance of Europe, from which have developed the universal values of the inviolable and inalienable rights of the human person,

freedom, democracy, equality and the rule of law." Treaty of Lisbon, Amending the Treaty on European Union and the Treaty Establishing the European Community (2007/C 306/01), Art. 1. *See* Haupt, *supra* note 46, at 993; Iordan Barbulescu and Gabriel Andreescu, "References to God and the Christian Tradition in the Treaty Establishing a Constitution for Europe: An Examination of the Background," *Journal for the Study of Religions and Ideologies* 8, no. 24 (Winter, 2009): 207–230.

48. "Vatican Resists European Secularism," *BBC News*, Feb. 11, 2005, http://news.bbc.co.uk/2/hi/europe/4253937.stm.

49. See "Europe's Irreligious," *The Economist* (online), Aug. 9, 2010, http://www.economist.com/node/16767758; Richard Posner, "Why Are Americans More Religious Than Europeans?," *Becker-Posner Blog*, June 28, 2012, http://www.becker-posner-blog.com/2012/06/why-are-americans-more-religious-than-europeans-posner.html.

50. The processes of secularization are most advanced in former Protestant countries such as Denmark and Sweden, and as Garreau finds, it is in these "parts of northern Europe, [that] this new [environmental] faith is now the mainstream" religion. Robert H. Nelson, "Rethinking Church and State: The Case of Environmental Religion," Pace Environmental Law Review 29 (2011): 127 (quoting Joel Garreau, "Environmentalism as Religion," *New Atlantis* 28 (2010): 62).

51. *See* Haupt, *supra* note 46, at 993 ("the strong ties between the Church of England and the state are gradually weakening").

52. William Faulkner, *Requiem for a Nun* (New York: Knopf Doubleday, 2012), Act I, scene 3. Quoted in *Lautsi*, Grand Chamber Judgment, Concurring Opinion of Judge Bonello, para 1.4.

53. *Lautsi*, Grand Chamber Judgment, Concurring Opinion of Judge Bonello, paras. 1.3 and 1.4.

PART THREE

THE CATHOLIC CHURCH, MORAL AUTHORITY, AND SECULARISM

Chapter 4

Public Religion, Secularism, and the Ethos of Love

HANS JOAS

For several decades after the Second World War, many scholars of religion claimed that religion was about to undergo a process of constant privatization. Although it remained rather unclear where the private sphere to which religion was allegedly withdrawing was exactly located—in civil society as distinct from the sphere regulated by government, in families and small circles of friends, or in the inner life of individuals—this assumption became hegemonic. This time is over, however. In sociology, a paradigm shift to a renewed interest in "public religion" is symbolized by the publication in 1994 of José Casanova's magisterial historical-comparative study of the United States, Brazil, Poland, and Spain.[1] This book was, of course, deeply influenced by the religiously inspired political movements in Iran, Poland, and Latin America and the rise of the Christian Right in the United States. In addition to the empirical debates about the "de-privatization" of religion, the normative debate about the legitimacy of religious arguments in the political discussions of democratic societies has become more and more intense. On the liberal side, from Rawls to Habermas, views began to change from a more exclusionary to a more inclusionary attitude. On the religious side, the question has therefore become more acute: How exactly should religiously inspired thinkers balance the commitment to their faith with the normative obligations of democratic discourse?

It is very instructive in this connection to compare two quite different but equally sophisticated contributions. In this chapter I will use the intriguing reflections of Douglas Kmiec (and my own sociological research) as a foil for the discussion of the position taken by the intellectual leader among the American Catholic bishops, Francis Cardinal George, particularly his most recent book, one that deals with the question (as its subtitle says) "how faith in God can address the challenges of the world."

The main title of the book is quite spectacular: "God in Action."[2] We are all used to viewing humans as the only beings able to act in the full sense of the term. Moreover, we live in a time in which biological reductionists claim that there is no such thing as a free will even in human beings. This is also a time when others experience economic or technological forces as so overwhelming that they offer little hope in human self-determination. Against such reductionism and against such pessimism Cardinal George defends the agency and sociality of human beings. Societies for him are not just aggregations of atomized individuals, and human beings are persons for whom their social relationships are constitutive. God—for the author of this book—is not just the creator of a clock-like universe nor a kind of authoritarian commander, but an actor himself who acts through us human beings (p. 193). In order for God to act through us, we have to open ourselves up to him and become, as Cardinal George writes, "in a limited but real sense" (p. 121) co-creators at least of ourselves. For those who know a little bit about the Cardinal's intellectual biography (his dissertation on George Herbert Mead, his reference to Josiah Royce in a preceding book) these views do not come as a surprise; the only surprising thing might be that in the new book the main philosophical reference is to Thomas Aquinas and not to those more modern figures of the specifically American, deeply democratic tradition of thinking about personal autonomy, sociality, and God—thinkers the Cardinal is so familiar with and who would make it easier to be part of the current intellectual discourse.

More important than such philosophical foundations are probably our assumptions about the present state and the future of Christianity. Let me first put my cards on the table and briefly refer to my own work in this area. Some of my contributions deal with sociological trends relevant to this future, others with crucial intellectual challenges for a contemporary reformulation of the message of the gospels.[3] The most important sociological trend I have identified in these writings is the enormous globalization of Christianity, a move that has led serious observers to speak of our time not as an age of secularization but as one of the most intense phases of the expansion of Christianity in history. This expansion partly has demographic reasons (e.g., rapid growth of the population in some Christian countries), but that is not the whole story. There are also some astonishing success stories of mass conversion to Christianity, mostly in Africa, but also in South Korea and parts of China. Through migration and a fundamental shift in the geography of power this will affect Christians in Europe and North America in many ways. A second important sociological trend is the ongoing dissolution of confessional milieus in those mostly Central European societies for which the co-existence of Catholics and Protestants in two clearly separated sociocultural milieus has long been characteristic. Many see this as a great danger for the transmission of Christian faith; I, however, am more optimistic because of indications that a smaller, inter-confessional but intensely Christian milieu is emerging. The third trend has to do with the growing importance of a rich variety of extra-ecclesial forms of religious activity and orientation. In my view, one should not overestimate the quantitative relevance here, but one can take these phenomena as symptoms of a growing individualization or "optionality" of belief.

When we look at Cardinal George's book against this backdrop, it turns out that he is extremely sensitive to the topic of globalization in general and to the globalization of Christianity in particular. Cardinal George is much less Americano-centric than other American churchmen. Chapter 8 of his book is on migration; it is perhaps the most beautiful in the book and ends with the almost poetic statement that "Faith gives us eyes to look at a stranger and see a neighbor, so that God will travel with both of us" (p. 178).

It is understandable that a book that focuses on the United States is less interested than I am in the erosion of confessional milieus although one should bear in mind that the American religious landscape is changing in comparable ways today. Most American Protestants pay little attention to the theological differences between different forms of

Protestantism, and new Christian churches emerge that cannot be assigned to any major historical denomination.[4] Instead, another topic becomes dominant in the Cardinal's thinking: The trend toward a legally enforced privatization of faith in America and the resistance against it. When the Cardinal defends the public role of religion—namely, the right of believers and religious communities to bring religiously based reasons into the public discourse—and when he resists the demands to privatize religion completely, I am on his side. What I find almost ironic, though, is that in certain European debates in which I have actively taken part,[5]—for example, on the preamble to the (failed) European constitution—I was among those who opposed the French "laicist" position by referring to the American counter-example of a separation of church and state that is not hostile to religion. Reading the Cardinal's book, the United States looks much more like France. I find his language here very strong. Should one really speak of a "nascent form of state tyranny" when one speaks of state-supported secularism? France, after all, is not a totalitarian state. And when Cardinal George writes that "in the U.S., the primary danger to democratic freedom comes not from religion but from philosophical secularism" (p. 32), I would object to that. The primary danger to democracy comes from the enemies of democracy, whether they are religious or not, and for the defense of democracy—I say that on the background of the German experience—the supporters, religious or not, have to fight together against its enemies, religious or not.

Douglas Kmiec here is much more moderate, not only in his tone but also in the substance of his argument. For him there are two main dangers that have to be avoided: "a democracy unattached from moral truth" and also one not protected from overstated claims of conscience.[6] The first danger is the one emphasized by Cardinal George. But the second is also serious. It arises when believers expect democracy to coincide with their own or their Church's understanding of moral truth. Kmiec writes: "Perfect coincidence of the two would not be democracy but a theocracy or heaven itself. Those who confuse earth with heaven will seldom be satisfied with a democratic outcome." For him no constitutionally mandated exemption from a generally applicable law can be deduced from such a situation and not even a justification for civil disobedience with respect to the law. While one might disagree with him regarding this last point—it could at least be specified by making clear when such a justification could be possible—his insistence that such a situation should not be "a signal for democratic withdrawal but for enhanced democratic engagement" seems to me to be fully convincing. In most European countries, perhaps because of much more widespread secularization, most Christians would share Kmiec's views.

All the sociological trends I have mentioned already pose questions about the self-understanding of faith in our time. When the nexus between the faith and homogenous social milieus is dissolved, when the Christian faith finds itself in competition with a vast number of partly secular, partly vaguely religious worldviews and lifestyles, when the faith is newly appropriated beyond the West, outside of cultures already long-marked by Christianity and under conditions of mass poverty and uprootedness, then Christianity clearly must be freed again from unconscious particularisms and articulated anew.

But in addition to the demands resulting from these changes there are others of a more purely intellectual character. Influenced by the great Protestant theologian Ernst Troeltsch,[7] friend and rival of Max Weber, I argue that the main challenges for Christianity in this sense can be found in four areas: (1) the ethos of love, (2) personalism, (3) communal worship, (4) the concentration of spirituality on Jesus Christ. The challenges to overcome lie therefore, in my words, in (1) an intellectual hegemony of assumptions that makes the ethos of love incomprehensible, (2) a conception of the human being that denies its specificity as a person; (3) an individualistic understanding of spirituality; and (4) the loss of the idea of transcendence because this blocks access to the idea of the Son of God as the mediator between immanence and transcendence. Obviously, a lot could and has to be said about all these problems, but again I will restrict myself to a few observations and questions that come up in relation to the Catholic thinkers under consideration here, Cardinal George and Douglas Kmiec.

I see Cardinal George's book as a strong defense of the idea of transcendence, for example, when he argues in the chapter on "God in American public life" that "God cannot be co-opted and remains always the primary actor in our history and our endeavors." This is directed against

those who claim God's will as a support for their own political strivings instead of submitting these strivings to the universalistic examination procedure of Christian reasoning. Cardinal George is an ardent
defender of a personalistic understanding of God (against mystical pan-
theism) and of human beings. He often refers to the thinking of Pope
John Paul II who was influenced, more than his successor, by twentieth-
century philosophical currents called "personalism," for example, the
philosophy of Max Scheler. He speaks of Karol Woytila's "personalistic
reading of the natural law traditions" (p. 122)—which probably is a fair
characterization of Woytila's thinking, but also a glossing over the tension that exists between personalism and natural law doctrines. This is
not the place to elaborate on these tensions in a more technical philosophical way. It must be sufficient to say that natural law doctrines have
often been tied to a fixed anthropology and an authoritarian claim to
define what human nature is and which human behavior goes against
this nature (e.g., homosexuality). Personalism is more willing to be part
of discursive attempts to understand the basic normative self-understanding of the contemporary world. It defends the ethos of love and the
message of the Gospel, but without further-reaching claims to a privileged access to the solution of moral problems. It is true that the natural law approach has resonance for some political contexts and need
not be juridical, as Kmiec's attention to guiding principles suggests. But
I am bringing this up because in some highly sensitive areas a consistently personalistic ethos of love and a natural law doctrine might come
to rather different conclusions. These areas are precisely those that religious persons seek to represent in public debates, but which also require
ongoing consideration within an intellectually engaged religious tradition. In the book under discussion here I find the long passages on abortion and the chapter on "God and Warfare" incomplete and the passage
on same-sex marriage not really plausible.

Why is that so? The discussion of abortion exclusively deals with
the role of the law in the formation or transformation of moral attitudes.
Cardinal George here draws parallels with the role of the law and the
courts in the overcoming of slavery, racial segregation, and racism in
this country. These parallels might easily offend the proponents of a less
strict position regarding abortion among Catholics because this makes

them look like the defenders of slavery in the nineteenth century, which I find not fair. The argument is incomplete here because a serious evaluation of the less strict position—a position I do not want to call "liberal"—has to be based on the values that motivate the proponents of that position. These are values of personal autonomy and self-realization that are crucial for a personalistic understanding of Christianity as well and not necessarily antithetical to such a personalistic orientation.

There is much more common ground between these approaches, I think, and the fact that the debate about this question is so polarized in the United States and much less so in most European countries should be taken more seriously in the American debates. It does not show that Europe simply is more secular than the United States (Europe is in this regard a rather heterogeneous continent), but that these moral questions have not become identity-markers in the political struggles there. Religious people in Europe often have great respect also for the ethos of self-realization that guides many feminists, and European secularist lawmakers often understand that religious people are indeed motivated by an ethos of protection for the weak. This has led to legal solutions that have become consensually accepted by all sides, distinguishing between the moral desirability of a certain behavior and the limited possibilities to influence behavior through strict legal regulations. Taking seriously these developments would be important not only for the debates between believers and non-believers, but also within the Catholic Church itself. It is an open secret that most Catholics deviate in their practice, and many also in their conviction, from the Church doctrines about contraception, for example. While it is true that the Church doctrine cannot be based on a majority vote among Church members, it is also true that the leaders of the Church have to take these facts more seriously. An ethos of mutual understanding and mutual respect—in the sense in which Douglas Kmiec uses these terms, derived from the Christian understanding of the human person—has to be the guideline for communication among believers and between them and others.

The chapter on warfare in the Cardinal's book is an interesting defense of the Catholic tradition of "just war" thinking even in the age of potential nuclear warfare and under contemporary conditions. I personally find this defense and the Cardinal's critique of the Iraq war convincing and would just like to mention two observations. The first is that Cardinal George seems to accept the highly controversial notion of a "war on terror"—though half-heartedly, since he puts it in quotation marks in some places (p. 167) and uses it without these in others. But this notion is not innocent: A war without a clear enemy, without any predictable end could serve as the ideal means to justify restrictions of fundamental rights and even the killing of people without the due process of law guaranteed by the US Constitution. The second observation is that the book remains totally silent about the death penalty, another question that a consistent personalistic ethic of life certainly has to debate. A rigorous defense of life is seen by most Europeans today, Catholics included, as the basis for denying the right of states to take the life of even the worst criminals. Here the difference between Europe and the United States is particularly conspicuous at the moment. Given that Cardinal George's predecessor Cardinal Bernardin and individual American Catholics like Sister Helen Prejean have played such a heroic role in this struggle, this omission can be called spectacular.

But the passage on same-sex marriage is, in my eyes, the most problematical of all. The Cardinal says beautiful things about the ways we grow in our relationships and into our relationships, "slowly disengaging (ourselves) from selfishness in order to become totally free to give (ourselves) generously without worrying about the risk" (p. 86). For me this means that an ethos of love makes "love" the important criterion for an evaluation of relationships, not an assumption about the naturalness of sexual orientations. I do not understand why the redefinition of marriage is said to "remove any logical basis for insisting on monogamy, fidelity, or permanence of marital commitment" (p. 78). On the contrary, an ethos of love would extend these crucial values to even more relationships. No empirical evidence is given for the thesis that same-sex marriage somehow threatens the stability of heterosexual marriage; the proponents of same-sex marriage do not argue for a "retreat of the law from family life," but for a different law! And even if there were such evidence, who could justify the suffering of homosexuals by the advantages this has for heterosexuals? I agree with New York Times commentator Frank Bruni[8] when he writes that he finds it "hardest to understand . . . why so many opponents don't see gay people's longing to be wedded as the fundamentally conservative, lavishly complementary desire it is. It says marriage is worth aspiring to and fighting for. Flatters it. Gives it reinvigorated cachet, extra currency, a sorely needed infusion of fresh energy."

I know that some Catholics, and again more so in the United States than in Europe, will very sharply disagree with me here and even find it offensive when I insist on this point. But I would courageously predict that in a few decades the Church will have moved in this direction that, in my view, is a necessary consequence of the Christian ethos of love. In my view, the Catholic Church could even be a leading force in contemporary cultural developments if it presented this core of the Christian faith as its main inspiration when it comes to questions of sexual morality, politics, or the style of discussion within its ranks and outside of it.

The comparison of Cardinal George's important book and Douglas Kmiec's innovative piece on the fundamental features of a less defensive and less polemical attitude of the Church with regard to the main challenges of our time demonstrates the wide spectrum of positions among contemporary Catholic intellectuals. For those outside observers who are surprised that there is such a wide spectrum of intra-Catholic controversy, let me end with a quotation from Ernst Troeltsch, a Protestant with a strong interest in Catholicism:

> Catholicism is not the miracle of rigid consistency as which it has often been considered. From its beginning on it has been an infinitely complicated system full of contradictions that has again and again in ever new ways attempted to combine fantastic popular religion and philosophical dogma, revolutionary individualism and absolute authority, profane cultural techniques and otherworldly asceticism, lively laymanship and priestly domination—a masterpiece of mediation that created in church authority only the ultimate regulator for the cases in which these mediations lead to frictions and a lack of clarity.[9]

In an age of rapid globalization of Christianity—as I have argued in my book *Faith as an Option: Possible Futures for Christianity*—this "masterpiece of mediation" can be said to be ideally suited for the new challenges of cultural diversity within states, global heterogeneity, mass migration, and gigantic urbanization. But this potential advantage can only be realized if the Church is not misled by an imaginary of administrative and doctrinal uniformity. When we confess *"una sancta Catholica et apostolica ecclesia,"* the *"una"* does not mean uniformity—as the "sancta" does not mean "free from all sins."[10]

NOTES

1. José Casanova, *Public Religions in the Modern World* (Chicago: University of Chicago Press, 1994).
2. Francis Cardinal George, *God in Action. How Faith in God Can Address the Challenges of the World* (New York: Image, 2011). (Page numbers in parentheses refer to this book.)
3. The most important source is my book: Hans Joas, *Faith as an Option: Christianity's Possible Futures* (Palo Alto, CA: Stanford University Press, 2014). A brief version of one of its chapters has been published in English: Hans Joas, "The Future of Christianity," *Hedgehog Review* 13 (2011): 30–39.
4. Robert Wuthnow, *The Restructuring of American Religion* (Princeton, NJ: Princeton University Press, 1998).
5. For an English-language publication, see my introduction to Hans Joas and Klaus Wiegandt, eds., *The Cultural Values of Europe* (Liverpool: Liverpool University Press, 2008), 1–21.
6. Douglas W. Kmiec, "Secularism Crucified?," See section "Two Essential Insights for Democracy to be Compatible with Faith."
7. Ernst Troeltsch, "Die Zukunftsmöglichkeiten des Christentums," *Logos* 1 (1910/11): 165–185.
8. Frank Bruni, "Value Our Families," *New York Times*, February 20, 2012.
9. Ernst Troeltsch, "Der Modernismus" (1909), in Ernst Troeltsch, *Gesammelte Schriften*, Vol. 2 (Tübingen, Germany: 1913), 52. (Abbreviated translation by author.)
10. See Joas, *Faith as an Option*; Cardinal Karl Lehmann, "Catholic Christianity," in *Secularization and World Religions*, ed. Hans Joas and Klaus Wiegandt (Liverpool: Liverpool University Press, 2009), 23–45.

Chapter 5

The Secularization of Sin and the New Geo-Religious Politics of the Vatican

MASSIMO FRANCO

Considering Europe as a place where secularism is going to be crucified would sound, in these years, at least paradoxical. The fact that in
September 2010 Pope Benedict XVI decided to create a ministry to re-
evangelize the Old Continent is quite telling. It meant that the pope had
a frustrating, even despairing, impression that among Europeans, and
overall among Western Europeans, Christianity is viewed as the faith
of a shrinking minority. Hence, his decision was an extreme reaction
and probably the strongest *geo-religious* gesture of his pontificate. Yes,
geo-religious. Since the end of the second millennium we have grown
used to rediscovering geo-politics and geo-economy. But there has been
a deep ignorance, or in any case undervaluation, of the impact of faith
on geography, and vice versa by most analysts and commentators who
orient states' policies.

The only reason for admitting the relevance of geo-religion was a
by-product of security concerns connected to Islamic terrorism. Government officials were focused mainly on the terrorism issue, due to the
dangers posed at the beginning of the Third Millennium by Al Qaeda.
Western governments were worried by the presence of strong Muslim
communities in most European countries. The United Kingdom especially was concerned about possible connections with fundamentalism

and Al Qaeda among the large numbers of North Africans, Arabs, and especially Pakistanis in Britain after the 9\11\2001 attacks on the Twin Towers in New York. From that point on, religion mattered but in a distorted way, as a consequence of national security concerns. Actually there was not any acknowledgment of religion as a political transformational factor, nor a cultural analysis and elaboration of the possible impact of faith—not just Islamism but faith in general—on political and social trends.

The result left the voice of religion to movements attempting to use Christianity as a label against immigrants, Europe, democracy, and tolerance, or to reaffirm an outdated "Western identity" at a time when practice of the Christian religion was declining just inside the West. Yet religion matters, and its decline does as well. It is reshaping the face and culture of the Old Continent and of the West as a whole: A process mirroring the radical changes in the Muslim and Christian world of the Global South. Even so, there is no automatic effect on legislation and interstate relations.

The problem is probably more debated in the United States than in Europe, a situation that arises from a number of sources: The widespread religiosity of this country and the historic identification between faith and freedom; the presence of a number of different faiths; a strong and aggressive "Bible lobby"; and, during the Obama administration, the uneasy relations between Catholic bishops, the White House, and the Democratic Party.

But key questions, such as "appointing Muslim or atheists to public office," are not so divisive in Europe, according to *New York Times'* former editor Bill Keller in one of his columns: Muslims were appointed as government ministers and Parliament members in France, Great Britain, and Italy. Nevertheless, Kmiec is right in asserting that in France "religion is widely seen as a source of trouble" and that "*Laïcité*, or secularism, is a principle enshrined in the French Constitution."[1] The prevalence of the Constitution when there is conflict with a public officer's faith can be a real problem. Can this officer follow his or her religious beliefs without violating constitutional laws? And if obliged to respect the law of his or her country, which consequences might he or she suffer inside his religious environment? Where is the compromise? The "conscience exception" is a painful bone of contention, especially, for instance, with families and doctors dealing with abortion. But so far such aspects are being overwhelmed by the debate on sex abuse scandals and gay marriages. And religion seems to be on the defensive.

Is secularization a positive trend? The different ways in which respected British clerics like the Archbishop of Canterbury Vincent Nichols and Cardinal Cormac Murphy O' Connor handle this issue are very telling.[2] They show quite contrasting visions of the threats posed to Christianity by secularism. But the fact that the lack of faith in Europe is not at all perceived as a public problem is starting to be viewed as a problem in itself. Can indifference to Christianity, and religious and moral values in general, be considered a positive signal for Europe's future? The answer is not unanimous. This growing indifference, and over time hostility, also stems from the delays and resistances of the churches in understanding the signals of the new times. But a desert of religious values is difficult to be viewed as an improvement.

The problem is that cultural paradigms have changed, but the Catholic Church, overall, is still struggling to update its mentality. The emergence of sex abuse scandals in 2002 in the United States should have been an alarm bell to papal Rome. The fact that they were brought to the surface at all, first in America, then in Europe and throughout the rest of the Western world, was something to pay attention to.

Why all of a sudden? And why the indignant reaction against sex abuses committed by Catholic priests after decades of indulgence and silence by the public? The shift in Western public opinion, compared to the past, is a milestone which confirms the cultural revolution that has occurred toward religion in general, and toward the Catholic Church specifically. More than his Regensburg speech on Islamism, and more than his controversial assessment on condoms in Africa, it's *this* scandal that shows the shift in the mood of the West against Benedict XVI's Vatican.[3]

What the Catholic Church is facing is mainly a cultural difficulty. It has to fight against the slippery enemy of what monsignor Rino Fisichella, the man appointed by Benedict XVI to revitalize European Catholicism, perceives as "the supremacy of the fragments." It is a cultural approach that tends to isolate and disperse Western societies: A sort of "grass root relativism."[4] Countries like France and Germany are experiencing a terrific decline in religious vocations. "When in a diocese you have just 15 priests aged around 72, it's difficult to keep the path," a French *monsignore* admitted in an interview in *Le Monde*, the French daily.[5] In France only 10 percent of the population regularly go to church, and more and more they are old people. Even in historic papist countries like Ireland, the government, although led by Catholic politicians, is at odds with the Vatican—up to the point of closing down the embassy of Ireland to the Holy See.

Officially, the decision was due to financial problems; de facto, to the scandals involving Irish Catholic priests and the tough reaction of the Archdiocese of Dublin, which infuriated the government. And when in June 2012 a Catholic congress was held in the Irish capital, a survey found that "just 38 per cent believe Ireland today would be in worse shape without its dominant church." The *Irish Times* said in its editorial: "Ireland will never again be a monolithic culture in which a single hierarchical institution can enjoy such power and prestige."[6] Why? The reason seems to be what I have called the "secularization of the sin."

It is the transformation, or better the revelation, of sex abuses as a crime: A by-product of the end of the Cold War. What once, just twenty years ago or so, was perceived as a terrible *sin*—to hide and treat secretly—now is valued as it actually is: A disgusting violation of the law. It's the symptom of a major cultural change. During the Cold War, the Vatican was considered the "moral arm" of Western values and, to some extent, a part of the anti-communist security system. The need for fighting the Soviet Union granted the Catholic Church some indulgence from civil authorities for the disreputable behavior of some of its officers. The fact that many communist regimes persecuted religion and mainly Catholic priests and bishops as pedophiles to defame them as "agents of the West" justified such an indulgence politically to some extent.

Even public opinion tended, if not to silence, then to tolerate and keep the secret, allowing the Church to handle these scandals in the shadow of dioceses. But now communism is over, as both an ideological and military enemy. Cultural paradigms have changed. American strategic military and financial unipolarism is strongly and dramatically disputed. And in parallel, the "moral unipolarism" of the Vatican is deeply under scrutiny as well, if not over. As a result, public opinion in the Western world requires the Vatican and Catholic bishops to treat sexual crimes for what they are and to collaborate with the judiciary. There has been a major historical shift, a changing view of the nature of sin. If it turns to be secularized, it means that its religious wrapping have been pulled away. The former sin remains as it is viewed in lay societies: A crime to be reported to the police or to the judiciary; and to be punished by the state. As a result, the role and power of the Church are diminished, and its behavior risks the appearance of unbearable self-indulgence.

The first signs of the "secularization of the sin" came in 2002 from the United States. The sex abuse scandals occurred in Boston. That led eventually to the resignation of Cardinal Bernard Law and to a number of huge compensation awards to the victims. The reaction of US authorities demonstrated that the Vatican culture of secrecy did not work anymore. But at that time the Holy See could not or did not want to understand that claim. It tried to dismiss and downgrade the scandal as an "American problem": Connected with the diversity (and perceived depravity) of US Catholicism and culture, and disconnected from the reality of worldwide Catholicism. And Cardinal Law was moved to Rome, as head of a major Roman basilica, out of the reach of the US judiciary.

Actually, what happened in Boston was the vanguard of the moral tsunami about to hit the Vatican at a global level in the years to come. What we are viewing now is just the long wave of the scandals that emerged at the turn of the millennium: A very old problem but perceived today in a totally different way. The reaction even of the Irish government against the Vatican is a symptom of this big cultural change in state-church relations. And the way the Holy See is reacting confirms a "clash of civilizations" of sorts within the Western world. The resistance of the Vatican to accept this new situation speaks volumes about the culture of secrecy rooted inside its mental universe. And it frustrates the courageous steps taken by Benedict XVI to fight the Curia's tendency to consider the scandals as "plots against the Church."

When still just "Cardinal Ratzinger," the pope tried to fight and eradicate this culture and to call crimes as they deserved to be called. But he was in the minority. The struggle will go on for a long time, and it will be a painful one. Anyway, if the Vatican does not come to terms with the "secularization of the sin," the foreseeable perspective is a unilateral rewriting of the relations between some states and the Holy See, and this with or without the Church's consent. If a lack of cooperation to fight the scandals continues, secular authorities will be tempted or even forced to act against the Vatican by infuriated Western public opinion. Together with the secularization of the sin we would view an acceleration of secularism as a whole, and a growing repulsion against the Catholic religion. That would be a negative outcome for the West as a whole.

So far this stress in state-church relations seems to be the predictable near future, at least in some European Western countries. Secularization is perceived as a strong trend in today's Europe. And Benedict XVI's attempt to revive religion represents a significant benchmark to measure the Vatican's capability to regain influence in what was once "its" Europe. The enemy is no longer communist ideology but consumerism and "do-it-yourself religion," which tends to isolate individuals in Western societies and to disperse traditional values.

Against Catholicism there is less hostility than something subtler and more dangerous: Indifference and estrangement. That is why the pope and his exegetes insist on a Catholic Church forced to view itself as a "creative minority," surrounded by growing religious dispersion, if not by a void; and Catholics are compared to Jews as a tiny but strong and united community. This fear of a victory by a secularized culture has many aspects. The first is an apparent difficulty of the Catholic Church to listen attentively and speak compellingly to the modern world. The force of tradition does not suffice any more, and religious language and gestures often seem outdated. There is a supermarket of secular celebrations capable of competing with Christian ones—celebrations that are more and more popular among the younger generations. That explains a widespread Catholic and more general Christian concern against feasts like Halloween.

These celebrations symbolize, in the Vatican view, the defeat of Christian values and the revenge of pagan rituals, which they fear will slowly conquer Europe. Whether the day is Christmas, or Easter, or All Saints, Catholic circles talk about a cultural-historic retort of paganism. Christmas, they state, has become the consumerist day of Santa Claus and not a celebration of Jesus's birth. Easter is going to be the feast of incoming spring, and All Saints the beloved day of "empty pumpkins," skulls, and witches: Halloween. Probably the Vatican attitude against Halloween is at the same time an exaggerated and a superficial assessment. It catches the phenomenon but doesn't explain its origin. If secularism seems to have laid siege to religion in Western Europe, it is because religions, and especially such centralized institutions as the Catholic Church, are condemned to follow and react, but rarely to anticipate facts or have a voice for today's problems.

And a quite striking observation is that Western Europe appears to be further from religion than some Eastern European countries. Tellingly, after a long struggle at the European Parliament on the ban of the crucifix in Italian public schools, resulting in the *Lautsi* case, the Holy See made an unpleasant discovery. It asked for help from all EU countries with Christian and Catholic traditions but in the end, the defenders of the Church's position were Italy, Russia, Bulgaria, Lithuania, Romania, Armenia, Greece, Malta, and Cyprus; later supporters were Albania, Austria, Croatia, Hungary, Macedonia, Moldavia, Poland, Serbia, Ukraine, and Slovakia. A strange alliance.

The map of Europe shows clearly that this religious coalition was composed mainly of Eastern European countries of orthodox tradition. Grégor Puppinck, director of the Christian lobby European Centre for Law and Justice, wrote in *l'Osservatore Romano*, the Holy See's official daily, that the Vatican must thank "the Patriarch of Moscow as a defender of religion against an advancing secularism."[7] The result is that Cold War Europe, split by the Iron Curtain between Christian and democratic West and communist and atheist East, today seems turned upside down. Religiously, a brand new secular iron curtain divides an agnostic West from the Vatican and from former communist Europe. According to Puppinck, "a great change has occurred in the building up of [the] European union. Everybody thought that unity would inevitably go from West to East, conquering eastern countries through economic liberalism and western culture." But the "war on the Crucifix" has provoked an opposite movement, from East to West. That's the reverse of John Paul II's plans and predictions.

He hoped Christian Europe would convert the former Soviet empire. Today, it is in traditional Western democracy, the Vatican asserts, where faith is receding. And secularism, far from being crucified, is gaining momentum. For the Holy See to prevail on the European Parliament, supported by Orthodox countries, sounds like a paradox. But the problem of the crucifix is just a symptom. What worries the Vatican is that the lobbying of pro-Church governments might confirm the breach between papal Rome and the most influential Western democracies. The battle risks being a pyrrhic one: A win in the *Lautsi* case by the Holy See and political elites among the general indifference of Western public opinion.

And a point must be kept in mind. The victory of the Vatican and of its allies in the *Lautsi* case depended on a shrewd legal strategy, not on the open acknowledgment of the crucifix as a legitimate religious testimonial. It was considered a symbol of Italian traditions, culture, and values: In a word, of Italian (and Western) identity. This argument had to do with faith only as a side effect. This confirms a basic difference between Europe and the United States. As the eminent historian Daniel Boorstin has said, individual faiths are not important in American life, but religion is enormously so.[8] The political philosopher Jean Bethke Elshtain observes that "the separation of church and state is one thing, the separation of religion and politics quite another."[9] From time to time in Europe, it sometimes seems the reverse. There, the presence of the Catholic Church especially deeply influences the relations between church and state, while religion seems to be less important.

That situation stems from the completely different history of the two continents. The United States was founded by people who fled religious persecutions, had a strong respect for minority rights, and harbored a profound hostility toward any religion trying to impose itself and its beliefs on the state. The second aspect of secularism crucifying religion, and not the reverse, stems from a deep crisis in the government and legitimacy of the Vatican. The theory of a plot against the Holy See from outside has been ridiculed after the revelations, in the spring of 2012, of secret documents and conflicts inside the core of papal power. The image not just of the Roman Curia but of the pontiff's inner circle has been shattered. Right or wrong, Rome is being viewed as a corrupt and rotten place, where power games prevail on ethic concerns and religious activity. And distracted by their internecine wars, Roman cardinals seem incapable of understanding what is going on in the rest of the world. They are not in control of the dynamics of the Catholic Church outside the Holy See's geographical borders.

The novelty is not just that scandals happen: There is a long history of internecine and bloody conflicts inside the Vatican. The true novelty is that these conflicts are leaked and offered with saucy details to the lay press. At the end of 2011 the news of a menacing letter against Cardinal Tarcisio Bertone, Vatican Secretary of State, was published by Italian newspapers. The reaction of the Vatican was to downplay it, declaring anonymously that such things are everyday routine in the Curia: Dozens of "dirty letters" arrive daily against this or that. But it missed the point that this time the *routine* had become hard news, due to the intensified struggle for power inside the Holy See.

The effects of such a situation will be clear only in the long run. But all the struggles and misunderstandings connected to the child sex abuse scandal and to the so-called Vatileaks scandal are already posing a huge problem. They are dangerously decreasing the Holy See's international profile, and redrawing state-church relations. Furthermore, the financial crisis in the Eurozone is adding tensions between northern European countries and southern ones. And what appears surprisingly striking is that we perceive not just an economic divide but a geo-religious one. Nations with a Lutheran majority (read Germany, the Netherlands, Finland) tend to consider Catholic ones (Spain, Italy, and partly France) as fiscal sinners, not only debtors. In German, the word *Shuld* means both debt and guilt. So any judgment regarding public debts is given with a whiff of moral disapproval as well. There is a tendency to see "a religious faultline"[10] crossing the Eurozone. "Many Germans protested that too much had been conceded by their government—and it might not be too far-fetched to see this as just the latest Protestant criticism of the Latin approach to matters monetary, which has deep roots in German culture, shaped by religious belief," BBC's Chris Bowlby recently wrote.

Stephan Richter, a German Catholic editor of The *Globalist*, has suggested that the Eurozone's crisis would have been avoided if Martin Luther had been one of the negotiators of the Maastricht Treaty. According to Richter, Luther probably would have said the following about the inclusion of Italy and Spain in the single currency system: "Read my lips: No unreformed Catholic countries." He suggests that "too much Catholicism is detrimental to a nation's fiscal health, even today in the 21st Century."[11] One could say these are just stereotypes and prejudices. True, but they revamp old European ghosts. And they add uncertainty to the future of Europe. All debates on confessionalism, on the need for responding to growing divisive religious issues with a law, on democracy and secularism, on interfaith relations with Islamism overall, are the mirror of a changing or maybe already changed West. Kmiec acts as a rhabdomancer to discover how our societies' values will be shaped by religion, or by the lack of religion in the next years; and how states will react to the new cultural balance. It will be a long, difficult but fascinating search.

NOTES

1. Douglas W. Kmiec, "Secularism Crucified?," See section "The French Exception."
2. See "Baptism of Fire," *Tablet*, November 21, 2009.
3. Benedict XVI, *Faith, Reason, and the University: Memories and Reflections* (Vatican City: Libreria Editrice Vaticana, 2006). Peter Seewald and Pope Benedict XVI, *Light of the World: The Pope, the Church, and the Signs of the Times* (San Francisco: Ignatius Press, 2010).
4. Massimo Franco, "Can the Pope Recapture Europe?," *Guardian*, September 27, 2011.
5. Stéphanie Le Bars, "La stratégie de l'évêque de Fréjus-Toulon contre le déclin des vocations de prêtres," *Le Monde*, June 22, 2012, 10.
6. "Church at a Crossroads," *Irish Times*, June 9, 2012, 17.
7. Grègor Puppinck, "Un'alleanza contro il secolarismo," *l'Osservatore Romano*, July 22, 2010, 7.
8. In Tiziano Bonazzi, "The Notion of America as an Antithesis to Europe," *Il Regno Quindicinale di Attualità e Documenti* 6 (2004): 18–23.
9. Quoted in Massimo Franco, *Parallel Empires: The Vatican and the United States—Two Centuries of Conflict* (New York: Doubleday-Random House, 2009), 119.
10. Christ Bowlby, "The Eurozone's Religious Faultline," *BBC News Magazine*, July, 18, 2012.
11. Stephan Richter, "Martin Luther and the Eurozone: Theology as an Economic Destiny?," *Globalist*, May 14, 2012.

PART FOUR

SECULARISM
AND INTERNATIONAL
AFFAIRS

Chapter 6

Religion, Secularism, and Social Justice beyond the Nation-State

ERIN K. WILSON

At its heart, the secular political project is bound up with questions of justice and equality. In democratic societies that are highly diverse and plural with regard to both immanent and transcendent worldviews, secularism in its various guises attempts to manage the relationship between these competing worldviews in order to provide the best circumstances for pursuit of the common good. Its purpose, in its ideal form, is to protect religious believers from undue coercion and influence from the state while at the same time preventing one religion from having greater power and control over public life than others.

Douglas Kmiec's thoughtful essay draws attention to this through his discussion of the tensions between ensuring as far as possible a neutral public sphere yet one that provides space for religious actors to intervene on issues relevant to the common good. He points out, following Talal Asad, that in its original nineteenth-century incarnation, secularism was not hostile to religion but rather offered a means through which believers could be given sufficient freedom to resolve moral questions according to their own conscience, without unnecessary interference from the state.[1]

As Kmiec notes, however, much has changed since then, with regard to religion, secularism, and society as a whole. New challenges have emerged that highlight the shortcomings of secularism and raise questions regarding its utility in its current form, whether secularism needs to be entirely reconceived or indeed whether the very concepts of the "religious" and the "secular" need to be done away with completely. In short, these challenges hint at something of a "crisis of secularism." Kmiec's chapter touches on a number of these challenges and changes, providing a detailed and thorough overview of the ways in which secularism has altered and almost reversed from this nineteenth-century version. Yet there are other crucial developments—in particular, impacts from increasing globalization—that are important for further understanding the nature of this crisis of secularism and thinking about ways to move beyond it.

The first development is the emergence and subsequent recognition of secularism as an ideology.[2] While Kmiec hints at the ideological dimensions of secularism, his chapter for the most part focuses on the judicial arrangements for managing the relationship between religion and the state—that is, secularism as statecraft. Yet arguably, secularism's ideological dimensions underpin the varieties of judicial arrangements across different states. These ideological dimensions have been just as, if not more, influential and their impact has spread far beyond the formal institutional arrangements for managing religion and national public life. Within political philosophy, religious studies, and international relations, scholars now widely recognize that secularism is not the neutral, universal arbiter of reason and political deliberation that it once claimed to be.[3] Rather, it is a highly specific, culturally embedded model for managing the relationship between religion and politics, albeit one that has now become very influential across many diverse regions of the world.

When we recognize these dimensions of secularism, we realize further that secularism is not just about the judicial and political arrangements for managing religion's relationship with politics; it is underpinned by an ideological agenda that makes assumptions about the worth of religious belief and practice in relation to other human pursuits, about the existence and value of immanent and transcendent realms, about the very nature of religion itself. These assumptions impact the way states engage with religious actors, interact with other states where religion is far more central than it is in Western secular worldviews, and carry out their policies. Indeed, the ideological dimensions of secularism are embedded within the solution that Kmiec puts forward to deal with the crisis of secularism—a clearer delineation of the boundaries between the public and private realms and the central role of the rule of law.[4] The rule of law relies on clear public and private spheres, and yet this understanding of how society may be divided up is inherently secular and, arguably, also carries implicit influence from the Judeo-Christian tradition. It affects the ways that "religion" is understood and defined, leading to an emphasis on belief (predominantly individual belief) and choice over and above rituals, practices, and the significance of community.[5] This leads to excluding certain practices and traditions from protection because they are not understood as "religion." Further, as seen in the *Lautsi* case but also in the *Salazar v. Buono* case in the United States, secularism, even in an inclusive form, imbues the state the power to define not only what "religion" is, but what religious traditions themselves do and do not stand for.[6] Therefore, proposing this "inclusive secularism," as Kmiec terms it, entrenches the ideological dimensions of secularism further, rather than addressing them and moving beyond them. Indeed, any proposal for reform that continues to operate within the confines of public and private spheres and the assumptions of secular ideology, as Kmiec's does, will do little to resolve the inequalities and exclusions that are produced by current secular political and judicial arrangements.

In international affairs, the ideological dimensions of secularism have affected understandings of religion's role in conflict, peacebuilding, and international aid and development, to name but a few. Only now are scholars beginning to explore how secularism as an ideology has affected different areas of global politics and to reexamine assumptions about religion's role in global civil society, and about religion itself. To make sense of the current context, we need to appreciate the changes that have occurred in secularism as statecraft and their impact on religion's relationship with politics. However, it is equally critical that we appreciate the ideological agenda of secularism and the ways that ideological agenda is being increasingly questioned and challenged at the beginning of the twenty-first century, both within and beyond the nation-state.

The second development that deserves attention in the discussion of the current state of secularism is the impact of globalization, particularly neoliberal globalization, on the nature and reach of both secularism and the position of the nation-state in global politics. The state is still the primary actor in international politics, but a number of other significant actors and important changes are demanding attention, making a consideration of religion, secularism, and politics beyond the level of the state timely and necessary. Globalization contributes to increasing interconnections across state borders and the emergence of multiple public spheres that overlap and intersect at various levels of global civil society.[7] These multifarious and overlapping public spheres necessarily affect the nature of secularism, since secularism is both constituted by and constitutive of the public/private divide.[8] Numerous scholars have begun to question the utility of this divide in the face of the growing interconnections brought on by globalization. Indeed, it is a societal division that has arguably been applicable only within the "West" and the Western-centric international system.

While Kmiec offers five models for conceptualizing the relationships between religion and politics in different contexts, all five are still very much focused on the nation-state as the primary referent. Further, the democratically acceptable models he discusses—confessionalism, inclusive secularism, and exclusive secularism—all assume that a division between public and private realms and the establishment of secular political and legal institutions are essential for democracy to function effectively. Given the historical philosophical origins of this division in Catholicism (as Kmiec points out in his discussion of the Gelasian Thesis), Protestantism (in Luther's doctrine of the Two Kingdoms), and liberalism (especially John Locke), it is questionable the extent to which this division will make sense in societies where no clear designation between immanent and transcendent authorities is recognized. This does not, or should not, mean, however, that such societies have no hope of ever establishing stable functioning democracies. Rather, to do so requires creativity and thinking beyond the confines of public and private, immanent and transcendent binary oppositions and even perhaps the nation-state itself.

An additional impact from globalization has been the rise of neoliberalism as the dominant ideology governing state and interstate economics. Manfred Steger has argued that the growing power of neoliberalism at the global level represents a shift from the national to the global in ideological contestations.[9] At the same time neoliberalism has gained increasing power at the national and international levels, alternative forms of globalization have emerged in the form of grassroots resistance to the inequalities and injustices brought about by neoliberal globalization. Prevailing analysis of these dynamics has undervalued the role of religious actors and worldviews, affected by the ideological assumptions of secularism.[10] Indeed, there has been a dominant assumption that religion is incompatible with resistance movements, since these are associated with progressive politics, and religion is often assumed to be highly conservative. These assumptions are unfounded, however, as the plethora of religious organizations engaged with social justice issues attests. Further, as Richard Wolin has argued, religious worldviews may provide one of the few sources of resistance to the onslaught of consumerism and competition associated with the neoliberal worldview.[11]

In the next pages, I explore these dynamics and their significance for rethinking secularism in contemporary international affairs. I begin by highlighting the importance of thinking beyond the state in exploring the impacts of secularism as an ideology, and understanding, in turn, how the labels of "religious" and "secular" as distinct categories are increasingly unhelpful for exploring the rather more entangled ways religious and secular dynamics and actors work within international affairs. I do this with specific reference to international aid and development. Second, I explore the significance of religious grassroots actors, as part of broader transnational social movements, in challenging neoliberal modes of domination and exclusion that produce widespread inequality and injustice. I note in particular the important role that religious societal actors play in a number of progressive social justice movements—relating to poverty, climate justice, asylum seekers—and as part of the broader global justice movement against neoliberal globalization and dominant modes of exclusion and marginalization. This important role of religious actors leads me to my concluding remarks about the need for developing alternatives to the secular model of living together, in response to Kmiec's call at the conclusion of his chapter, but as an alternative to the inclusive secularism he suggests. I briefly discuss three possible alternative frameworks—postsecularism, relational dialogism, and multidimensional pluralism. These alternatives develop from the recognition that secularism does not have a monopoly on the best ways to pursue justice, peace, freedom, democracy, and equality—in fact, the secular may be a source of violence and exclusion.[12] The separation of religion and politics through secularism has not resulted in the justice and equality that was hoped for from the secular project. There is a need to rethink how the relationship between religion and politics is managed, but this must include a focus that goes beyond the level of the state to incorporate the dynamics at the grassroots and at the global level, given the increasingly transnational and global nature of contemporary international affairs.

THE IMPACT OF SECULARIST IDEOLOGY IN INTERNATIONAL RELATIONS

Secularist perspectives have significantly impeded understandings of religion and its role and influence in international politics. In part owing to influence from the secularization thesis and the assumption that religion was a "spent force" that would soon disappear from society,[13] the field of international relations and related sub-disciplines of peace and conflict analysis and development studies have for a long time viewed religion largely in institutional, individual, and irrational terms[14]—that is, religions are primarily observable through their institutions; they are mainly individual private belief systems, constituting a matter of personal choice;[15] and they are on the whole irrational. These last two characterizations in particular have fed the assumption that religion should be kept out of the public sphere, both at the national and at the international levels.

Numerous scholars in recent times have explored how these assumptions have impacted theory and practice in international affairs. Perhaps nowhere is their influence more observable than in the field of international aid and development. Approaches to development have been heavily underpinned by the principles of both modernization and secularization theory.[16] This situation contributed to the prevailing assumption that the only model for development was the

Western model, which included the secularization of society and the privatization of religion.[17]

As a result of these prevailing assumptions, religious organizations working in the development sector have often been viewed with suspicion by governments and secular non-government organizations; they are assumed to have an alternate agenda of proselytizing and conversion, and their approaches to development issues are assumed to be antithetical to the scientific modernizing spirit that has underpinned mainstream approaches to development.[18] This attitude may in part stem from the historical involvement of religious organizations in missionary activity, which nonetheless served as an important precursor to contemporary development.[19] Indeed, many faith-based development organizations have themselves internalized what are popularly understood as "secular" norms and values—human rights,[20] for example, or, more recently, neoliberal models for management, productivity, and efficiency[21]—highlighting the extent to which secular, modern values have become embedded within prevailing approaches to development. Yet, as Barnet and Gross Stein point out, secular humanitarian aid is its own kind of faith and in many ways resembles elements of religious commitments to serve those less fortunate, alongside a more cosmopolitan, transnational understanding of who we owe assistance to.[22] Barnet and Gross Stein refer to this as the "sanctification" of humanitarian aid and development, a complex entangling of sacred and profane in the development sector that increasingly undermines our understanding of "religion" and "secularism."[23] As a result, the view that "secularism" offers the most neutral, universal means for pursuing cross-cultural interactions and relationships is undermined.

This view of secularism is further weakened with regard to the role of religious actors in the development sector. Mainstream secular development organizations, including national governments but also intergovernmental organizations such as the United Nations, have for a long time either ignored or undervalued the role of religious actors in development. Influenced by Western secularist assumptions, these actors assumed that religion was a private matter and consequently should not form part of public sphere activities that relate to processes of development. Yet, the understandings of society as divided into public and private spheres, so central to contemporary secular models of state-craft, often do not make sense in contexts outside the West. In numerous countries in Africa, such as Nigeria and Ghana, for example, or in countries throughout Asia, rituals and beliefs that Western scholars and policymakers would associate with "religion" are a central part of public decision-making discourses and practices.[24] There is no clear division between public and private realms in many of these contexts, so secular approaches that attempt to limit the influence of religion and maintain a strict separation between religion and politics are meaningless. Religious beliefs, worldviews, and authority figures are extremely influential in these contexts, not because they use religion to gain political power or because they are attempting to manipulate politics to gain more influence for their religion, but because there is an entirely different understanding of the relationship between the two—often entirely different ways of understanding what Western scholars call "religion."

Scholars and policymakers are beginning to recognize that these divisions between religion and secularism, public and private, religion and politics, immanent and transcendent are unhelpful in many developing contexts. This awareness has led a number of typically "secular" organizations and approaches to become increasingly open to engaging with religion on development and social justice–related problems. Perhaps the most famous example is the establishment of the Office of Faith-Based Community Initiatives in the US State Department. Other notable examples include the UN High Commissioner for Refugees' Dialogue on Faith and Protection held at the end of 2012, or the Joint United Nations Programme on HIV and AIDS' interest in promoting the World Vision International Channels of Hope program as an example of best practice in challenging attitudes of stigma and marginalization on HIV/AIDS.

At first glance, these appear to be positive developments, an increasing awareness that religion can contribute to the pursuit of societal transformation and justice rather than simply being an impediment to equality. Yet, as Elizabeth Shakman Hurd has pointed out, often these engagements occur within the boundaries of the secularist worldview.[25] Religions are deemed "good" or "bad" according to criteria laid out by secularist organizations. Further, these organizations make decisions about who or what constitute "religious" actors that are worthy to engage with and support financially.

The decision in the *Lautsi* case provides one example here: The court decided that Christianity was primarily about charity rather than belief in God, making it less religion and more cultural heritage. Kmiec welcomed the decision, arguing that "the crucifix is let in to compete side by side with the idea of the secular republic." However, in the interpretation of other scholars, the ruling has seen the crucifix as symbolic of universal (read "secular") values. Beaman[26] and Gedicks and Annicchino[27] have made this point (albeit with different readings of the purpose of this move)—that confessional symbols such as the crucifix are able to remain in the public sphere only if they are presented as symbols that are secular and universal rather than specific to a particular religious tradition. Indeed, if the crucifix was permitted in the classroom to compete with the secular republic, why were not symbols from other worldviews—religious, indigenous, humanist, atheist, socialist—also present in the classroom? Secular political publics engage with "religion," but only on secular terms, according to their own criteria and understanding of what "religion" is and whether it is "good" or "bad" for the pursuit of secular political and ideological ends.

In many situations, the religious actors who are deemed "good" and worthy to be engaged with continue to be traditional religious institutions, often represented by men. This introduces a significant power dynamic that can disrupt societal relationships. It also risks neglecting equally important grassroots movements that are inspired by spirituality and religious belief. As such, scholars and policymakers need to move away from the ideas of a strict separation between religion and politics as laid out in secularist worldviews if they are to have a more nuanced appreciation of religion's role in international affairs.

RELIGIOUS RESISTANCE TO NEOLIBERALISM

There is a second area where I argue the impact of secularism requires greater analysis and understanding; this relates to the influence of neoliberalism in contemporary national and global politics and economics and the capacity of religions to offer a significant form of resistance to neoliberalism. As Steger has noted, neoliberalism, or as he calls it, market globalism, has become the dominant global political ideology, influencing the policy and practice of corporations, states, and both intergovernmental and non-governmental organizations.[28] Neoliberalism manifests in a growing emphasis on privatization of social services, deregulation of finance, liberalization of trade, and trickle-down economics—the idea that wealth creation among the elite will benefit everyone, eventually. There is also a greater emphasis on cost-benefit outcomes, competition, individualism, and consumerism. Neoliberalism is in many ways a form of hyper-economic rationalism and relies on the same assumption about the existence of a universally accessible form of reasoning that underpins all human behavior and decision-making as that which is found in dominant secularist worldviews. The emphasis on rationalism and the focus on individualism, competition, and consumerism suggest that neoliberalism and secularism are intimately connected and that the one may even facilitate the other.[29]

The impacts of neoliberalism can be seen across the world. States increasingly privatize social welfare services, resulting in the inability of entire groups within society to access basic necessities, including water, electricity, and healthcare. The economic gap between the wealthiest and the poorest in many societies is continuing to widen. These incidents, alongside the global financial crisis of 2007–2008 and the ongoing fiscal crisis in the European Union, demonstrate that neoliberal economics has not generated the wealth and prosperity for all that was promised.[30]

Grassroots transnational social justice organizations and movements have been critiquing and resisting neoliberalism for decades. Religious organizations such as Caritas International and the World Council of Churches have been at the forefront, participating in spaces such as the World Social Forum (WSF), declaring that "another world is indeed possible." Their participation in the WSF is particularly interesting, since the WSF is explicitly non-confessional and secular.[31] A number of organizations within the movement explicitly state that they see religion as anti-democratic and as encouraging discrimination and exclusion; these organizations strongly promote assumptions of secularist ideology where religion must be excluded from national and global public spheres.[32] Yet religious organizations are active and also respected by key organizations like the Transnational Institute as part of this "movement of movements,"[33] again demonstrating that the ideology of secularism is being increasingly challenged and undermined, not just at the level of the state but in grassroots transnational movements as well. The World Council of Churches has been conducting research to establish a "greed line," a level of wealth that it is unacceptable to live above, to complement the poverty line; it has engaged in a dialogue with the World Bank in an attempt to encourage the bank to move away from neoliberalism as a guiding framework.

As Kmiec discusses in his chapter, Pope Benedict the XVI also strongly urged reform of neoliberal market economics to address global inequality. The dramatic impact of Catholic liberation theology in Latin America provides an important precursor and model for much of the resistance to neoliberalism that has emerged in that part of the world, in many cases leading the way in the global movement against neoliberalism.[34] Other examples of what Western scholars typically conceptualize as "religious" and "secular" organizations working together to challenge inequality and injustice include movements around rights to asylum such as City of Sanctuary in the United Kingdom, De Vluchtkerk (Refugee Church) in the Netherlands, the New Sanctuary movement in the United States, and campaigns on asylum seeker rights in Australia. These movements provide important forms of welfare support for asylum seekers, the homeless, and numerous other marginalized groups within society that have found themselves increasingly unable to access social support given the neoliberalization of the nation-state.[35] As states have increasingly privatized social welfare, utilities, and other essential services, leading to the disenfranchisement of vast sectors of society, religious organizations have frequently stepped in to breach the gap. Whether these organizations possess the political strategy, organization, or coherence to push back against the growing tide of neoliberalization, however, remains to be seen.

It seems to me that the strict separation of religion and politics that secularism calls for is neither desirable nor possible, since the reality on the ground within and across states is that confessional and non-confessional organizations are and have been for a long time work-ing together to challenge prevailing forms of domination and exclusion. It is equally true that religious and secular organizations have worked together to maintain the status quo that excludes and marginalizes people, privileging corporations and entrepreneurs often at the expense of the poor.[36] As such, secularism does not provide the defense against exploitation and oppression that many of its advocates argue or hope for. If we are to have a more nuanced analysis of the relations between religion and politics across different levels of society, and if there is to be greater cooperation, understanding, and inclusion, secularism re-quires at the very least reform, if not the development and implemen-tation of alternative ways to manage the relationship between religion and politics. In the final section, I discuss three possible alternatives— postsecularism, relational dialogism, and multidimensional pluralism.

BEYOND SECULARISM?

Postsecularism has gained increasing traction in academic discussions regarding the relationship between religion and public life. William Connolly was the first to articulate the idea,[37] but the recent work of Jurgen Habermas has arguably been the primary catalyst for engage-ment with the idea. Recently, Mavelli and Petito have identified two main ways in which the postsecular has been utilized.[38] The first is to describe the circumstances in which we find ourselves in late moder-nity of the early twenty-first century. Contrary to dominant theories of secularization, so the argument goes, religion has not declined and disappeared but has "re-emerged," or, in Jose Casanova's words has de-privatized.[39] This revitalized presence of religion in the public sphere suggests that perhaps we are witnessing the emergence of a postsecular society, requiring us to address the exclusion of religion and rehabilitate it into the public realm (Habermas 2006, 2008).

This particular understanding of the postsecular, however, has been critiqued for re-inscribing the Western-centric gaze within which "re-ligion" has traditionally been analyzed. Further, as Pabst emphasizes, Habermasian postsecularity still defines religion "in essentialist or epiphenomenal" terms.[40] In contrast, Pabst argues if we are to move beyond secularism to a truly postsecular form of analysis and framework for societal organizations, we must incorporate metaphysics into our everyday theorizing about politics and our everyday legal and political practices.

How to do this remains distinctly challenging, though perhaps the recognition of alternative rationalities is a good place to start. Both Pope John Paul II and Pope Benedict XVI offered one means of beginning the process of recognition, emphasizing that faith and reason are not the opposite of one another, nor does secularism have a monopoly on reason. Rather, the reasoning of faith simply begins from foundational assumptions that are different from those of the reasoning found within secularism.[41] Kmiec extends this line of thinking by positing the benefits of religious (in this case Catholic) reasoning for public debate. He highlights the important connections between religious traditions and the establishment of the rule of law in his chapter. While this tradition provides an important starting point for rethinking the political and legal arrangements that manage relationships between religion and politics, it does not go far enough. It maintains the problematic distinction between the religious and the secular, the transcendent and the immanent. Kmiec also seems to equate "religion" and "faith" with "morality" and argue that without religion, secular publics run the risk of losing their sense of virtue and piety.[42] Yet morality is not the sole purview of religion, and while religion has provided a source for the law in many if not most countries, it is not the only source of the law.

Mavelli and Petito's second argument is that the postsecular has emerged as "a form of radical theorising and critique prompted by the idea that values such as democracy, freedom, equality, inclusion, and justice may not necessarily be best pursued within an exclusively immanent secular framework. Quite the opposite, the secular may well be a potential site of isolation, domination, violence, and exclusion."[43] From this critical perspective, the secular becomes a mode of Foucauldian governmentality and control for the state, providing the criteria against which all actors, logics, and rationalities are legitimized or excluded. The postsecular critique destabilizes categories of "religious" and "secular," "public" and "private," "rational" and "irrational," emphasizing that such categories are largely historically, socially, and culturally constructed.[44] What we have come to understand as the secular has arisen out of a specific cultural and historical context (European Christendom); therefore, it is not the neutral, universal form of reason that it has often been assumed to be.[45] As Joseph Camilleri notes, however, this postsecular critique has largely been limited to a focus on the state,[46] which is why it is so important for us to turn our attention to the impact of secularist ideology across grassroots transnational networks and issues.

Thus, at present, the postsecular critique remains just that—a recognition of the problems of secularism, but without an alternate proposal for organizing our social relations across the traditional divides of public/private and secular/religious, among others. The problem with any kind of alternative is how to avoid simply inscribing new divides and hierarchies in place of the old. I suggest that part of the problem with secularism is its assumption that religion's place in political and social life has been "settled" once and for all. The challenge to secularism has arisen because events in the late twentieth and early twenty-first centuries make manifestly clear that this is not the case. Rather than trying to develop an alternative mode for managing religion and politics that seeks for a new settlement, we must pursue multiple alternatives that are always open to new possibilities, that avoid settlement altogether and instead enable us to live with openness, uncertainty, and insecurity on these questions. Part of the problem with Kmiec's proposal of inclusive secularism that clearly delineates between public and private spheres is precisely that it seeks settlement, closure, and finality on these issues. My suggestion is that the boundaries between public and private do not need to be more clearly delineated; instead, they need to be done away with entirely and new forms of understanding the entanglement of religious and secular, sacred and profane, immanent and transcendent explored.

I have elsewhere proposed a combination of Bakhtinian dialogism and relational thought—relational dialogism—as one possible framework through which these relations between religion and politics can be negotiated while acknowledging the continual possibility of alternative outcomes.[47] This framework attempts to move away from the traditional assumptions implicit within secularism that something can be—must be—either public or private or religious or political; instead it proposes a "both-and" model. This both-and conception offers a means for holding differing conceptions of the nature of reason, existence, politics, and religion, maintaining them in tension with one another instead of insisting on settlement and closure.

A third alternative to dominant conceptions of secularism is William Connolly's notion of multidimensional pluralism.[48] For Connolly, multidimensional pluralism encourages deep, sincere engagement and understanding across traditional dividing lines of religion, ethnicity, nationalism, class, and gender, among others—though Connolly is particularly focused on religion. Secularism, in his view, promotes a shallow tolerance, a "live and let live" kind of attitude that does not encourage understanding and inclusion but instead fosters marginalization and exclusion. It encourages the majority not to engage with minorities but to "leave them alone" in their separate enclaves and societies. From this perspective, Kmiec's proposal to strengthen the divisions between the public and private spheres would serve to entrench ignorance of others, to enhance marginalization and exclusion rather than understanding and inclusion. In Connolly's view, secularism also does not acknowledge the implicit subjectivity of a secular public realm and the assumptions about the nature of belief and human existence that go with that, maintaining the illusion of neutrality and universality. Again, from this perspective, the central role for the rule of law that Kmiec advocates is problematic, because the law contains within it certain assumptions about the nature of religion itself that then inform how the relationship between religion and politics is managed.[49] It also maintains the centrality of the state as the main arbiter of the relationship between religion and politics, when both politics and religion transgress the boundaries and authority of the state. Multidimensional pluralism, by contrast, promotes profound respect of diversity and difference through engagement and understanding across multiple boundaries, including those of the state. In practice, the application of multidimensional pluralism could result in political and legal institutions that take seriously claims about the existence of alternate realities and cosmic orders, institutions that are imbued with both transcendent and immanent sensibilities, working through these different belief systems and understanding them in an attempt to reach reconciliation and consensus across differences. Such deep respect and understanding, rather than shallow, disengaged tolerance, is an alternative means to addressing the seeming conundrum that presents itself to public life as a result of the unexpected persistence of religion.

These are but a few of many possibilities for addressing and moving beyond the problems of contemporary secularism. Douglas Kmiec offers us one suggestion, but in my view, inclusive secularism does more to entrench than to alleviate the problems we are encountering with secularism. Postsecularism, relational dialogism, and multidimensional pluralism all offer preliminary alternative directions for the conversation. Given the important ways in which the Catholic Church has and will continue to challenge established ideological, political, and legal power structures, it seems to me imperative that the Catholic tradition, among others, pursue discussion of alternatives to secularism that truly go beyond the binary assumptions of public/private, secular/religious, sacred/profane, immanent/transcendent that color so much of our present theorizing on these issues. In today's increasingly interconnected world it is critical that we explore these and other alternatives further—not just at the level of the legal and political arrangements within states, but also the assumptions and frameworks that shape interactions at the grass roots and in transnational and global relations.

NOTES

1. Douglas W. Kmiec, "Secularism Crucified?" See section "The Different Forms of Secularism."

2. José Casanova, *Public Religions in the Modern World* (Chicago: Chicago University Press, 1994).

3. Christopher Eberle, *Religious Conviction in Liberal Politics* (Cambridge: Cambridge University Press, 2002); Elizabeth Shakman Hurd, *The Politics of Secularism in International Relations* (Princeton, NJ: Princeton University Press, 2008); Ahmet Kuru, "Passive and Assertive Secularism: Historical Conditions, Ideological Struggles, and State Policies toward Religion," *World Politics* 59, no. 4 (2007): 568–594; Daniel Philpott, "Has the Study of Global Politics Found Religion?," *Annual Review of Political Science* 12 (2009): 183–202; Luca Mavelli, *Europe's Encounter with Islam: The Secular*

and Postsecular (London: Routledge, 2012); E. K. Wilson, *After Secularism: Rethinking Religion in Global Politics* (Basingstoke: Palgrave, 2012); Simon Glendinning, "Japheth's World: The Rise of Secularism and the Revival of Religion Today," *European Legacy* 14, no. 4 (2009): 409–426.

4. See, for example, Kmiec's essay sections "Religion and Politics—yet Again" and "Secularism in Relation to Public/Private Spheres of Decision Marking."

5. Benjamin Berger, "Law's Religion: Rendering Culture," *Osgoode Hall Law Journal* 45, no. 2 (2007): 284.

6. See, for example, the ruling from the ECHR Grand Chamber on the *Lautsi* case: "In Christianity even the faith in an omniscient god is secondary in relation to charity, meaning respect for one's fellow human beings. It follows that the rejection of a non-Christian by a Christian implies a radical negation of Christianity itself, a substantive abjuration; but that is not true of other religious faiths, for which such an attitude amounts at most to the infringement of an important precept" (13.3 of Administrative Court Decision in *Lautsi II*, quoted in Lori G. Beaman, "Battles over Symbols: The 'Religion' of the Minority versus the 'Culture' of the Majority," *Journal of Law and Religion* 28, no. 1 (2012): 135). The *Oregon Employment Division v. Smith* case in the United States from 1990 provides another example: two Native Americans claimed discrimination on the basis of religion because they were denied unemployment benefits after they were dismissed for using peyote, a drug used in traditional Native American rituals but deemed illegal under the laws of Oregon. The case was dismissed; the court ruled that peyote had not been made illegal to discriminate against Native Americans. See Phillip E. Hammond, *With Liberty for All: Freedom of Religion in the United States* (Louisville, KY: Westminster John Knox Press, 1998), 42–45. In *Salazar v. Buono* (2010) the Court ruled that a cross erected by private parties on National Park Service land could remain, with the majority opinion stating that the cross' meaning was not solely religious.

7. Nancy Fraser, "Transnationalizing the Public Sphere," *European Institute for Progressive Cultural Policies*, March 2007, http://eipcp.net/transversal/0605/fraser/en.

8. Charles Taylor, "The Polysemy of the Secular," *Social Research* 76, no. 4 (2009): 1143–1166; E. K. Wilson, *After Secularism*.

9. Manfred B. Steger, *The Rise of the Global Imaginary* (Oxford: Oxford University Press, 2008).

10. Peter Jay Smith and Elizabeth Smythe, "Faith, Global Justice and Forums of Resistance: From the World Social Forum to Occupy!," paper presented at the 2013 International Studies Association Conference, San Francisco, CA (2013).

11. Richard Wolin, "Jurgen Habermas and the Post-Secular Societies," *Chronicle of Higher Education* 52, no. 5 (2005): 16.

12. Luca Mavelli and Fabio Petito, "The Postsecular in International Politics: An Introduction," *Review of International Studies* 38, no. 5 (2012).

13. Jonathan Fox, "Religion as an Overlooked Element of International Relations," *International Studies Review* 3, no. 3 (2001): 53–73.

14. Wilson, *After Secularism.*

15. Berger, "Law's Religion."

16. Alberto Arce and Norman Long, eds., *Anthropology, Development and Modernities: Exploring Discourses, Counter-tendencies and Violence* (London: Routledge, 2000).

17. See, for example, Walt W. Rostow, *The Stages of Economic Growth* (Cambridge: Cambridge University Press, 1971); Jacob Bercovitch and Richard Jackson, *Conflict Resolution in the Twenty-First Century* (Ann Arbor: University of Michigan Press, 2009); Neil Cooper, Mandy Turner, and Michael Pugh, "The End of History and the Last Liberal Peacebuilder: A Reply to Roland Paris," *Review of International Studies* 37, no. 4 (2011): 1995–2007.

18. Cecelia Lynch, "Religious Humanitarianism and the Global Politics of Secularism," in *Rethinking Secularism*, ed. Craig Calhoun, Mark Juergensmeyer, and Jonathan VanAntwerpen (New York: Oxford University Press, 2011); Michael Barnet and Janice Gross Stein, "Introduction: The Secularization and Sanctification of Humanitarianism," in *Sacred Aid: Faith and Humanitarianism*, ed. Michael Barnet and Janice Gross Stein (Oxford: Oxford University Press, 2012).

19. Lynch, "Religious Humanitarianism"; Barnet and Gross Stein, "Secularization and Sanctification."

20. Liliane Voyé, "Secularization in a Context of Advanced Modernity," *Sociology of Religion* 60, no. 3 (1999): 278.

21. Lynch, "Religious Humanitarianism."

22. Michael Barnet and Janice Gross Stein, "Introduction," in *Sacred Aid: Faith and Humanitarianism*, ed. Michael Barnet and Janice Gross Stein (Oxford: Oxford University Press, 2012), 13.

23. Ibid., 25.

24. Maia Green, "Confronting Categorical Assumptions about the Power of Religion in Africa," *Review of African Political Economy* 33, no. 110 (2006): 635–650; Ruth Marshall, *Political Spiritualities* (Chicago: University of Chicago Press, 2009); Ebenezer Obadare, "Religious NGO's, Civil Society and the Quest for a Public Sphere in Nigeria," *African Identities* 5, no. 1 (2007): 135–153.

25. Elizabeth Shakman Hurd, "International Politics after Secularism," *Review of International Studies* 38, no. 5 (2012).

26. Beaman, "Battles over Symbols," 67.

27. Frederick M. Gedicks and Pasquale Annicchino, "Cross, Crucifix and Culture: An Approach to the Constitutional Meaning of Confessional Symbols," *European University Institute Working Paper RSCAS 2013/88* (Badia

Fiesolana, Italy: European University Institute, 2013): 7–8, available at http://cadmus.eui.eu/bitstream/handle/1814/29058/RSCAS_2013_88. pdf?sequence=1.

28. Steger, *Rise of the Global Imaginary.*

29. E. K. Wilson and Manfred B. Steger, "Religious Globalisms in a Post-secular Age," *Globalizations* 10, no. 3 (2013): 484–485.

30. Manfred B. Steger, James Goodman, and E. K. Wilson, *Justice Globalism: Ideology, Crises, Policy* (London: Sage, 2013).

31. World Social Forum, "Charter of Principles, no. 8" (2002), available at http://www.tni.org/detail_page.phtml?page=socforum-docs_charter.

32. See, for example, Articulacion Feminista Marcosur, "About the Current Campaign – Against Fundamentalisms" (2009), available at www.mujeres-delsur-afm.org.uy/index_e.htm.

33. Steger, Goodman, and Wilson, *Justice Globalisms.*

34. Ibid.

35. Wilson and Steger, "Religious Globalisms."

36. Ibid., 487–489.

37. William E. Connolly, *Why I Am not a Secularist* (Minneapolis: Minnesota University Press, 1999).

38. Mavelli and Petito, "The Postsecular in International Politics."

39. Casanova, *Public Religions.*

40. Adrian Pabst, "Realism beyond Secular Reason: Religion and the Revival of Grand Theory in IR," *Review of International Studies* 38, no. 5 (2012): 996.

41. Pope John Paul II, "Fides et Ratio (Faith and Reason)," *Encyclical Letter of the Supreme Pontiff John Paul II to the Bishops of the Catholic Church on the Relationship between Faith and Reason* (1998), available at http://www. vatican.va/holy_father/john_paul_ii/encyclicals/documents/hf_jp-ii_ enc_15101998_fides-et-ratio_en.html.

42. See Kmiec's chapter section "Two Essential Insights for Democracy to Be Compatible with Faith."

43. Mavelli and Petito, "The Post-secular in International Politics," 931.

44. Luke Bretherton, *Christianity and Contemporary Politics* (London: Wiley-Blackwell, 2010), 15.

45. Eberle, *Religious Conviction.*

46. Joseph A. Camilleri, "Postsecularist Discourse in an Age of Transition," *Review of International Studies* 38, no. 5 (2012): 1019–1039.

47. Wilson, *After Secularism.*

48. William E. Connolly, *Pluralism* (Durham, NC: Duke University Press, 2005).

49. Berger, "Law's Religion."

Chapter 7

A Strategic Perspective for a New Era in Euro-Mediterranean Relations

Religion, Immigration, and a Post–Arab Spring World

STEPHEN CALLEYA

In "Secularism Crucified?" in this volume, Douglas Kmiec provides a thought-provoking perspective of the complex debate on efforts that have been made to separate political decision-making from the doctrines of faith. As a crossroads of civilizations, the Mediterranean is clearly important in any analysis focusing on the relationship between religion and democracy. This area is home to a diversity of distinct religious cultures such as Christianity (Catholic, Orthodox, Protestant), Judaism (liberal and orthodox), and Islam (orthodox and fundamentalist).

As a framework of analysis to help clarify the complex variables in the role of religion in contemporary international relations, Kmiec's chapter is extremely timely. The profound questions he raises go a long way toward mapping out the parameters of an effective interfaith diplomatic strategy that is essential if twenty-first-century global relations are to be peaceful. Are all religious faiths, including Islam, compatible with democracy? What is the role of religion in the current transition taking place across the southern Mediterranean? How do the events of the Arab Spring connect to the problem of immigration, particularly the religious dynamics of these events? Will these events stop or exacerbate religious dynamics of immigration? What is the intersection between religious ideas/groups and current migrant integration efforts in Europe?

This brief analysis cannot address such an exhaustive agenda, but it does provide insight into contemporary regional dynamics in the Mediterranean area, particularly those security and integration concerns generated by the movement of migrants from majority Islamic countries in Africa to Europe. Kmiec's chapter "Secularism Crucified?" is inspiring in identifying policy measures to manage more effectively the challenge of irregular migration in the Mediterranean; it highlights the importance of focusing more on promoting an interfaith dialogue to reduce conflict between the southern and northern shores of the basin. Moreover, the specific reference to the speech delivered by President Barack Obama in June 2009 at the University of Cairo is especially indicative in this regard:

> I've come here to Cairo to seek a new beginning between the United States and Muslims around the world; one based upon mutual interest and mutual respect; and one based upon the truth that America and Islam are not exclusive and need not be in competition. Instead, they overlap, and share common principles— principles of justice and progress; tolerance and the dignity of all human beings.[1]

Kmiec correctly stipulates the importance of nurturing harmony between Christianity and Islam after relations suffered a significant setback following the tragic events of September 11, 2001. The trend for Europe's laws to treat Christianity and Islam unequally reflects European unfamiliarity with non-Christian religions. As Kmiec states, this unfamiliarity leads to an inability to understand how religious traditions could have different conceptions of religious freedom, precluding closer relations between the countries concerned.

The heterogeneous nature of the Mediterranean can be problematic in managing the security challenges in contemporary international relations. The Mediterranean Sea connects three continents. As Fernand Braudel observed, the Mediterranean is not even a single sea; it is a complex of seas; and these seas are broken up by islands, interrupted by peninsulas, ringed by intricate coastlines.[2]

Historically, the Mediterranean divided the old Byzantine and Ottoman and Holy Roman Empires, and today it is the most proximate fault line between the West and the other civilizations.[3] For four decades the European Union has projected policies promoting democracy in the southern Mediterranean without achieving a common outcome. While the Euro-Mediterranean Partnership succeeded in engaging most of the Arab states in this catchment area, it had little influence in creating democratic systems of governance. The Mediterranean also contains distinct political systems of governance—liberal democracies, monarchies, and authoritarian regimes.[4] A decade into the new millennium, while southern European states have become more deeply integrated into the European sphere of influence, similar to their counterparts in Eastern Europe since the end of the Cold War, no similar pattern of unity is noticeable across the other Mediterranean sub-regions. Actually, several Arab states in the Maghreb and Mashreq resisted embracing the global trends of democracy and liberal values until the Arab Spring of 2011 changed the equation completely.

THE RELIGIOUS AND POLITICAL CONTEXT OF THE SOUTHERN MEDITERRANEAN

The struggle of radical Islamists against the powerful forces of modernization, capitalism, and globalization is not a new phenomenon. Resistance to change has occurred at regular intervals. The Arab Spring of 2011 is actually the third awakening of its kind in modern Arab history. The first episode was the political-cultural renaissance of the late 1800s when scribes, lawyers, and other intellectuals sought to reform political life, separate religion from politics, emancipate women, and do away with the legacy of the Ottoman Empire. The chronicler of this movement that was led by Beirut and Cairo was George Antonius whose 1938 book "The Arab Awakening" remains the main manifesto of Arab nationalism.[5]

The second awakening took place in the 1950s and 1960s when Pan-Arabism flourished, led by Gamal Abdel Nasser in Egypt and Habib Bourgiba in Tunisia. These leaders were no democrats, but they did succeed in ridding their people of the inferiority complex that they had inherited from the Ottoman Empire and colonial relations. When they failed to address the challenge of changing demographics and to harness their authoritarian tendencies, they faltered and were replaced by police states and political Islamic movements.[6] The third awakening commenced with the revolution in Tunisia in 2011 that quickly spread to Egypt, Yemen, Libya, Bahrain, and Syria.

The election of al Nahda, an Islamist Party, in the constituent assembly elections of October 2011 in Tunisia and the Muslim Brotherhood in the presidential elections in June 2012 in Egypt has ushered in a transitory period of new Islamic thinking where political Islamic movements have to date been able to abide by the principles of democracy. Yet is it possible to apply universalist principles such as democracy and human rights to particular regions of the world? Can democracy, a concept that emerged in Hellenic Greece, be transposed to the Arab Middle East? Or is democracy a phenomenon that is rooted in "Western" political culture?

Democracy has been functioning successfully in non-Western parts of the world such as Asia. While there are different interpretations of the teaching of the Qur'an there is no denying that Islamic *Sharia* (consultation) underlines the basic idea of a desire for good governance. Similar sentiments are echoed in the Qur'anic principles of *ijtijad* (independent reasoning) and *ijmà* (consensus). Moreover, the Qur'an does not forbid parliaments, freedom of the press, or political parties.[7]

In any case, the current awakening of Arab democracy is clearly coinciding with a revival of anti-democratic Islamic movements. The rise of Islamism and the emergence of Islamic rejectionists who oppose democracy because of its association with a "liberal ethos" are already increasing anxiety among secular elements of society in different Arab states, as witnessed in Tunisia in deliberations on the Code of Personal Status that has guaranteed women's rights in recent decades. Radicalization and social regression could result in a more profound division between secularists and religionists in the respective Arab states.

Avoiding such an outcome is one of the main challenges Arab democrats must address if the Arab Spring of 2011 is not to be hijacked by anti-democratic forces. Most Arab states remain allied to the United States. Morocco, Tunisia, Jordan, Egypt, Saudi Arabia, the GCC states, and now also Iraq—all Maghreb and Mashreq states that are also aligned to the European Union through its numerous regional initiatives including the European Neighbourhood Policy, the Euro-Med Partnership, and the more recent Union for the Mediterranean.

Managing the Challenge of Irregular Migration in the Mediterranean

Yet the Mediterranean continues to be a source of instability in international relations. It is the home of the conflict between Israel and Palestine that has existed for more than six decades and that continues to hold the attention of Euro-Mediterranean regional actors and international great powers. The Arab Spring of 2011 unleashed a period of upheaval that has further attracted international attention to the Mediterranean.

Since the end of the Cold War and especially after the September 11, 2001, attacks on the United States, there has been a continuous unease in Europe and the perception of a threat from the Middle East. Alarming headlines in the international media focusing on instability in the Middle East and the regular arrival of hundreds of illegal migrants from the southern shores of the Mediterranean to Europe undergird this perception.

The flow of news coming from the Middle East predominantly features threatening images such as extremists preaching hatred against the West, or terrorists displaying contempt for human rights, or brutal dictators seeking to acquire weapons of mass destruction. Such reports portray the Middle East as an alien, hostile, and backward region. They also focus attention on the large migrant communities across Europe from these countries. Xenophobia toward migrant communities across Europe has strengthened and given rise to large right-wing political movements in France, Britain, and the Netherlands. In reality, the economic affluence and military supremacy that Europe enjoys when compared to its southern neighbors make the suggestion that the Middle

East is a threat to Europe seem nonsensical. Yet, since the end of the Cold War, there has been an increasing perception in Europe and North America that the new enemy after communism would come from the Middle East. Alarmist propaganda fueled by the media has focused on the emergence of an Islamic jihad against the West, particularly after the 9/11 attacks against the United States. In reality, the Middle East is not an alien, backward, and hostile region, but the media's portrayal of it in this way has allowed such a perception to emerge and gain ground.

This perception has been further bolstered by the ever-increasing number of illegal migrants who have sought a better life in Europe by crossing the Mediterranean. A "migration invasion" syndrome gained ground throughout the 1990s when tens of thousands of migrants from North and sub-Saharan Africa opted for maritime trafficking that more often than not ended up in a futile attempt to arrive in Europe.

Economic stagnation across much of Africa and the lack of any serious political reform throughout the continent has served as a major push for millions of young Africans to pursue a different lifestyle elsewhere. However, the international economic downturn since 2008 is certain to lead to more stringent administrative procedures in Europe for dealing with applicants seeking political asylum, especially when the clear evidence proves that such would-be asylum seekers are economic migrants in search of a better standard of living.

The European Union's inadequate response to this large flow of people seeking political asylum or refugee status has also underlined the hollow commitment of advanced countries when it comes to humanitarian policies and welfare resources. Falling birthrates in Europe coupled with the large number of arrivals from the southern shores of the Mediterranean led many pundits to question what impact such phenomena would have on the future identity of the different nation-states of Europe.

The revival of Islamic extremism in countries along the Mediterranean easily provokes fears across Europe of a resurgence of the Islamic faith seeking to make up for past battles lost. Political sensitivity to migrant communities is easily amplified as a result of long-term high levels of unemployment in Europe. Deeply rooted folk memories in Europe of the long and bloody battle between Christianity and Islam continue to resonate. Whether real or myths, this history can easily be revived as a political resource by anti-immigrant movements; this happened during the 2009 referendum that resulted in a majority voting against the construction of minarets in Switzerland. If not addressed in a concerted manner, the Huntingtonian clash of civilizations theory could become a reality in Euro-Mediterranean security discourse in the decades ahead. This is an outcome that would have catastrophic consequences for all peoples of the Mediterranean and is therefore a scenario that must be fiercely rejected.[8]

As highlighted in Kmiec's chapter, an increase in the number of Muslim believers will inevitably lead to increased debate about intercultural and inter-religious respect and rights. European governments in general and the European Union Commission in particular must take more seriously the extent to which the separation of political and religious practices will continue be manageable as demands increase for the inclusion of Islamic religious practices. The reference in Kmiec's chapter to the crucifix as more than a religious symbol but also embedded in the cultural identity of a country offers a way forward in this regard. If interfaith respect and understanding is to become a bedrock of future Euro-Arab relations within the EU and across the Mediterranean, then EU governments must adopt more neutral policies that invite inclusiveness of different religions. "Inclusionary secularism" as described in Kmiec's chapter, with its focus on seeking to assimilate sensitivities of the different religions, must be sought. In practical terms, for the European Union to adopt a less restrictive visa regime toward neighboring Arab countries in the Mediterranean would help dispel the sense that immigration exclusion and religious exclusion seem to be one and the same. Despite policy pronouncements claiming to desire closer Euro-Mediterranean relations since the launching of the Barcelona Process in November 1995, the EU has actually tightened visa restrictions toward its so-called partner countries in North Africa and the Middle East, especially following the September 11 terror attacks in the United States.

In the first decade of the new millennium, the Mediterranean has increasingly become a frontline area for irregular migration from the African continent to the European Union. Since 2002, the central Mediterranean has experienced a growing influx of migrants predominantly from the Horn of Africa, practically all of whom departed Africa through Libya. Even though, in absolute terms, the total number of seaborne migrants crossing the Mediterranean from Africa has not been massive, the flow is continuous and has become a permanent security challenge. Boat migration across the Mediterranean has also become an increasingly pressing humanitarian challenge. In recent years, several hundred would-be immigrants have died every year in the Mediterranean trying to reach the EU from the south.

The challenge of managing illegal migration has had an enormous impact on the state of Malta, given the country's small size and very high population density.[9] Consequently, illegal immigration has become one of Malta's top policy priorities, nationally as well as at the EU level, where Malta has been calling for burden-sharing mechanisms and support from other EU countries to cope with this flood. About 11,500 illegal migrants arrived in Malta between 2002 and September 2008. Relative to population size, this equates to around 1.72 million immigrants arriving in France or the United Kingdom, 2.35 million in Germany, 1.6 million in Italy, and about 1.15 million in Spain. While on a per capita basis Malta has experienced one of the largest—if not *the* largest—influx of undocumented immigrants among EU countries over recent years, Malta's total foreign-born population—estimated at around 2.7 percent—remains very small by comparison with other European countries. Among EU countries, only Slovakia with 2.3 percent and Poland with 1.8 percent have smaller foreign-born populations; in most Western European countries, the foreign-born population ranges between 7 and 15 percent. The challenge for Malta and also Italy has thus not really been one of coping with a comparatively large immigrant population but rather with a population of (irregular) immigrants that has increased dramatically over a very short period of time.[10]

As ambassador of the United States of America to Malta, Doug Kmiec was instrumental in fostering a more effective policy of respect and inclusion toward irregular migration. Instead of perceiving the arrival of migrants as a threat to society and labeling migrants as aliens, Ambassador Kmiec encouraged providing support toward assimilating migrants into the daily life of Maltese society, in one way by supporting several educational programs for the newcomers. Another effort was to offer a large number of migrants the opportunity to relocate to the United States. Ambassador Kmiec's legacy during his appointment in Malta was to help everyone appreciate more clearly the human dimension of irregular migration. By supporting efforts to improve the conditions in which the migrants lived, Ambassador Kmiec was able to demonstrate that the influence and solidarity of the United States in such circumstances is not restricted by geographical distance or geopolitical representations in international organizations. Leadership in contributing to a better future comes from individuals who are able to identify the human dimension of international relations and take action to improve the outlook of people who are marginalized by society.

In his chapter, Kmiec highlights how essential it will be for a policy of inclusionary secularism to be adopted during this embryonic stage of the "Arab Spring." It will require strong leaders in both the Muslim world and the international community to comprehend that the policy of exclusionary secularism, where Islam is not part of the governing structures, is not a feasible perspective.

Thus far, the European Union has not yet developed any comprehensive policy on integration of immigrants. For the last few years it has tended to turn a blind eye to what happens to these individuals after their period in detention. But the reality is that the numbers living and working (or wanting to work) in communities across the EU are growing. Continuing with the current policy of neglect in integrating immigrants runs the risk that many EU countries will see an increase in a new form of immigrant ghetto characterized by extreme social marginalization and exclusion.

Contemporary immigrant ghettos, sometimes referred to as "hyper ghettos," are much more extreme as they have little of the social solidarity and civil society that used to characterize "traditional" ghettos These new ghettos are places of extreme social fragmentation and exclusion, whose inhabitants are often focused exclusively on sheer survival. Needless to say, for the countries where they are, such enclaves pose a broad range of severe social and other problems.

To avoid such a scenario from occurring across the EU there is a need to develop a comprehensive, long-term integration plan that addresses every aspect of the integration issue holistically on a national basis. Consideration must be given, inter alia, to employment and economic consequences (both positive and negative); to the social consequences as children grow up and begin to make inter-marriages; to the need to allay racist and xenophobic fears among the native population; to the educational implications; and to the positive and negative consequences for the national health and social security and housing systems. These are the material realities of migrant life amid a European social transformation of which Kmiec's chapter mainly addresses the cultural and constitutional aspects. Beyond careful weighing of religious minority rights in a secularized Europe, a comprehensive integration policy will also require more efforts to integrate immigrants into the national labor market. Policy measures in this sector would include the development of skills enhancement programs and the creation of job placement centers for immigrants. Moreover, young immigrants must have adequate educational programs to facilitate their access to the labor market.

The great majority of undocumented immigrants landing in the European Union apply for political asylum (between 70 percent and 80 percent). In the EU context, the so-called Dublin Convention provides that the EU member country the asylum seeker enters first shall be responsible for processing the application. While the main rationale of the Dublin Convention is to prevent "asylum shopping" within the EU, it imposes a disproportionate burden on small countries, such as Malta and Cyprus, which happen to be located at the EU's external borders.

The status of persons crossing an international boundary without appropriate papers or visas depends on a number of factors. A person who is accorded refugee status has specific rights in the admitting country, including rights of residence, employment, social security, and others. Persons who apply for such a status are usually referred to as asylum seekers and should be treated in the same manner as refugees until their status is finally decided. The most problematic issue refers to the status of those individuals who are not granted the status of refugee (or humanitarian assistance status) or who do not apply for such a status. Such individuals are usually referred to as economic migrants, and international law has not, at present, provided them with adequate protection or assistance. They are usually considered to be criminals since most states have strict penal rules concerning unauthorized entry into their territory. The criminalization of such persons frequently persists throughout their stay. If they are employed, it is in the black economy (thus again falling foul of employment laws); they are accused by locals of taking jobs from them although mostly these jobs are menial ones that local residents will not do.

In reality, EU southern states such as Malta, that are less developed and secularized than other northern EU member states, are also less prepared to accommodate irregular migrants. A major factor contributing to the poor management of irregular migration in Malta is the lack of sophisticated policy coordination between the different ministries responsible for ensuring that the welfare of these people is safeguarded. An effective migration policy in any country requires that the ministries of home affairs, foreign affairs, health, education, and social services work together. Southern European states are also less equipped and less experienced from an educational standpoint to confront the challenge of irregular migration. This reality must be addressed more constructively by the EU if it is serious about adopting a more effective management policy toward the migrants who enter its borders.

Another major challenge in the management of illegal migration is to combat negative attitudes generated by the media about illegal migrants. The growth in irregular immigration into Europe has often been accompanied by a rise in anti-immigrant and racist attitudes and activities. Even in Malta where such political manifestations are a complete novelty, there has been a rise in attacks against organizations and individuals working to protect the rights of immigrants, or against people denouncing racism.

The media, in their role as educators of public opinion, bear a responsibility in this regard. Efforts should be made, if necessary with the help of EU financial support, to implement a sustained information exercise in the media through which professionals can articulate the plight of illegal migrants and the challenges that all countries in the world are facing as a result of displaced persons. Such a campaign needs to air regularly so that everyone concerned becomes more familiar with the socioeconomic and sociocultural reality these people are facing and the ways in which countries of destination should deal with them— humanely and in a properly managed manner.

The indifference toward migrants in Europe is also due to the dominance of secular decision making in ministries of European governance. Since its creation in 2004, the European Parliament Working Group on the Separation of Religion and Politics (now the EPPSP) has focused on the meaning and interpretation of the institutional provision of what has become Article 17 of the Lisbon Treaty.[11]

During the debate on the Draft European Constitutional Treaty, the Holy See lobbyists in Brussels worked very hard to have a reference to God and to "Europe's Christian roots" included in the Preamble of the Constitution. The decision was taken that the EU, unlike its member states, is the result of modern European post–World War II secular politics. It has never had any institutional or ideological footing on religion. Its authority and legitimacy were founded on the principles of modern democracy, with its citizenry as the ultimate source of legitimacy and authority, not God or any other entity. Created for economic purposes, the EU has developed over the past decades into a complex and comprehensive political reality. Where it becomes involved in the debate on values, principles, and ethics it must represent the plural reality of Europe.

The EPPSP was created to monitor developments taking place in Europe and to alert EU decision makers and citizens about any attempts by religious groups or other organizations to impose their position on public policies and seek privileges that go against basic principles and values of modern Europe. Now that the Lisbon Treaty is in force and its provisions are legally binding, the EU is unable to embrace a leading role in religious affairs. This reality has stifled the EU's ability to participate in religio-legal debates and undermined any initiatives that have sought to give the EU a voice when it comes to promoting a policy of interfaith dialogue.[12]

Politicians, church leaders, and opinion-formers more generally have a responsibility to counteract these racist tendencies, and the earlier action is taken, the easier it will be to avoid a real "racist backlash" which some European countries have had to confront in recent years. This will require that politicians and other opinion leaders generally avoid language that could incite racism or aggravate tensions between communities, and also highlight the potentially positive effects of a managed immigration scheme. This issue underlines—if it needed underlining—the vital need for a properly coordinated and structured integration policy to be put in place by EU governments.

In the case of Malta, given the very recent nature of irregular immigration, the country has not had much time to develop adequate institutional structures and policies, as they exist in other European countries which have long been confronted with immigration flows. This has also been reflected in the still rather ad hoc and piecemeal approach to immigration in Malta, where a comprehensive and long-term strategy that addresses all facets of the immigration issue is now crucially necessary.[13]

If one lesson can be learned from the experiences of the older immigrant countries of northwestern Europe, it is that neglecting the issue of integrating immigrant communities into their societies will, in the long run, come at a severe cost to the host country. Most of these countries, back in the 1960s and 1970s, assumed that immigration would be a temporary phenomenon only, and that few if any of their immigrants would remain in the country in the long run. The reality, however, was that the large majority of these immigrants, even if their original intent was to come only on a temporary basis, settled in their host countries, and that even after policies of active recruitment had come to an end, the immigrant communities continued to grow (through family reunification, higher birth rates, and in other ways). The unstable short-term outlook in countries along the southern shore of the Mediterranean and in sub-Saharan Africa indicates that migrants arriving in Europe are going to be seeking long-term residential arrangements.

If the European Union wants to increase security in the Mediterranean at a human level it needs to decide whether it is going to export more jobs to its southern neighbors or it is prepared to absorb within its borders some of the excess employment capacity that is due to grow further in the next decade. Current projections estimate that the population of North Africa and the Middle East is due to increase from 200 million to 300 million by 2020. Unless the countries along the southern shores of the Mediterranean are able to significantly enlarge their economic growth to above 6 percent per annum, unemployment figures in this part of the world are scheduled to increase rapidly in the next ten years. This demographic time bomb is therefore certain to be a source of instability in the Euro-Mediterranean area if not addressed in a concerted manner in the near future.

THE PROSPECT OF THE FUTURE

The Arab Spring triggered in 2011 has unleashed high expectations of change in all countries of the southern Mediterranean, particularly those that have deposed authoritarian rulers. Political participation, economic growth, and freedom of expression concerning faith have been driving forces behind the upheavals that have taken place. Failure to demonstrate progress in any of these areas, or even worse an attempt to hijack this process of reform, could result in a counter-revolution movement that would seek to deny the peoples the rights they have been fighting for. In such uncertainty it is easy to envisage a situation where a mass exodus of migrants would seek a more stable future in Europe. While conflict and the persecution of minorities have been leading factors influencing the increase of migratory flows across the Mediterranean, a continuous period of instability in North Africa would further exacerbate the flow of migrants northward.

During the next decade the Arab Spring countries must make progress on delivering the promises of a better political, economic, and human security agenda; otherwise, these countries will remain in turmoil. In such a volatile situation, what policy measures will the European Union introduce to manage more effectively the extremely fluid pattern of relations unfolding in its southern neighborhood? Will the EU unveil a comprehensive migration policy that seeks to integrate and assimilate migrants arriving from the southern Mediterranean? Will it seek to implement a foreign policy migration strategy that focuses more on respecting and seeking to understand the principles and values of the Islamic faith? Will the EU successfully establish a modus operandi with the numerous Islamic political movements that are reshaping the geopolitical landscape of the Mediterranean? Or will the EU become more introverted and develop a fortress mentality that results in legislating against the rights of Muslims already in Europe and against those trying to arrive?

To date, the European Union has largely been a bystander in the unfolding events of the Arab Spring. While it is to be expected that the EU would concentrate its resources on dealing with the serious euro crisis, it is nevertheless astonishing that it has shown no sign of launching a more engaging and dynamic policy toward the Mediterranean that seeks to nurture a stronger relationship with the Muslim world. This is especially the case when it comes to promoting interfaith understanding and dialogue. It is clear that religious leaders have a responsibility to move such an important agenda forward, but governments must also contribute to facilitating interaction between different religions in the Euro-Mediterranean region if peaceful relations are to be sustainable. As Kmiec stipulates, civil peace can only be fostered through policies of respect and inclusion. In this regard, Europe's tendency to disfavor Islamic belief and practice undermines initiatives that aim to strengthen peace and stability in the Euro-Mediterranean area. To develop closer cooperative relations across the emerging Mediterranean a policy of inclusionary secularism centered upon the premise that all faiths are equal before the law is necessary.

Kmiec's reference to "mutual interest and mutual respect" in President Obama's Cairo speech must be at the heart of any Euro-Mediterranean policy that seeks to adopt a functional and viable way of managing the challenge of irregular migration. More focus on the human dimension of this phenomenon and a diminution of the criminal perspective needs to guide policymakers mapping out strategies to accommodate the different aspirations of the peoples across the northern and southern shores of the Mediterranean.

Professor Kmiec is correct to indicate that a good deal of hard work will be necessary to achieve an interfaith understanding and to arrange governing institutions so that shared moral authority based on different moral conceptions is respected. Any attempt to suppress faith symbols and practices will not result in harmony or integration but in division between native and migrant populations.

During the past forty years the EU has sought to implement a comprehensive Euro-Mediterranean policy that seeks closer cooperative relations between the different states around the Mediterranean basin. The Euro-Mediterranean Partnership went some way toward formalizing this process of regular interaction and creating the context within which sensitive issues such as interfaith dialogue could take place. If the EU's policy toward the Mediterranean is to provide the foundation upon which a *Pax Euro-Mediterranea* is to be established over the next few decades, it is essential that the EU focus on advancing initiatives that promote mutual respect for the different religions and different systems of governance that exist in the Mediterranean. This must result in E.U. policies that ensure a fairer distribution of prosperity's benefits with its neighbors in the south. The Mediterranean Sea must not become a wall of religious intolerance and widespread poverty along the EU's southern periphery. This is the ultimate challenge facing the international community in the Mediterranean.

NOTES

1. President Barack Obama, "Remarks by the President on a New Beginning," Cairo Univesity, June 4, 2009, Cairo, Egypt, http://www.whitehouse.gov/the_press_office/Remarks-by-the-President-at-Cairo-University-6-04-09.

2. Fernand Braudel, *The Mediterranean and the Mediterranean World in the Age of Phillip II* (New York: Harper and Row, 1973[1949]), originally in French in 1949. See Bo Huldt, *Euro-Mediterranean Security and the Barcelona Process*, Strategic Yearbook 2003, (Stockholm: Swedish National Defense College, 2003).

3. David Abulafia, *The Great Sea* (New York: Penguin Books, 2011), xxiii.

4. Indra de Soysa and Peter Zervakis, "Culture and Governance in the Mediterranean: A Rationale and Overview," in *Does Culture Matter, The Relevance and Governance in the Euro-Mediterranean Zone*, ed. Indra de Soysa and Peter Zervakis, ZEI Discussion Papers (Bonn: Centre for European Integration Studies, University of Bonn, C111, 2002), 11–16. See Jurg Martin Gabriel, "The Mediterranean: Clashing Patterns of Governance," in *Mediterranean Perspectives on International Relations: A Collection of Papers on the Occasion of MEDAC's 20th Anniversary* (Malta: Medac Publishing, 2009), 305–332.

5. Fouad Ajami, "The Arab Spring at One, a Year of Living Dangerously," *Foreign Affairs* 91, no. 2 (March/April 2012): 56–65.

6. Ibid.

7. John L. Esposito and James P. Piscatori, "Democratization and Islam," *Middle East Journal* 45, no. 3 (1991): 427–440.

8. Samuel Huntington, *Clash of Civilizations and the Remaking of World Order* (New York: Touchstone, 1996).

9. Stephen Calleya and Derek Lutterbeck, "Managing the Challenge of Irregular Migration," *The Today Public Policy Institute* (Malta: Today Public Policy Institute, 2006).

10. British Council and Migration Policy Group, *Migrant Integration Policy Index*, October 2007, http://www.mipex.eu. See Commission of the European Communities, "Green Paper on the Future Common European Asylum System," European Union: European Commission (June 6, 2007), COM (2007) 301 final, http://www.refworld.org/docid/466e5a972.html; European Employment Observatory, *Undeclared Work in Malta* (Malta: Centre for Labour Studies, University of Malta, 2007); European Union Agency for Fundamental Rights, "Report on Racism and Xenophobia in Member States of the E.U.," European Union (2007), http://fra.europa.eu/sites/default/files/fra_uploads/11-ar07p2_en.pdf; European Network against Racism, *ENAR Shadow Report 2005: Racism in Malta* (Malta: ENAR Malta, 2005).

11. See *The Lisbon Treaty* (2008), www.lisbon-treaty.org.

12. James L. Heft, "The Necessity of Inter-Faith Diplomacy: The Catholic/Muslim Dialogue," in *MED Agenda Occasional Paper Series* (Malta: MEDAC Publishing, November 2011).

13. Government of Malta, *The National Policy on Irregular Immigrants, Refugees and Detention*, final draft (Malta: Government of Malta, 2007). See also Stephen Calleya, *Evaluating Euro-Mediterranean Relations* (New York: Routledge, 2005); Jesuit Refugee Service, Emigrants Commission and Maltese Red Cross, *Joint NGO Position on Detention of Asylum Seekers*, 2005; Katia Amore, *Active Civic Participation of Immigrants in Malta* (Oldenburg, GR: European Research Project POLITS, 2005), country report; Ministry of Justice and Home Affairs of Malta, *Irregular Immigrants, Refugees and Integration Policy Document* (Malta: National Legislative Bodies, 2005), http://www.refworld.org/docid/51b197484.html; Mario Vassallo, *Racism in Malta* (Malta: Allied Malta Newspapers Ltd., August 2005), study report.

Epilogue

The Future of Secularism in Public Religious Life: The Author's Response

DOUGLAS W. KMIEC

No greater respect can be given an author's work than for his writing to engender thoughtful written commentary. In the pages that follow is my brief response, given in gratitude, to the commentaries of Michael Anderheiden, Massimo Franco, Hans Joas, Stephen Calleya, Geoffrey Watson, and Erin K. Wilson.

The question of how to reconcile democracy with diverse religious beliefs remains ever prominent, even as the hope of accomplishing that essential task is obscured on any given day by the related horrific violence in Syria, the tribal/Al Qaeda challenges to civil order in Libya, the injustice of mass trials and disproportionate (sometimes death) sentences for acts of protest in Egypt, and the ever unsettled (or is that settlement-contested) continuation of the Arab-Israeli impasse over a two-state solution, a solution that is affirmed publicly but privately resisted.

The 2012 US presidential re-election of Barack Obama was less divided over religion and politics than the election of 2008, but only nominally. The clash lurked right behind the repeated effort of the Republicans to repeal the Affordable Care Act in part over whether the mandated insurance requirement provides public money for abortion. Relatedly, there was the drafting and redrafting of a waiver for religious organizations opposing artificial means of contraception. Despite very troubled economic times, the presidential contest involved close attention to the respective views of President Obama and the Republicans over how best to handle issues of moral and cultural dimensions.[1] Going into the final weeks of the 2012 campaign, it seemed that the president might have failed to drive home his religious sensitivity, leaving many young, progressive (and progressive Catholic) voters undecided. When the votes were counted, young people in their twenties and thirties overwhelmingly favored the president and he retained a slight majority of the Catholic vote, down 3 to 4 percent from the 2008 contest.[2]

Yet the numbers hardly tell the whole story. The boundaries or topics of dispute varied among voters. If secularism is thought to be a means by which the common peace can be achieved by cordoning off religious insight (or in a more fundamentalist sense, condemnatory judgment) over the moral perplexities of the moment, the message that believers must be timidly deferential to science and other empirically based normative sources has failed to penetrate any aspect of the constitutional republic—executive, legislative, or judicial. Secularism as ideology does seem to lead the competing political parties in the United States to different approaches. For example, Democrats continue to insist that abortion is a matter of privacy—or more particularly, the private sphere—a decision for the woman alone. By comparison, Republicans tend to place the issue on the public side, though hedging the impact or intrusiveness of its moral judgment by having it imposed by a lower level of government. Relying on state and local governments also allows for some variation of result even if the political actor thought the issue black and white or self-evident.

Yet, the complex nature of moral judgment with assumed, if not always provable, ill-effects if that judgment is not observed, did not always allow the Republicans to trust localism for the answer they desired. For example, the Republican answer to gay marriage was to defend traditional marriage at the federal level, casting aside any sensitivity for the intimacy of the question or any compromise tolerance for differing state answers. Ironically, the Republican-appointed members of the United States Supreme Court would lead the effort to invalidate a key section of the Defense of Marriage Act (DOMA) that defined marriage for purposes of federal law as only between a man and a woman. The justices found this effort to define marriage for *federal* law purposes to trespass on issues reserved to the *states*; the non sequitur in legal reasoning of the local determining the national was simply left awkwardly unexplained. Conservatives were caught having to choose between what was claimed as moral baseline (that marriage is limited to husband and wife) and locally exercised democratic choice that could go in various directions, but often affirmed same-sex marriage.

Of course not every state, even notably liberal ones like California, has as a matter of democratic choice approved same-sex marriage. Indeed, California's controversial Proposition 8 reasserted traditional marriage by public referendum after the Supreme Court of California had followed the progressive path. This case too made its way to the US Supreme Court. This time, however, the Court seemed less than enthusiastic about getting involved, perhaps to keep the Court from becoming the object of attention in presidential debate. Stepping aside by jurisdictional means, the US Supreme Court found that there was no one left in the case sufficient to defend the anti-gay position taken by the majority of the people of California when elected officers of the state of California refused to defend the people's reaffirmation of traditional marriage. For now, the anti-gay marriage position is simply being disregarded even though it was democratically chosen.

It is perhaps not too surprising that the justices did not expound on whether any given conception of secularism motivated their clever dodge—however temporary—allowing the Supreme Court of the United States to avoid having to rule definitively on the legality of same-sex marriage. The nature of popular voting could not officially disclose whether the people of California had adopted its opposition to same-sex marriage out of prejudice or deeply held religious belief, though it is reasonable to speculate both as present. But as I say, in this tangled tale, secularism as a means of avoiding or mitigating the clash of ultimates made no noticeable appearance. Has secularism truly been crucified? And if so, are the nail marks being driven by a prevailing religious conception of the human person? After all, this religious conception appears, however passively, on the walls of Italian classrooms and suggests that faith is the only source capable of aiding human reason to understand the most profound challenges to human life.

Or maybe not.

Staying in metaphor, the ideological view of secularism may not be a neutrality that allows equality of religious symbol on those Italian classroom walls. Rather, secularism could be the hammer blow that leaves the religious idea of humanity in the tomb. Dr. Erin Wilson instructs us to think of secularism as an ideological concept. I offer a few additional comments about her insights later but it is useful here to inquire about alternative ideological conceptions of secularism. Is secularism an ideology that demands public discourse to be religion-free or is the ideology of secularism one that invites religious and non-religious ideas to compete for our allegiance?

In America these competing conceptions of secularism as an ideology are worked through in the interpretations of the religion clauses in the First Amendment, and in particular, the establishment clause. The First Amendment to the American Constitution reads, in relevant part: "Congress shall make no law respecting the establishment of religion or prohibiting the free exercise thereof." When the essay that prompted this volume was first written, the US Supreme Court was still maintaining precedent from the midpoint of the twentieth century that "no establishment" meant the exclusion of all religious reference, except that which might have additional non-religious justification, such as reference to history or tradition whereby a cross could be part of a larger monument to, for example, remember the sacrifices of military service. A recent case decided as the final manuscript of this volume was being readied for publication suggests the high court in America has been tentatively fashioning a view more congenial to religious belief as a basis for a public decision.

The establishment clause case of note is *Town of Greece v. Galloway*, dealing with the constitutionality of prayer before local decision-making bodies, such as town or city councils that normally concern themselves with matters of land-use planning, traffic congestion, building safety, and other permitting or licensing matters related to common occupations.[3] A lower court had interpreted the no establishment clause as denying a local council the right to begin proceedings with a prayer—at least under the circumstances where the prayers offered were overwhelmingly Christian in content and the lower court had felt the council had made little effort to be inclusive of other faiths.

The US Supreme Court, 5 to 4, reversed this decision, allowing prayer except where it was used to denigrate other beliefs, or as a proxy for a hidden favoritism, or to manifest coercion or a desire to proselytize. While prayer before state legislatures had long been allowed as a matter of history and tradition, it was argued that town councils, which involve more give-and-take between citizen and official, presented a context that inherently coerces non-believers. On the record before them, the Court found none of this subtle coercion though it admitted that the matter was "fact sensitive." That fact sensitivity, however, should not be taken to mean that the Court will involve itself as a censor to remove even particular sectarian reference to pray to Jesus or Yahweh or Allah (praise be unto him), for example.

Does fact sensitivity and a new appreciation for the tradition and history of prayer in public places mean that the United States and Europe are now in the same inclusionary category? Would the United States and the European Union now decide a particularistic religious symbol case such as *Lautsi* in the same way? Not quite. It is still premature to place the United States in a category different from the exclusionary one suggested in the main essay.

Nevertheless, there is little question that the decision represents a course correction for the Supreme Court aligning it more closely with the side of US culture that welcomes an inclusionary attitude more easily. Where or when or over what topics might this more inclusionary attitude manifest itself and where will it be resisted? Its manifestation will be found in the symbolic matters and not the perennial trouble spots of abortion, divorce, bioethics, and embryonic stem cell research.

To recap, the divergence between the United States and the European Union over religious displays in public has narrowed in favor of including even particularistic religious reference. The US Supreme Court is likewise in agreement that the no establishment principle does not demand neutrality between religion and no religion. That is not neutrality at all but disguised anti-religious secularity. That said, the dissent by Justice Kagan should not be overlooked. It raises the commitment behind the First Amendment protection of religious freedom that in the republic of the United States all citizens are equal. That equality, even the dissent conceded, "did not necessitate that town councils be a 'religion free zone,'" but it did require sensitivity to the promise of the First Amendment that "every citizen, irrespective of her religion, owns an equal share in her government." This is a principle of great importance, as journalists pointed out that all of the justices in the majority of the recent opinion were Catholic and the dissenter Jewish. Thus far, this mention of the denominational personal preferences of the justices is only a softly spoken point of interest and not a matter of public alarm, nor should it be.

No one in the majority disagrees with the proposition stated by Justice Kagan that the Constitution does not permit test oaths. In this regard, Justice Alito writes only of his concern that Justice Kagan's dissent will result in a misimpression among religious minorities that they are denied equal benefits of citizenship. "Nothing could be further from the truth," writes Justice Alito. He continues, "All that the Court does today is to allow a town to follow a practice that we previously held is permissible for Congress and state legislatures. In seeming to suggest otherwise, [Justice Kagan] goes far astray."

The revised judicial thinking of the US Supreme Court still leaves the United States and Europe in somewhat different places. The US Supreme Court makes clear that the classroom filled with young impressionable students would produce a different outcome from that occurring in the town council meeting attended by adults. Justice Kennedy for a plurality reaffirmed that the government must be sensitive to the kind of implicit coercion associated with peer pressure. The greater sensitivity described by Justice Kennedy presumably would invite different, less inclusionary, treatment of religious symbols and prayers in the schoolhouse and it is reasonable to suppose that the crucifix, as in the initial *Lautsi* rulings, would still be excluded from an American public school classroom.

What is highly commendable even in this somewhat fractured opinion is the discernment that religious practice in the form of invocation is consistent with the nation's history and tradition and that this history and tradition is continuing into the present. The decision eliminated unnecessary hostility toward religion in general, reflecting as Justice Douglas once said that our institutions presuppose the existence of a supreme being.[4] At the same time, the most recent decision embraces the principle given slightly different emphasis by the majority and the dissent of the need to be cognizant of any perception or reality of public decision or benefit going to a favored faith. Such favoritism would be contrary to both the protection against being coerced to give support to a faith not of one's choosing and the recognition that all citizens regardless of belief or unbelief are guaranteed equal protection of the law. A previously blunt-edged judicial device led to religion's unnecessary exclusion and engendered its own tangled jurisprudence trying to distinguish between acceptable and unacceptable public assistance—as if it was all right for the fire department to let the church burn but not the schoolhouse. The refinement of this legal device has its own embarrassment and provocation to dispute the relationship between religion and politics. The intensity of dispute over matters of religion and politics is a global phenomenon. It cannot be otherwise as church and state are natural competitors for the formation of the larger culture and the people who make it up. To expect these matters to disappear is to expect agreement over what makes up a life well lived. As the divide between Western and non-Western religions illustrates, this is not the nature of the human condition. For this reason, disputes over exactly what constitutes the good life are inescapable. It was the intrinsic bias of secularism—indeed, its conceit—that in the pretense of neutrality it could exclude the religious sources that inform human beings of the content of happiness pursued. A concept of secularism that implicitly took the side of one set of interests over another is not surprisingly absent from judicial deliberations steeped in a commitment to equal justice under law.

Without deifying the US Supreme Court, the insight of exposing secularism as a form of false neutrality allows the Court to share in the praise for the outcome of the ECHR in *Lautsi.* The US and EU courts differ on whether a school classroom is intrinsically coercive, but the recent opinion in *Town of Greece* illustrates why the secularist claim in *Lautsi* was appropriately crucified. Given the harmony and civil peace promoted by these judicial outcomes, it seems especially worthwhile to inquire, still in the "Arab Spring" push for democracy, whether there are additional mechanisms or models for advancing religious freedom and civil order. In this, let me suggest, as the first chapter of this volume does, that there should be a new appreciation for the need for statecraft (as illustrated by the various models of governance). The comparison of governance models in the first chapter illustrates the ingenuity of humanity to administer complex body politics like those in North Africa with their multi-sourced conceptions of man. Significantly, the chapter reveals why a successful new democracy will need to transcend either a commitment to secularism or its twin: The coerced establishment of a particular religious majority. While diplomacy is readily accused of interference if it associates too intimately with the internal affairs of another nation, one can argue that the West's timidity to appreciate the various ways in which other democratic regimes accommodate competing religious beliefs unnecessarily handicaps the democratic project. Failing to explore alternatives for accommodating divergent religious belief in Western and non-Western ideas has too frequently left the coerced "accommodation" associated with the use of weaponry, detention, mass trials, and disproportionate sentencing.

There have been other significant religious, political, and diplomatic events that relate to the core themes of the original essay that gave rise to this volume. Keeping the dynamic nature of the subject matter in mind, the reader will find that the thoughtful commentaries included in this volume address a number of these developments, and in making my response, I will comment upon these developments as well.

MICHAEL ANDERHEIDEN

Michael Anderheiden assesses my inquiry into how well any theoretical model of a democratically organized political system accommodates the great diversity of religious beliefs. As Anderheiden sees it, my prescription for guaranteeing religious accommodation turns on a distinction between public and private. He suggests an alternative by calling on the insights of the late Winfried Brugger, who situated religion in neither a public (he uses the word political) sphere nor a private one. Rather, like John Courtney Murray, Brugger places religion within a separate social sphere. As Anderheiden suggests, this affords faith and religious practice greater breathing space in which its influence can be proposed and freely embraced. In other words, it should not just be thought that it is the individual versus the state—as my private/public terminology might suggest—but the individual through his faith influencing first his or her community of believers and then, if persuasive, the larger social milieu.

I cheerfully accept this improvement of my terminology. In doing so, however, I am less sanguine that Anderheiden fully appreciated that, no matter how one divides up the universe, there are additional prerequisites for successful accommodation including the full, uninhibited, and equal participation of believers of every type[5] in the polity as well as the opportunity to bring religious argumentation into public discussion, always understanding that a democratic outcome may resolve matters contrary to one's preferred religious belief.

The best designed democratic structure, as I see it, has structural off-ramps to avoid a premature vote on matters that are obviously divisive and would engender the breakdown of the democratic polity. That sensitivity would be actualized by super- or extra-majority votes or procedures that would make it difficult to trigger a vote that would carry the message to a losing cultural or religious minority to "get out of here," or in the words of Albert O. Hirschman, suggest that the only alternative for the proponents of the losing view is exit rather than voice. In most cases, propositions that are profoundly divisive are easily recognized; for example, electoral results that consistently favor or disfavor one religion, or even an index derived from the last half decade of 5–4 votes in the US Supreme Court. It is not that these issues are off the table forever; it is just that, especially in new democratic governments where a certain amount of operational success is necessary to keep one invested, the democracy does not run roughshod over minority beliefs to the point of early disaffection and a return to mass protest and violence. Relatedly, the various gerrymanders that are used to entrench winners over losers must be guarded against. Secularism in its most demanding, exclusionary posture has none of this sensitivity; indeed, to the extent that secularism denies the significance of faith in private and social spheres it produces a form of disinterested and disinteresting government not likely to command much loyalty or longevity in the clinches.

Anderheiden's proffered alternative models based on Brugger do add a different view, and I am grateful for them, but they do not necessarily clarify the issues I address. Brugger, we are told, has three models: strict church-state separation; equality of treatment, which depending on the strength of that egalitarian commitment, is some variant of inclusionary practice; or a third "feel-good" category where faith and reason or religion and politics inform each other as the lion lies down with the lamb.

There is nothing particularly wrong with a polity premised on strict separation except that its achievement of peace among faiths is in disregard of them all. Separationism either resolves nothing or puts the citizenry to a choice: Your religious self or your civic self. Because many are likely to pick their religious selves, the consequence is a form of ghettoization that is likely to leave the state far less of a community than human nature seeks. Nevertheless, in the pre-incorporation stage of a democracy, which one would hope is short and not so vulnerable as to necessitate the repeated interventions of the military, there can be a place for such strict separation to convey that there is no inside favoritism in constitutional drafting and other acts of formation. Anderheiden indicates that Brugger thought this separationist model was one that would be particularly important at a time when there are "dangerous religious contentions." One suspects that when the European Court of Human Rights (ECHR) adamantly refuses to accommodate any aspect of Islamic belief in democratic governance that it sees itself as following this model. Of course, since only Islam has been categorically declared incompatible with democracy by the ECHR, the separation is decidedly unequal. In fairness to the ECHR, I suspect the court would posit that it is an inequality of Islam's own making, at least to the extent that it is unwilling to concede the rights of those holding competing faith beliefs.

The second model drawn from Brugger is one of equal treatment. Aside from whether equality can be conditioned on a faith tradition's willingness to foreswear violent forms of conversion, and for the prospect of civil order and human rights there can be no other choice, Anderheiden notes some immediate awkwardness with this model. Like John Rawls's difference principle, digging into the concept of equality immediately raises all manner of discussion regarding how one characterizes certain natural advantages. Just as Rawls thought it necessary to neuter the notion of natural ability and merit by the provocative claim that no one has an entitlement to one's distribution of abilities, so too, adjusting for the incumbency advantages of a majority religion's influence on the law and culture can be daunting. Are Sunday closing laws a religious advantage written into law for a majority faith? And how many are celebrating Kwanzaa over Christmas or Chanukah? Moreover, public support for treating radical minority creeds the same as more predominant or mainstream creeds is surely thin, as the US Supreme Court revealed by backing away from guaranteeing a strict look at all general laws that substantially burden religious belief or practice.

Even Catholicism's plea that it not be burdened with a direct or indirect support of an artificial contraceptive subsidy seems to have tested the limits of tolerance of the larger polity. The topic of contraception saw the Church hierarchy so desirous of securing its imposed moral perspective against contraceptive usage that the bishops of the American Catholic Church were willing to forsake the Church's own far more Christ-centered teaching on social justice and its long-time advocacy of health care as a human right.

Accommodating competing secular and sectarian worldviews is complex enough, but it can be downright mind numbing not only when there are competing sectarian views (as one would anticipate), but also differing realities of belief and practice within the faith. The contraceptive objection is principally with the Catholic hierarchy and not with other religions. Moreover, the objection is largely unobserved by Catholics themselves in their own practices.

When the conservative voices in the Church hierarchy objected to having a Catholic employer supply the contraceptive option to employees, the president and the secretary of Health and Human Services offered to remove the issue from employer obligation into what might reasonably be thought to be the public (or secular) sphere altogether. Specifically, the proposed accommodation would place the obligation upon insurance companies to provide "free" condoms.[6] When this too was said to interfere with the free exercise of religion, the president's advisors were perplexed. Many could not see any remaining offense to sectarian interests or religious freedom, but the accommodation left unaddressed theological theories arguing that the public or secular accommodation of private choice is itself participation in a moral evil. This broad conception of moral complicity essentially exploded the distinction between public/private spheres altogether and seemingly made impossible the location of the secular-sectarian divide along the usual division of public/private concern.

In litigation, the Catholic Church is effectively taking the position that religious freedom of Catholic employers cannot be observed by the secular facilitation of private choice, but only by the public adoption or observance of the sectarian perspective held by the Catholic hierarchy—that is, the law had to be compliant with the Catholic position or it was unsatisfactory. With rather deliberate irony, the legal advisors to the Church hierarchy sought to characterize the presidential choice to leave contraceptive usage up to the married couple as the real denial of religious freedom, not of the Catholic couple, but of the Catholic employer who would be mandated by the health care reform to supply the contraceptive option. There is little sympathy for pushing the Catholic objection so far that not only Catholic churches and all the wonderful Catholic nonprofit healthcare and social service institutions, but any for-profit entity (well, at least those that are not publicly traded) that has an objecting Catholic directing the firm be immune from the contraceptive coverage responsibility of other employers. Of course, the notion that a single faith would dictate the terms of a public program is problematic, and in this instance, incompatible with the actual practice of millions of the adherents of that faith.

Similarly, attempts to equalize subsidies to public and private schools in the United States (as feeble as that effort has been) have proven complicated. Most of those complications are associated with pre-*Town of Greece* exclusionary ideas of no establishment. Thus, it may not be fair to hang them on Brugger's equality model. Indeed, the better comparison may be the US case law that has been protective of religious speech and expression, even in the context of public environments. That equality—when coupled with protection against favoring one faith over another and the avoidance of real or genuinely perceived coercion—is very much part of the inclusionary model favored in Chapter 1. There are lessons to be learned from Anderheiden's commentary, however, including being alert for how different faith traditions either orient themselves toward the congregation or the individual, or the influence of public law, and ensuring equal treatment of these apples and oranges may again be problematic.

The third model suggested by Brugger's writing is described by Anderheiden as one of "connectedness" or a complementary relationship of public and religious morality. This is a happy place, but it also seems a bit utopian. The notion that a citizen is compatibly shaped by expressions of public as well as private or faith-based morality is, with respect, to wish away the real-life difficulty that prompted the *Lautsi* case and the entire inquiry of Chapter 1. Issues from abortion to same-sex marriage to divorce to in vitro fertilization to embryonic stem cell research to the obligation (or not) to set limits on corporate compensation just aren't resolvable in the same way in faith as in "public morality."

The idea of "public morality," while attractive in the language of common good, is likely to be perceived as displacement of an authentic faith insight with a diluted and unsatisfactory minimal substitute. Moreover, as Anderheiden writes, "a meaningful part of the community's shared morals is heavily formed by a majority religious tradition." Yes, and that is the rub. Anderheiden holds out the first paragraph of the German basic law that "the dignity of man shall be inviolable," and so it should be for any polity that sees humanity as consisting of those made in God's image, or at least, redeemable in that direction. As the conflicts around the globe reveal, this is not a universal concession. Nevertheless, the reference to the third model is useful as a reminder that the often assumed aim of a mature democracy is indeed the transmission, when and where there is significant consensus, of religious teaching into legal precept binding on all. The maturity of that democracy allows for "religious tolerance for political reasoning," and is likely for that reason stable even in its underlying diversity of belief. Anderheiden claims that all three models posited by Brugger depend on political tolerance. My comments about the emptiness of strict separation would challenge that proposition with respect to the first model, since the coercion needed to maintain that separation is far less than an act of toleration, if not its opposite. Anderheiden writes, "the goal of integration may also be unrealistic if the majority religion is not itself moderate enough to allow for other religious views and services." In the end, Anderheiden and I may not be far apart as he is right on target in that telling observation. The heart of the problem to be solved is the extent that the role played by the state can result in moral decision making that is contrary to religious belief. Brugger's three models, while an interesting restatement, leave the resolution to be found elsewhere. The devil, as they say, is in the details—or is that God?

MASSIMO FRANCO AND HANS JOAS

Massimo Franco and Hans Joas get quickly to the heart of the constitutional difficulty facing Arab Spring nations seeking to transition successfully to democracy. Whether Tunisia, Egypt, or Libya, majority Islamic populations in each have been and will continue to be reflected at the ballot box both in terms of candidates and the commissions formed. Once again, there is no escape from the question, "Is Islam compatible with democratic governance?" The ECHR decision abolishing Turkey's Islamic Refah Party said it was not, and some events since the Arab Spring raise the question anew. In Egypt, the election of Mohammed Morsi of the Islamic Brotherhood initially was greeted with cautious optimism, especially since Morsi seemed well positioned to calm Israel. When Morsi was unable to fully implement a redrafted constitution that had been approved by plebiscite, thousands of protestors started to defy curfews and other police measures.[7] Morsi was arrested and by *coup d'etat* displaced by military strong man, Abdel Fattah al-Sisi. An attack on a police station led by Morsi supporters in the city of Minya led to forty-three police deaths; several hundred Morsi supporters were killed. Under al-Sisi, the Egyptian courts have begun mass trials with

thousands being tried and receiving a death sentence, sometimes com-
muted to life, for what would appear to be non-violent, though disor-
derly, protest activity. Morsi himself has been sentenced to death along
with Mohamed Badie, one of the spiritual leaders of the Brotherhood.
Most obviously, none of these "judicial" proceedings fulfill any conception of human rights or due process, and while a number of nations have
written to General al-Sisi to urge that he put a stop to the carnage, the
lack of effectiveness of these objecting voices is perhaps best illustrated
by the Obama administration's completion of fighter jet and weaponry
transfer agreements while at the same time decrying the disregard of
international standards of justice.[8]

Joas writes that whereas immediately after World War II, there was a
period of time in which religion was thought to be solely a private matter,
that has not been the modern experience almost anywhere on the globe
for the last twenty years or more. Today, concludes Joas, the question
has become acute: "how exactly should religiously inspired thinkers
balance the commitment to their faith with the normative obligations
of democratic discourse?" Drawing on his sociological research, Joas
identifies additional trends that on the surface suggest an even greater
"clash of civilizations." At the same time the enormous evangelization of
Christianity into significant portions of Africa, South Korea and parts
of China highlights, there has been a decline in confessional states, particularly in Central Europe. Yet, a fully engaged clash of civilizations in a
Huntington sense is not inevitable to Joas since he also finds evidence of
religious practice becoming "extra-ecclesial"—with more people adopting an individualization or optional approach to faith beliefs.

Individualization may avoid conflict, but as Joas notes, leaders of
the American Church like Cardinal Francis George are likely to say, "At
what price?" If the price is widespread cafeteria Catholicism, or worse,
indifference, the price is too dear. Neither Joas nor I would disagree, but
here is where something curious happens. Joas and I applaud the American constitutional arrangement with its acknowledgment of the transcendent source of human rights in the Declaration of Independence
and a constitutional promise that each individual citizen has complete
freedom to believe or not believe what he or she likes about that Creator. Joas reports that he frequently made reference to this philosophical

foundation to make, as it turns out, a losing argument to include a non-hostile reference to faith in the EU charter.

Why didn't the European Union follow the US example? If a scholar of Europe like Joas is baffled, this American constitutionalist diplomat is in no position to hazard an answer. Like Joas, I directly experienced in an unexpected way a similar European rejection of what I would have seen as a noncontroversial but important reference to the Divine. Having concluded my service as ambassador to highly Catholic, indeed constitutionally Catholic, Malta, the president of the Republic asked me to return to the country as a scholar who could assist him in his role as convener of a periodic re-examination of the Malta Constitution. Valuing my friendship with the president and indeed Malta as a whole I invested heavily in page upon page of fine-tuning that would not change the meaning of the constitutional provisions but make them more succinct and less dependent on an understanding of idiosyncratic facts. For example, Malta is a deeply religious Republic. It is no accident that John Paul II visited twice and Benedict XVI made a visit to some forty-plus local parishes.

My pride of authorship in legal recalibration, however, was dashed when a suggestion I thought would be accepted by acclamation unleashed a torrent of newspaper concern over something that I would have never predicted for Malta. And what was it that created a clamor so deafening that the bulk of my polishing was ignored? It was a greeting to the assembled audience that suggested adding a preamble to the Malta Constitution that thanked the Creator for the blessings of liberty (*pace* Thomas Jefferson) and acknowledged God as the ultimate origin and guarantor of human rights. To my surprise, this nation—that treated the Holy Father as a rock star and that regularly and joyfully processes in prayer on every feast day (and some that only exist there), carrying about with pride and effort Catholic icons—treated this suggestion like a suggestion to disenfranchise followers of the World Cup or at least the return of the Inquisition. I rationalized the unexpected reaction to be a by-product of the smallest nation in the European Union not wanting to contradict the "big" players, but frankly to this day I am puzzled.

Joas seems less surprised by the European rejection of such reference, even as he indicates his personal support for similar language to be added to the Treaty of Lisbon. What does surprise Joas is the discovery of how the American proposition which—said the US Supreme Court—presumes that the existence of a Supreme Being was described by the present leadership of the American Catholic Church (most notably, Francis Cardinal George, until recently the president of the US Conference of Catholic Bishops) in unbelievably dark and pessimistic terms. Joas quotes George as writing that American democracy is endangered by "philosophical secularism." Joas rightly thinks this exaggerated, and it is. In this regard, Joas is quite correct that the enemies of democracy are the enemies of democracy and not solely or maybe even primarily an atheistic cabal seeking to efface reference to the Divine.

Joas notes my dual concerns about maintaining democracy: First, establishing in constitutional foundation that democracy and moral truth of the human person must be linked, and second, understanding how different religious traditions see the moral truth differently. To me, the enemies of democracy are most likely to attempt to subvert the cultivation of ways in which we give respect, even when we cannot give affirmation, to the claims of conscience made by others. That respect entails not making overstated claims of conscience, but it also means leaving enough constitutional space that even unusual claims will not feel easily or readily pinched. Moreover, when the squeeze or the clash does come, as it will in any pluralistic state, it will prove useful to have anticipated this in advance by the construction of by-ways that allow for opt-outs, or cooling periods in which to attempt greater understanding or consensus. Indeed, I am not certain how Joas explains his efforts to have the European Union make reference to a transcendent source or at least to philosophical principles larger than the EU itself. My reason for proposing this to Malta relates directly to the point that a general acknowledgment of the transcendent promotes tolerance for all religious beliefs and practices that can then be comfortably accommodated within its generous scope. The preamble I proposed fit not only because it mirrors who the Maltese are (and constitutions, said Madison, are best when they are excellent reflections of human nature as it actually is), but also because by making a reference like that in our Declaration of Independence to "the law of nature and nature's God," it could embrace an extremely wide swath of belief systems, particularly those with common Abrahamic roots.

As I read him, and as I would concur, Joas has a refreshing confidence in different concepts of faith to find their way to a satisfactory end without violence. Joas writes eloquently: "when the nexus between the faith and homogenous social milieus is dissolved, when the Christian faith finds itself in competition with a vast number of partly secular, partly vaguely religious worldviews and lifestyles, when the faith is newly appropriated beyond the West, outside of cultures already long-marked by Christianity, and under conditions of mass poverty and uprootedness, then Christianity clearly must be freed again from unconscious particularisms and articulated anew." There is so much wisdom packed into that sentence that this brief response cannot do it justice. For the rising generation of Catholic or Jewish or Islamic scholars, it is the gift of a research table well aimed at meeting the modern tragedies of life— poverty and uprootedness—not with endless theological searches for the error of the other, but in common offering of the best of ourselves in the service of love of neighbor. Having taken Cardinal George to task for indulging a rigid judgmentalism, Joas properly praises the cardinal for his thoughtful treatment of migration which becomes an example of the kind of wisdom Joas and I would both encourage—a wisdom that relies upon the "eyes of faith to look upon a stranger as a neighbor."

Likewise, those searching for the materials needed to construct those constitutional byways or off-ramps to avoid collisions of faith with respect to public duties will find ample insight in John Paul II's personalism. Personalism promotes acceptance of the individual and the "ethos of love." Joas is right that, in their absence, the answers the Church gives to naggingly difficult modern controversies is incomplete and unsatisfying by the Church's own measures of faith. Even John Paul II, a personalist survivor of the Polish underground as the Nazis sought to decimate everything brilliant and unique about his ancestral personality, had difficulty consistently applying the great commandment to imperfect beings like ourselves. In similar fashion, Joas finds Cardinal George's engagement of these challenges—the excesses of the "war on terror," same-sex relationships, stem cell research, abortion—to be incomplete. It was as if doors of inquiry were slammed shut behind a barricade marked "intrinsic evil." The clear import of the barricade was, of course, not to make more understandable that which is morally difficult to resolve, but to increase the difficulty with a corresponding discouragement of inquiry. "Trust us" is not really an answer for a Church celebrating the fiftieth anniversary of *aggiornamento*.

When different faiths interact over contentious matters in public discussion, it is reasonable to suppose that some, perhaps many, will be more open to accommodation or even acceptance of the view of a religious body if it is delivered with charity. Is it charity or gratuitous cruelty to proclaim one's fellow citizen to be "intrinsically disordered," to proclaim those who like all of us wish merely to love and be loved within an orientation said by the science we ourselves accept to be anything but freely chosen? Joas suggests that when the Church reacts in these harshly categorical ways without a dialogue honoring the dignity of others who disagree, it disregards "values of personal autonomy and self-realization that are crucial for a personalistic understanding of Christianity."

The reader should not understand Joas to be writing as an apologist for the popular progressive figures of the day. Joas joins Cardinal George in expressing skepticism over the meeting of the so-called war on terror in disregard of the juridical structures traditionally applied to threats and acts of violence. With an eerie perspicacity now more clearly appreciated in the still fragmentary legal and ethical considerations implicated by the use of drones, Joas levels a broadside at President Obama, identifying him not by name, but by condemnation of governmental action involving "restrictions of fundamental rights and even the killing of people without the due process of law guaranteed by the US Constitution."

Not everyone will find Joas persuasive, but they cannot help viewing his assessments as well aimed at some of the most troubling places where not only fundamentalist Islam but traditional American Catholicism will find itself in a dissenting position. To raise that dissent, which Joas certainly encourages, the only pre-condition should be to follow the path of civic virtue outlined by Aristotle and in turn Aquinas of a citizen bringing argument to the polis. Hans Joas's own writing is given with so much courteous and joyful civility and intelligence that his contribution to this volume easily ranks as an exemplar of how to conduct the conversation he urges. Indeed, Joas brings to our attention a quotation from the Protestant historian Ernst Troeltsch that warrants the emphasis of repetition. Catholicism is not "the miracle of rigid consistency" that some claim it to be; rather, Catholicism from the very beginning has been "an infinitely complicated system full of contradictions that has again and again in ever new ways attempted to combine fantastic popular religion and philosophical dogma, revolutionary individualism and absolute authority, profane cultural techniques and otherworldly asceticism, lively laymanship and priestly domination – a masterpiece of mediation that created in church authority the ultimate regulator for the cases in which these mediations lead to frictions and a lack of clarity."

That quoted reference is a fascinating statement possessing for this volume—containing a main essay and responses seeking to define how contrasting faith belief gets resolved in the public democratic space—only one overstatement: Namely, that the Catholic faith cannot assume that its beliefs will be conceded to be the "ultimate regulator" on a contested public matter. The Catholic Church like all others can expect that its voice will be heard and responded to positively or negatively. When appropriate democratic means have been used to resolve a public matter (or even an internal matter if it threatens public order or a serious crime) and the resolution is contrary to the teaching of the Catholic Church or any other, the participants sharing in the democratic system will have a reasonable expectation of compliance, or in the alternative, a persuasive argument for exemption, or as Joas comments, nonviolent civil disobedience. Were all to truly grasp how a democracy functions in a manner whereby a prevailing majority can be said to expect, but not necessarily *deserve,* compliance from an entity with contrary belief, we would have traveled a good distance down the road of religious freedom as it must be understood in a democracy. No one faith a priori can be given the latitude to proclaim the definitive meaning of life we are all given to live.

How well equipped is the Catholic Church to engage where private belief and public rule or law are at odds? Returning to the remarkable commentary of Massimo Franco, the ability of the Catholic Church to constitute this authority must be conceded to be in some genuine disarray—at least within itself—by virtue of the fuller disclosure of documents related to the priesthood and the worldwide sex abuse scandals. Indeed, here in Los Angeles as this is written, documents of near unbearable shame have been made public. Few institutions other than one founded upon the rock of Peter could withstand the sorrow, the pain, the acrimony, and now the continuing suspicion these documents cannot help but engender. The nature of abuse against innocent children and their families by delegates of Christ's authority is repugnant and no amount of repetition of that repugnancy, accompanied by contrition and, however imperfect, remediation, can ever say differently.

Franco raises the scandal to reflect on how these acts committed by priests and covered up by the hierarchy are not just sins but crimes, serious crimes. That they were so even during their commission is not fully brought out in Franco's essay, but to the extent that other external threats in the world, such as communism, allowed the gaze of responsible prosecutors and public officials to be turned away from this inexcusable criminal behavior, it is a present reality. It is commonplace to comfort oneself in the belief that God allows us to find good even in as unlikely a place as this scandal. What possible good might there be in the context of our present inquiry? This is not to suggest that the Church ignore its teaching as a means of redressing the injury of scandal; it is to suggest that if the Church fathers have not been given a level of genuine empathy for the harms rendered by this sinfulness of others by what has transpired and made public, the concept of empathy is either without meaning or the Church fathers are uneducable.

Franco is right that the scandal has withdrawn some authority from the Church without its consent. In California, hundreds of abuse cases were transferred from the confessional to the courts by the unorthodox decision of the state legislature to re-open the civil statute of limitations. The release of personnel files kept by now retired Cardinal Mahony runs deeply against the long-standing desire and practice of religious and clergy for self-discipline under Canon law. There is renewed pressure to lift procedural statutes again, suggesting that the Church may presently command less respect under the general laws than the average criminal. Whether or not the Church fathers have greater humility, the Church's present ability to have the larger culture meld to it, rather than vice versa, is reduced. In this context, it is almost miraculous that the Church has wrung additional concessions from President Obama with respect to the Catholic objection to the mandatory inclusion of contraceptive services in his national health reform. To many, it seems beyond brazen that a weakened Church would now demand even more—insisting that the law exempt not just the Church and its auxiliaries, but as already noted, any private, closely held business that has an objecting Catholic as its CEO.

Franco writes that European secularization is alive and well. Even though it may be invidious to compare the status of the Church in America with the Church in Europe, Franco gives the definite impression that the persuasive sway of the Church in Europe is more greatly diminished than in the United States. To me, it is unclear. On the one hand, the openness to religious symbol in school settings represented by the judgment in *Lautsi* is far more accommodating than that afforded similar displays in the United States. As noted earlier, the United States has drawn closer to the European Union on this with a somewhat broader conception of acceptable prayer before local public meetings. There are still differences. Yet, the difference has more to do with the exclusionary nature of our no-establishment jurisprudence—which Europe lacks in law altogether—so it is difficult to see it as a measure of respect or influence. And Franco is correct that the legal victory for the cross in *Lautsi* was premised on legal strategy that protected the symbol as an aspect of tradition more than faith. As my former colleague Professor Watson points out, even in the face of a constitutional command of no establishment in the US Constitution, clever lawyering promoting historic preservation and the like has left some religious symbols on display in open forums in America.

Franco's commentary about how the different countries within the EU view each other is an aspect that escapes the attention of the American press, but it is certainly interesting to hear the view expressed that national economic irresponsibility within the European Union may dredge up religio-cultural antagonisms of the long, distant past. This happens all the time in marriages when the most recent spousal tiff becomes the basis for a more extensive bill of indictment raising failings thought long forgiven. My general impression is that rehearsing these failings is unhealthy for personal as well as national unions. Franco is right that old fault lines along religious difference may predict how the European Union will respond to the challenges of fundamentalist Islam. As a sometime denizen of Europe, I applaud the EU not only for its promotion of economic and regulatory efficiencies but also because the idea of union for regulatory and monetary purpose always held the promise of further growth in cultural affinity. When travel restrictions are eased and business can be conducted among a single union with twenty-seven different cultural histories, the result is almost certain to be the formation of a human community of rich diversity in food, art, architecture, song, and everything else that human beings do to ascertain the good life. Seen this way, the E.U. refusal to have an explicitly religious preamble or reference is not an uppity denial of the Divine but a reservation to individual nation-states for each to decide how best to express that Divinity in relation to the secular work of government. In not accepting a diluted recital of religious value, the EU may not be endorsing a secularism that is indifferent to faith, but rather endorsing a secularism where all faiths are welcome. If that interpretation is more than wishful thinking, Islamic thought should not be categorically left out of this ongoing vibrant discussion. As Franco concludes, "all debates on confessionalism, on the need for responding to growing divisive religious issues with a law, on democracy and secularism, on interfaith relations with Islamism overall, are a mirror of a changing or maybe already changed West." The active verb, "changing," is the hopeful one, for in this dynamic, the accommodation of Islamic believers is likely to occur with less resistance—unless of course, those first resident in Europe choose to demonize the newcomer and deny him or her the same latitude of inquiry into human purpose that the European continent has been indulging without conclusion for centuries. The burden of Franco's response, I suspect, was to demonstrate the triviality of the *Lautsi* outcome, and in so doing, to defend secularism or at least suggest how the hanging of a cross leaves it unscathed. I concede that one judicial outcome does not remake the European mindset, but isn't it fascinating how it has provoked this discussion and many others like it? The result of that dialogue may yet reveal the power of the person hung upon the cross to reorient our perspective away from all things trivial.

Let me begin to conclude this response to my interlocutors by remembering the late Ambassador Christopher Stevens, the US diplomat assassinated in Benghazi, Libya, on the anniversary of 9/11 in 2012. Ambassador Stevens was a friend and colleague in diplomatic work and it was my pleasure to know his devotion to the establishment of a democratic state in Libya with adherence to the rule of law, religious freedom, and gender equality.

The progress of Libya toward a democracy observant of religious freedom has been framed in the United States by his assassination, and that of three other embassy personnel, in Benghazi, Libya. When the war in Libya broke out in February 2011, it fell to my embassy in Malta to rescue 338 people, including roughly 100 US nationals caught behind the shooting lines in Tripoli and elsewhere in Libya.[9] The ambassador who preceded Chris Stevens in Libya had been called home for consultation. Chris who had served as deputy chief of mission in Libya until 2009 was away from post in 2010 completing a master's degree at the Naval War College in Washington, DC. Within the next year, however, our embassy hosted then-special envoy Stevens when he went to Benghazi in April 2011 to evaluate the likelihood of success of the rebel forces aligned against Gaddafi. Our embassy in Malta, being closest to the Libyan mission, helped meet Chris's resource needs and facilitated his coming and going.

With the loss of Ambassador Stevens, it would be a natural human reaction to expect to see hatred or suspicion. It is perhaps not well known that the purpose of Chris Stevens's visit to Benghazi in September was in large part to begin a US-to-Libya medical assistance program. How natural it would be to let that idea lapse after his assassination. But the Stevens family, being of selfless American nature, is salving their great personal loss by arranging medical care for the country that took their brother's life. In February 2013 the "J. Christopher Stevens Initiative on Health Education across Libya for Children" was fully launched. This initiative, designed to honor Ambassador Christopher Stevens's goal of improving relationships between the citizens of Libya and the United States, is a joint venture involving Seattle Children's Hospital (SCH), Massachusetts General Hospital (MGH), and Benghazi Medical Center (BMC). The aim of the initiative is to improve the health and safety of children and families in Libya by providing training and strategic support to Libyan doctors and healthcare professionals on topics collectively identified as national and regional priorities. And those needs and priorities are great, as this city the size of Seattle has no basic or advanced emergency care for children; no accident, injury, or illness prevention programs for children; no "911" system nor ambulance service; and much more. In short, the goal of the Stevens initiative is to offer doctors and healthcare professionals in Libya resources and expertise from two of the finest health centers in the United States so they can develop effective emergency care programs for children and families of Benghazi and beyond.

This may seem irrelevant to the considerations of secularism versus religious tolerance, but it is not. Without progress on mutual understanding of competing faith norms, there will not be sufficient mutual respect on which to sustain the embryonic democratic impulse in the Mediterranean. Loving one's enemy is not easy. And despite the lack of a comparable verse in the most popular Qur'an translations in the United States, anyone visiting the region quickly learns that just as Islam is not our enemy, neither are the Libyan people. The enemy that threatens their freedom, threatens ours. For as the inaugural poet Richard Blanco said so well: It is under "one sky" we live.

Ambassador Stevens is loved still by many friends and greatly missed, and those of us who admired his efforts want them to succeed. Indeed, he has even inspired this senior, or at least retired, ambassador to volunteer to take up his work. Whoever is privileged to continue the effort, will be assisted by the insight and writing of Stephen Calleya, Geoffrey Watson, and Erin K. Wilson that I turn to next.

STEPHEN CALLEYA

Stephen Calleya is the director one of the finest diplomatic schools in Europe and certainly the one most prominent in the study and analysis of the Mediterranean region. During my ambassadorship in Malta, where the school is located, my days were especially enriched by invitations to interact with his distinguished faculty and students from every point on the globe. Often, guests of the school are those who will be indispensable in addressing the most difficult aspects of harmonizing a plurality of faith in nascent democracies. Among the leading religious and scholarly visitors were Father James Heft, S.M., the president of the Institute for Advanced Catholic Studies at the University of Southern California; Admor Ha'Cohen, the chief rabbi of the region; and Imam Mohammed el Sadi, whose devotion to promoting reasoned dialogue with all is well known. Dr. Calleya wrote that

> the election of al Nahda, an Islamist party, in the constituent assembly elections of October 2011 in Tunisia and the Muslim Brotherhood in the presidential elections in June 2012 in Egypt has ushered in a transitory period of new Islamic thinking where political Islam movements have to date been able to abide by the principles of democracy. Yet is it possible to apply universalist principles such as democracy and human rights to particular regions of the world? Can democracy, a concept that emerged in Hellenic Greece, be transposed the Arab Middle East? Or is democracy a phenomenon that is rooted in 'Western' political culture?

No one yet knows the answer, but much will turn on it. What is needed? First and foremost, the ability to convey that there is no singular constitutional form that can be dropped over the Libyan, Tunisian, or Egyptian personality. If accountable governments are to result, they will need to be reflective of the religious and cultural practices and potential of the respective nations, and these differ. In Libya, given the absence of intermediate governing structures—these entities having been deliberately suppressed by Gaddafi—one would expect a significant bottom-up effort emphasizing, as Calleya reasons, that Sharia itself contains within it a desire for good governance. In Egypt, where constituent assemblies are numerous at the top, there will probably be a top-down effort to get buy-in from enough of a coalition to govern. We should not expect these democratic forms to resemble the presidential or parliamentary models so common in the West, since those are based on a population of largely Protestant orientation who had common ground.

Every Arab Spring nation for the near term should expect to have an open, ongoing constitutional convention. The transitional or early draft constitutions should not seek to close off public debate prematurely; instead, they should be transitionally secular and plain vanilla. The draft or transitional constitution should contain the structural provisions needed to allow certain avenues for monetary investment, premised upon enforcement of contract; title rules that promote the allocation and alienation of property; and the pledge of a police force/military willing to back up these structural avenues of interaction with enforcement and adjudication of disputes before a neutral judge or magistrate. These are the operational aspects of constitutional governance. They are fair and will entice external investment (both of which a new democracy needs on an expedited basis); but they do not represent the emotional or normative side of governance that stirs the soul and that for millennia have prompted religious wars over the meaning of human life, whether it is sacred, and how we can lead a good life.

In short, to get a new government on its feet economically and politically, a transitional draft of a constitution ought to stay clear of what divides people within their fundamental core. In this regard, compare the US constitution. The provisions the Arab Spring nations most need to calm matters in the street are really elaborations of the statement: "we will pay you back if you lend us money." In US constitutional terms, it is the protection that life, liberty, and property will not be taken without due process; security against the impairment of contract; protection against the confiscation or "taking" of property at least without a good public purpose and compensation and the housekeeping matters of currency—a bank to keep it in and lend it out; and appropriations for executive, military, and judicial personnel.

Notice, I have not included the legislative or law-making body in the transitional constitution. However, one could include them, except that during the initial constitutive stage, the people should speak as directly as possible in plebiscite and initiative. As the democracy further transitions and matters of fundamental philosophy have been satisfactorily stated and settled, the elaboration of codes will be given to a legislative assembly. Ideally, this assembly should commit to meet regularly but not constantly (Montesquieu's recommendation in the *Spirit of the Laws*). That way it will not overwhelm the system early or wander into religious and culture topics that need to come forward, if at all, only when a persuasive consensus has emerged that these issues cannot be resolved within religious congregations because a religiously pluralistic outcome is undermining the continuation of the state itself. Most present-day controversies over cultural or religious difference are not of that order. When resolution of cultural or religious difference warrants uniform public action, the normatively oriented provisions of a constitution related to free expression, freedom of religion, and guarantees of equality of treatment—as well as the promise of privileges and immunities and the law of nations ("human rights")—is what will determine the ultimate success of the polity.

Is the constitutional drafting proceeding in this way? Partially. In Libya, which is the last nation of the Arab Spring revolt, there is a "draft constitutional charter for the Transitional Stage." There are operational or process provisions protecting property. For example, Article 16 provides that "property shall be inviolable. No one owner may be prevented from disposing of his property except within the limits of the law." Power is located in a more or less executive arm of the transitional national council, which is elected from local councils, with the voting strength of the local councils determined by population. There are provisions for fair trial and independent judges, though the appointment of these is a bit unclear. Most noticeable is the following: "Islam is the Religion of the State and the principal source of legislation is Islamic Jurisprudence (Shari'a)." Perhaps this is not surprising, but it is a proposition that Turkey has rejected, with the affirmation of the ECHR. It is also a radical departure from the 1951 constitution when the pre-Gaddafi country was clearly a democratic parliamentary system. Article 21 of the old constitution stated: "Freedom of Conscience shall be absolute. The State shall respect all religions and faiths and shall ensure to Libyans and foreigners residing in its territory freedom of conscience and the right freely to practice religion so long as it is not a breach of public order and contrary to morality."

The draft constitution—not for better, but only for worse—thus inserts itself unhelpfully and divisively into cultural matters. At a time when more prosaic legal infrastructure is still under construction and basic civil order is still in doubt, the draft constitution presumes to referee competing faith traditions from a Sharia-based perspective in preference to all other faiths. Meaning no disrespect, observe that many differences exist among and within Christian and Judaic denominations or sects (the other Abrahamic descendants), and trying to resolve the definitive meaning of one's faith tradition has frequently complicated its usefulness to address the secular philosophical claims of utility, libertarianism, and autonomy and corresponding duties to families and the public community that swirl about public debate. It remains to be seen how this will work out and whether the weak promise in the transitional document allowing "non-Moslems the freedom of practicing religious rituals" ensures religious freedom for all.

There has always been a vibrant debate about the relation of constitutionalism and justice. The American constitution recites as one of its purposes the establishment of justice, but it does little to define the concept. If one took the call for justice seriously, however, governance would be anchored, in Catholic terms, less on the material (maximizing wealth) or the libertarian conceit (maximizing freedom from—usually obligations to another) and more on what Aristotle and Aquinas would associate with governing structures, namely, the pursuit of friendship, the common good, virtue, and a life well lived. American legal education, unfortunately for the last thirty or more years, has been dominated by the law and economics nostrums of *laissez-faire*, trickle down, and similar reasons to disfavor distributive justice. Libertarians have made efforts, most recently through the Tea Party, to confine human freedom to the Revolutionary slogan of "don't tread on me."

There is a counter-push. John Rawls made a decent run, for example, at justifying greater equality by cleverly appealing to life's uncertainty and thereby securing our willingness to be put behind a "veil of ignorance." Not knowing whether we would be the son of Mitt Romney or the daughter of a homeless, single mother would ensure our own minimum care or resource fairness along with others who are less fortunate if that be our lot. Note, however, that none of these prevailing worldviews address virtue in the Aristotelian sense. Rawls in his later work even prohibits discussion of virtue from a religious perspective, or at least boxes it in, to prevent belief from being relied upon directly. Instead, he urges that we speak in the secular terms of so-called public reason. Rawls, of course, meant well in intending the exclusion of religious insight as a means of avoiding religious hatreds. As discussed in Chapter 1, however, this also results in censorship and too great a loss of the capacity of faith to guide and enrich this life.

Is there a constitutional structure that can avoid the secular and sectarian extremes? Frankly, there has to be a better alternative than either the favoritism of one faith or the exclusion of them all. Libya's draft secures the vesting of property and contract rights, while also proclaiming the establishment of Islam as the religion of the country, with Sharia "the principal source of legislation" while guaranteeing for non-Muslims "freedom of practicing religious rituals." On the surface, this may turn out to be comparable to Malta with its establishment of Catholicism and robust guarantee of religious freedom for non-Catholics, but it remains to be seen if the freedom of "religious ritual" is broad enough to secure religious pluralism. Quite obviously, neither Libya in transition nor Malta has chosen the American model of a dual security for religious freedom—with the government neither establishing nor prohibiting matters of faith. This is not to proclaim the American constitution best for all times and circumstances. In this regard, Robert Kennedy once thoughtfully questioned why the GNP, "counts nuclear warheads and armored cars for the police ... [but] does not allow for the health of our children, the quality of their education, or the joy of their play."[10] These aspects of human happiness are what we dearly desire, but we have created constitutional governments that measure and give us much less. Could this inquiry into human happiness or satisfaction be more directly addressed in the newly drafted constitutions, rather than imposing Sharia—or for that matter, the Catholic Catechism—on those who do not believe?

This is not the place to make detailed findings of the constitutional drafting efforts in the Arab Spring nations, but Calleya reveals that democracy has been transplanted outside the West, pointing to the existence of democratic regimes in Asia where Western ideas do not dominate. Perhaps by attempting to anchor constitutional democracy on something nobler than wealth and autonomy, the higher calling and expectation would be the nutrient necessary for democracy to take root in Arab lands and avoid the violent ineffectiveness of near failed states.

It is not just the fate of the Arab Spring nations that depends on successful constitutional drafting. President Obama in Cairo launched an interfaith initiative to promote mutual understanding and respect. Much remains to be done, and this can be witnessed (as I have) in the distress and persecution felt by migrants from Eritrea, Somalia, and Nigeria as they flooded into Malta. Efforts to integrate these migrant populations into larger Europe has encountered resistance, in part traceable to the sour economic conditions in parts of the EU. As a matter of humanitarian assistance and goodwill, the US State Department authorized us to resettle roughly 800 migrants and their families in the United States.

Economic and cultural integration will always meet with resistance, especially in times of scarcity. Would it not be better to establish the rule of law, thereby attracting economic trade and investment to these African nations? Their populations would not desire to leave behind dear family and the familiarities of home if that home were transformed into a venue of economic opportunity and personal freedom, including that of the religious kind.

GEOFFREY WATSON

Geoffrey Watson, a highly regarded, international legal scholar at the Catholic University of America, supplies a clear-eyed, practical, review of the legalities surrounding the state of secularism in Europe and the United States. He concedes that the American law, framed as it is by a non-establishment principle, has been more exclusionary toward religious symbols than the present jurisprudence in Europe, as exemplified by the *Lautsi* decision. Watson is equally right to point out that the outcome in *Lautsi* may have been reflective of the unique doctrine of margin of appreciation that exists within the jurisprudence of the ECHR. In this regard, deference to displaying the symbol may be less about secularism versus faith than about favoring local traditions over international decision making.

Watson acknowledges that there has been harsher ECHR treatment of Islam than Christianity, writing, "A Muslim citizen of Europe could be forgiven for wondering why it is acceptable to display a crucifix in a classroom but not a Muslim headscarf." Nevertheless, Watson's scholarly recalibration or reexamination of the American and European cases does suggest that the protection of free exercise has been reasonably robust on both sides of the Atlantic and Islam has not always been on the losing side. Moreover, there are multiple cases where Christianity has asserted a desire to continue a community-forbidden practice and lost.

Watson concludes his commentary by applauding the effort in Chapter 1 to categorize constitutional systems along the linear spectrum from compelled theocracy to compelled atheism. He finds these to be useful and sensible divisions and suggests adding an additional dimension that would measure the specific facts of individual cases in both Europe and United States. Watson's reformulation would include subtle assessments of various alternative and complementary ways of promoting freedom of religion for individuals.

On the general question of whether secularism has been crucified in Europe by a single lopsided decision in favor of an important religious symbol, Watson has caught on that this former colleague and dean was merely provoking a fresh examination of the necessity of religious freedom. Watson sees secularism as occupying an important seat at the table of worldviews. Yes, secularism has a seat. Whether it is an important seat is a matter of debate and of freedom. By my lights, the more important seat at the table must be freedom—in this case, freedom of religion. Which jurisdiction does a better job advancing this freedom? Borrowing from John Rawls's "veil of ignorance," Watson observes, might help us compare American and European jurisprudence. That is a better use of the philosopher than Rawls's own push to exclude religiously grounded argument from public decision making, which is a denial of freedom of thought and expression.

The title of Chapter 1 playing off the decision in the ECHR was most certainly intended to provoke a lively and serious, non-ideological examination of the comparable permissibility or impermissibility of religious symbols in public spaces in the United States and Europe. Having accomplished that minor task, we could then inquire why jurisprudence in Europe and the United States resolves the question in opposite ways. There are differences in judicial methodology (how much deference to give local decision making, for example), but it is clear that the stakes are much higher than indicated by these nuances of constitutional law. The true inquiry of Chapter 1 and the splendid challenges and affirmations of the responses made by Michael Anderheiden, Massimo Franco, Hans Joas, Stephen Calleya, Geoffrey Watson, and Erin K. Wilson deal with the underlying philosophy of the human person. While the US Supreme Court has found a way to mitigate its previously mistaken establishment clause jurisprudence that had resulted in manifesting a hostility to all religions, Watson believes both Europe and the United States have manifested something even more vital: A comparable protection of free exercise. For the most part, that legal protection is capable of opening the human mind to religious belief, notwithstanding an occasional, if idiosyncratic, hostility toward the display or other manifestations of faith in the United States, or the ill effects of hubristic secularism in Europe. Europe, after rejecting explicit reference to God in its basic charter, has found a way to return God to the classroom. The United States, which explicitly acknowledged the Creator in its founding document, labors under a jurisprudence that keeps God out of school and courthouse. Which is the more lost?

Meanwhile, new democracies that are greatly influenced by Islam wonder what to make of all this. The "all this" includes levels of consumerist anxiety and familial and marital disintegration and gun violence, none of which the citizens of Libya, Tunisia, or Egypt want any more than the people of America or Europe do. The Arab Spring countries have an opportunity to draft constitutions for themselves that neither extoll disbelief nor oppress freedom. It would be a shining legal and political result were the Arab Spring nations to construct a new constitutional order focused more directly on what gives the human heart and mind the greatest satisfaction: Being of service to others, engaging in productive work that is illustrative of an educated mind and natural talent, and living a life worthy of the love and trust of one's family and others.

ERIN K. WILSON

Erin Wilson invites us to contemplate secularism not in the context of institutional means to accommodate the relationship between religion and politics, or if you will morality and law, but as an ideology. In truth, as my earlier reference to Wilson observes, I have always assumed secularism to be a competing worldview. She adds to the mix that the worldview represented by secularism denigrates the worth of religious belief and practice in its relation to human pursuits. Wilson observes accurately that in international affairs, the ideological dimension of secularism has often dismissed the understanding of religion's role in conflict resolution, peace-building, and international aid and development. She then enriches this consideration by adding yet another: Namely, that the ideology of secularism allows for the assessment of the role of the nation-state in global politics. In this regard, she notes that by means of globalization and increased interconnection across state borders, entities beyond the nation-state affect the way we perceive the public-private divide. Most intriguingly, she suggests that attempts to differentiate what is public and what is private are almost senseless when considered through the lens of non-Western religious perspective.

Taking each part in turn, I find myself in total agreement with Wilson that secularist perspectives have significantly impeded understanding of religion and its role in international politics. She is uncomfortably accurate in her comment that the secularist ideology assumes that religions "are mainly individual private belief systems . . . and they are on the whole irrational" When secularism is thought about in this way it reveals its exclusionary or hostile side. Moreover, the enemies of religion flying beneath this secularist banner are often close at hand, in one's own foreign ministry, state department, and the culture at large. They think of themselves not in terms of enemy but in the terms of modern sophisticates who have long ago given up seeing the human person as created facts.

Wilson reports that this disregard of religion by the secularist ideology is not confined to the US State Department or any other single government but includes intergovernmental organizations such as the United Nations. The consequence of such disregard is a lack of effectiveness in numerous countries of Africa and Asia where religious rituals and beliefs are central part of public decision making and discourse. If that is true, one would need to ask the question that Justice Kagan suggests in her dissent, Is one being judged unequally in light of a favored or disfavored religious belief? Once that question is asked, the need for statecraft to harmonize and accommodate different religious beliefs in order to maintain fairness is quite apparent. Thus, I would suggest that to the extent Wilson claims that secularism as an ideology is a deeper explanation than that which inhabits the discussion of the relationship of church and state, I agree. Yet I would not want that agreement in any way to suggest further agreement with the proposition that the necessity for statecraft and diplomacy to harmonize disparate religious perspective is secondary. Quite the contrary, unlike the secularist perspective that demeans all religious belief as irrational, the effort to devise means by which a state of pluralistic belief can advance the common good and honor our common humanity becomes uppermost in consideration.

Wilson finds encouragement in the establishment of the office of faith-based community initiatives in the US State Department. The incumbent president of the United States more than any other national or international leader, other than the pope, sees the interrelationship between religion and politics as critical to the understanding of the human being. Indeed, he shares intuitively, if not consciously, with the pontiff an understanding of how the world does not turn on the deregulation of finance or trickle-down economics or any of the things that consumerism and materialism deliver to our doors. The rejection of these false goods (gods?) transcends any difference between Western and non-Western ideology, illustrating exclusionary secularism to be the fraud, materialism to be the aider and abettor of the fraud, and the pretensions of society that are built upon these frauds to be embarrassments of first rank. To think that these distinctions characterize and perpetuate the North-South divide, allowing for the consumption of trivialities when a good portion of the world's population is starving, is a state of affairs the soul finds difficult to accept and, one suspects, a final judgment will find difficult to overlook.

I do not doubt, as Wilson opines, that grassroots transnational social justice organizations and movements have voiced their criticism of neoliberalism for decades. But their voice is still dimly perceived, and this is no credit to the acuity of the democratic process and the institutions we have fashioned thus far. So then the question becomes, "Is there a way to get beyond the false idol that secularism represents?" It is statecraft that holds the promise of bridging the differences of religion and politics in the public realm. The Muslim Brotherhood in Egypt erected a bridge for purposes of electoral politics but rather quickly disassembled it in matters of practical governance and constitutional drafting. The net result is the *faux* democratic affirmation of the military dictator—hardly the success story anyone wanted for the Arab Spring nations.

It may well be as Wilson argues that bridging differences among religious beliefs is a Western-centric idea; perhaps, it largely is. However, the tradition of the Ismaili Muslims to resolve disputes amicably through the intervention of elders suggests both that it is not a bad idea and it is one that crosses over into the East. By contrast, the alternatives of secularist suppression of all religion or fundamentalist religious imposition are far less in keeping with the truth of the human person. At the moment, bridging differences is an academic contemplation that allows the Western view to be transcended. I do not denigrate my own profession, but I also recognize its limits make a difference in people's lives. And late in life I now recognize how it also can mean the difference between life and death for those who take ideas seriously if not too seriously.

Yet, this writing should not end in this unhappy way. Wilson mentions recent papal efforts to unite faith and reason as not in opposition but in collaboration, acknowledging that this is the beginning of the way toward truth. Whatever statecraft or model of governance we choose must not get in the way of this. As with all good academic inquiries, Wilson proposes that the discussion not end in a definitive statement as to what form of government is to be preferable but that instead we engage or simply promise to be engaged in the inquiry as to what new possibilities may exist to manage religion and politics in a more effective manner. Amen. This book is about dialogue, but a dialogue informed by an accurate understanding of where we've been and where we need to go, and an assessment of the means to those ends that doesn't presume to embrace the non-Western merely because the Western has come up short. I agree that we can contemplate if not engage in new forms of multinational or multidimensional pluralism. Yet, I am suspicious that the call for such multidimensional pluralism may be an academic ploy for putting off the tough issues for another day.

A FINAL WORD

The crucifixion of secularism? Admittedly the terminology is awkward and provocative, but it is also intriguing. Before one arrives at the alleluia of the empty tomb there are dark moments that must be endured. One of those moments, the dialogue between Pontius Pilate and the masses, illustrates the limits of democracy. Pilate's wife had been warned in a dream to have her husband stay clear of it, but Pilate did not see how that was possible. Even then, the secular and religious were interrelated. Pilate does seek to build caution into the choice of the majority, inquiring whether there is any secular law violation and announcing that he has found none. But Pilate discovers that the crowd before him has no mechanism by which to apply his differentiated inquiry—they see a threat to what they understand and they are not about to stand on the formalities of jurisdiction. Without any edifice constructed in law and observed by the majority in advance, Pilate fears that he will be held accountable for disorder.

Pilate settles for the half measure of letting the crowd decide and indulging the symbolism of washing his hands. In a form of reverse Hobby Lobby, Pilate—the government administrator—seeks to distance himself from what he perceives to be a wrongful imposition by the majoritarian mob upon his freedom to govern. That sounds quite odd to the modern ear since we are used to defending David against Goliath. The proponent of religious freedom as an individual standing courageously against a majority hostile to his specific religious ethics is our usual hero. But that is a two-dimensional view and vastly understates the value of democracy that comes to the aid of the individual; it also defends the collective or the majority against individual dissenters who would deny the efforts sought to be made on behalf of all. Goliath sometimes needs protection from David. If democracy is to have meaning it must be possible to at least envision the case where the individual claim of David does not warrant majority accommodation. We know these cases exist, and they are difficult, whether it be the polygamous practices of the Church of Jesus Christ of Latter-Day Saints ruled out of bounds by the territorial powers of the United States or the harsh fundamentalist punishments called for by individual imams in an Islamic tradition ruled to be contrary to the human rights enforceable before the European courts. As this epilogue is finalized in early 2014, it is unclear whether the majority will prevail over the individual claimants known as Hobby Lobby. If the majority prevails, the ruling's legitimacy will depend on whether the majority's insistence on minimum contraceptive coverage is perceived *not* as an effort to exclude altogether categorically the Catholic mind on the subject, but as merely the rejection, at this moment, of the conclusion of that mind.

Secularism as an ideology is far too unnuanced and far too exclusive of the necessary dialogue between church and state. For the proper balance to be achieved in this dialogue, ideological secularism needs to be identified for what it is: Not an ethic of neutrality but of authoritarian exclusion. As Pope Francis has commented about capitalism, so too for ideological secularism: "It is no longer simply about exploitation and oppression, but something new [—exclusion]. Exclusion ultimately has to do with what it means to be a part of the society in which we live; those excluded are no longer society's underside or its fringes or its disenfranchised—they are no longer even a part of it. The excluded are not the exploited but the outcast, the leftovers."[11]

The luxury of looking down upon Tahir Square from the ivory tower is no longer available. The blood is flowing into that square and many others around the globe. The tourniquet needed to stop the bleeding is at least, in part, the hard work of creating an edifice of a government that doesn't presume to know the answer to why we are here and where we're going, but is encouraging, in freedom, of every religious tradition that is willing to instruct and to propose on these perennial matters of humanity without coercion or violence. It is by means of statecraft and resulting governing structure that we are able to check secularism's effort to reduce the faith to triviality, irrationality, and privacy. The private sphere is essential not because that is where religion is to be consigned, but that is where its persuasiveness can be assayed in relation to human truth in its continuing dialogue and influence upon the public sphere.

NOTES

1. See Douglas W. Kmiec, Edward M. Gaffney, and J. Patrick Whelan, *America Undecided—Catholic, Progressive, and Social Justice Perspectives on the Re-election of Barack Obama* (Kindle Amazon, 2012).
2. Fr. Joe Borg, "For U.S. Catholics Obama Is Still the One," *Times of Malta. Com*, November 18, 2012, http://www.timesofmalta.com/articles/view/20121118/opinion/For-US-Catholics-Obama-is-still-The-One.445770.
3. *Town of Greece v. Galloway*, 572 U.S. (2014).
4. *Zorach et al. v. Clauson et al.*, 343 U.S. 306 (1952).
5. Anderheiden remarks that I rule out both compelled atheism and compelled theocracy as incompatible with a successful accommodation of church and state in a democracy. In particular, he notes that the combination of radial atheism with democratic procedure in France led in the eighteenth century to terror. This is an astute observation. However, as suggested by Bill Keller, quoted in Chapter 1, compelled theocracy—in addition to being intrinsically contrary to the very idea of faith (that is, beliefs embraced or accepted in freedom)—raises serious concerns about oppression and censorship. Nevertheless, it is interesting to ponder how democracy neither rules out political participation by either of these extremes, though were they to take hold of the majority they would be democracy's own undoing. Again, Keller of the *New York Times* was anxious to make certain that the rights of non-believers were not in any way threatened by believer-candidates, and by his very skepticism, he was suggesting that believers bordering on the theocratic ought to be closely watched and questioned. It is notable how Anderheiden discerns the terror that historically resulted from a democracy without the compass of belief, but most modern progressive writers like Keller omit that concern altogether. It may be that the pinch or denial of freedom is felt more quickly under a compelled theocracy, whereas the anarchy that rules the soul of the non-believer is seen as unthreatening—well, at least until it is too late. While a successful accommodation will not be at these polarities, it must be remembered that to be true to their democratic ideal, the adherents of neither extreme can be ruled out of bounds from participation, and extremism can from time to time win electorally—especially in a parliamentary democracy where governing coalitions are needed for the government to function.
6. There is the difficulty of religious entities like the University of Notre Dame which self-insures, but presumably an existing or newly legislated third party entity that was publicly funded could handle the self-insured segment of the Catholic employers.
7. David D. Kirkpatrick, "Chaos in Egypt Stirs Warning of a Collapse," *New York Times*, January 30, 2013, A1.

8. "Egypt Sentences 683 Morsi Supporters to death," *Russian Times*, April 28, 2014, http://rt.com/news/155284-egypt-court-death-penalty/.

9. Stanley Pignal, "American Evacuees Reach Malta," *Financial Times*, February 26, 2011. http://www.ft.com/cms/s/0/999c5288-4117-11e0-bf62-00144feabdc0.html#axzz2RzWhyM4o. As recounted in my recent book, *Lift Up Your Hearts* (Embassy International Press, 2012).

10. Robert F. Kennedy, "Remarks at the University of Kansas," March 18, 1968 http://www.jfklibrary.org/Research/Research-Aids/Ready-Reference/RFK-Speeches/Remarks-of-Robert-F-Kennedy-at-the-University-of-Kansas-March-18-1968.aspx.

11. Pope Francis, "Evangelii Gaudium" (Vatican City: Vatican Press, 2013), para. 53. http://www.vatican.va/evangelii-gaudium/en/.

INDEX

Note: The letter 'n' following locators refers to notes

INDEX

Libya, 47, 55, 82, 203, 213, 226, 236, 240, 242, 245; doctors in, 237; revolution in, 199
Liechtenstein, Catholicism in, 56, 56n114
life, unborn, 100
Lift Up Your Hearts [book], 252n9
Lincoln, Abraham, 37
Lisbon, Treaty of, 147, 150n47, 207, 229
Locke, John, 180
Longinqua [encyclopedia], 104n258
love, 155–164: "ethos of,"230
Luther, Martin, 173
Lutheran: community, 130; EEOC, 90n218; nations, 147, 173
Lynch v. Donnelly, 59n119, 62n124, 70, 71n164, 149n33

Macedonia, defended Church position, 171
MacIntyre, Alasdair, 110–111
Madison, James, 74n178, 229
Maghreb, 198: allied to the EU, 200
Magisterium, 33n43, 117
Malta, 203–208, 229, 242: Catholic, 228; confessionalism in, 120; Constitution, 228; Catholicism in, 45, 56, 82n199; Christianity in, 58n117; confessionalism in, 40, 82, 109; defended Church position, 171; divorce in, 45, 45n79–84; interfaith initiative at, 36n54; population of, 110n276; Maltese Red Cross, 212n13; racism, 212n13; size of, 110; United States Ambassador to, viii, 18, 30
marijuana, 75n180
Maritain, Jacques, 110, 113
Marrakesh, 143
Marriage: in California, 215; differences in, 234; in France, 67; in Tunisia, 48; same-sex, 10, 63n125, 88n215, 100, 104, 160, 162, 230; in U.S., 67
Marshall, Charles C, 100, 100n246, 101, 103
Mashreq, 198: allied to the EU, 200
Matthew [7:5], 26n25

Mavelli, Luca, 188–189, 194n12, 195n38, 195n43
Mead, George Herbert, 156
media: mass, 201, 234; migrants, 206
mediation, Catholic, in the U.S., 163
Mediterranean, Europe and the, 18, 197, 211n2, 212n13
Mennonite, 114
menorah display, 62n124, 149n33
Menschenwürde, 125
Middle East, population in, 208
migration, 157, 230: from Africa to Europe, 201; Catholic, 87; into Europe, 76, 207; in the Mediterranean, 200
minarets, 202
Minneapolis, 93
minorities, religious, 132, 223
Miranda warnings, 75, 140
modernity, rise of, 7
Moldavia: Christianity in, 58n117; defended Church position, 171
monogamy, 162
Montesquieu, 239
morality, 10, 12, 25, 39–40, 64n129, 107n271; faith, 29, 189; public and religious, 35, 37, 39–40, 131, 189, 225; religion, 189
More, Thomas, 23, 117
Morsi, Mohammed, 226–227, 252n8
movements, social, 247: resistance of neoliberalism, 181; religion, 181
Mubarak, 61
Murray, John Courtney, 6, 44–45, 221
Muslim Brotherhood, 51, 83, 199, 227, 238; in Egypt, 248
Muslims: and Catholics, 68n156; circumcision, 128; differences among, 50; election of, 24; in Europe, 68n153, 211; in France, 66n143, 67n152; in public office, 166; migration to Europe, 76; in U.S., 67n152; women and equality, 25n19

Nahda, revolution in, 199
nationalism, 17: Arab, 198